CW01651511

PHOTOGRAPHIC EXPOSURE IN PRACTICE

PHOTOGRAPHIC EXPOSURE IN PRACTICE

Leonard Gaunt

DAVID & CHARLES
Newton Abbot London North Pomfret (Vt)

An Element technical publication
Conceived, designed and edited by
Paul Petzold Limited, London

First published 1987

British Library Cataloguing in Publication Data
Gaunt, Leonard
Photographic exposure in practice.——
(Photography in practice)
1. Photography——Exposure——Amateurs' manuals
I. Title II. Series
770'.28'2 TR591

ISBN 0-7153-9060-0

Copyright © Paul Petzold Ltd 1987

All rights reserved. No part of this publication may be reproduced, stored in a retrieval system, or transmitted, in any form or by any means, electronic, mechanical, photocopying, recording or otherwise, without the prior written permission of the copyright owner

Typeset by ABM Typographics Limited, Hull
and printed in Great Britain
by Butler and Tanner Limited, Frome, Somerset
for David & Charles Publishers plc
Brunel House Newton Abbot Devon

Published in the United States of America
by David & Charles Inc
North Pomfret Vermont 05053 USA

CONTENTS

INTRODUCTION

Why do we need a book on exposure when in-camera exposure meters are able to take care of every conceivable subject? There is even a camera meter that decides whether the subject is 'average' or not and reacts accordingly.

Well, not everybody owns a camera with that type of meter and even those who do will not find it completely infallible. Exposure meters, no matter what their construction, believe what their designer tells them. In most cases, what they are told is that every subject consists of a collection of tones that average out to a mid-tone of about 20 per cent reflectance. In other words, if you mixed all the tones together, they would produce a mid-grey tone that reflects about 20 per cent of the light falling on it, compared with the 90 per cent of a brilliant white surface and the one per cent or less of a deep black. That is the photographic 'average subject'.

The meter is also told that it must reproduce the scene in the same way, so that all the tones in the image on the film mix to a similar mid-tone. The snag is that comparatively few subjects do mix in such a way. So the meter is working from a false premise. It has been misinformed. It cannot know that, so it carries on regardless and tries to make the image an average one even though the subject is not. With a predominantly snow-covered scene, for example, the result is underexposure and grey snow.

How, in that case, do exposure meters work so well, and why is automatic exposure so successful? There are two main reasons. First, although few subjects actually average out to a mid-tone, most are reasonably close to it. Secondly, there is no one exact exposure for any subject. All films can tolerate a certain amount of 'error', and the most commonly used black and white and colour print films are very tolerant. They have, in the jargon, a fairly wide exposure latitude.

Those who habitually use colour print film and send it to a budget processing lab for prints of about 6 x 4in should, with reasonable care, get successful results most of the time with a simple auto-exposure camera. They may fail only when they shoot subjects that depart noticeably from the norm – when they are not average subjects. That could be, as we have already indicated, a snow scene, a shot against the light (ie, with the light behind the subject), a smallish subject against a very light or very dark background, a night-time scene, particularly with light sources in the picture area, an extreme close-up, and many others.

These subjects are not particularly rare and, now that cameras are so easy to use and the most astonishing claims are made for many of them, owners of even the most simple cameras tend to expect too much of them. Gone are the days when the amateur photographer operated only in sunlight and with the sun behind him shining on the front of the subject. Any photographer now expects to be able to take pictures in almost any lighting conditions. The 'average' subject is not so average any more, and failures are beginning to creep back onto the scene.

The result could be disillusionment for the enthusiast. The equipment and the manufacturer's claims for it become suspect. That is a pity, because modern cameras and films really are capable of producing excellent pictures in almost any conditions. It just needs a little knowledge on the part of the operator as to how the film reacts to exposure to light. Then, the exposure meter's trusting 'brain' can be re-programmed to come up with the right answer every time.

1 MATTERS MECHANICAL

The film you load into your camera is coated with a substance that is sensitive to light. When it is exposed to light it undergoes a chemical change. The effect is not visible but it can be amplified until it is, by immersing the film in a solution known as a developer. The parts that have been acted on by light are then further attacked by the developer, which has the effect of turning them black. If the whole film has been exposed to light, it all goes black. If only certain areas of it have been exposed, such as by projecting an optical image on to it via the camera lens, then only those parts that the light has reached will go black.

How tones are produced

The light-sensitive layer has thickness and, scattered through this thickness at different depths, are minute particles of silver compounds known as silver halides. It is these particles that become black on development. Where the light level in the optical image is very low, only a few particles, mostly those toward the surface of the film, are affected. With a little more light, more particles are affected (made developable); with more light, more still are affected, and so on. Where particles at all depths through the emulsion are struck by light, those particles tend, in effect, to overlap and form a continuous maximum density. Where comparatively few are struck, there is little overlapping and the density is less.

Thus, there is a different amount of blackening across the film according to how much light reaches the various parts. If very bright light reaches part of the film, all the particles are affected and, on development, the film in that area becomes almost completely opaque. Where little or no light strikes, the film remains nearly transparent. Between those two extremes, the various tones of the subject, reflecting differing amounts of light, are represented by varying densities on the film. A 'negative' image is therefore built up, with a large range of densities or 'tones'. It is a negative image because the film blackens to a greater extent where more light reaches it, so that the image is darker where the subject was lighter, and vice versa.

All this is true even of a colour film. The difference is that colour films have three separate light-sensitive layers, each made to react to different parts of the spectrum of white light – in the red, green and blue regions. The black silver image is still formed in the same way as with a black and white film. The difference is in the processing. The colour film has dye substances incorporated alongside the silver halide grains. The developer used is formulated to release the dyes along with,

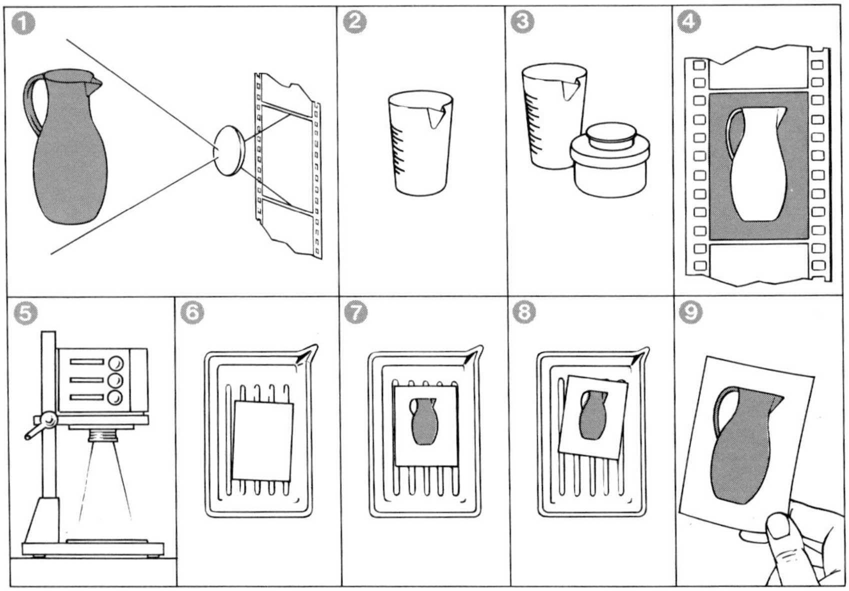

1.1 Image formation. 1 The camera lens projects an image on to the film. 2 Developer. 3 Fixer. 4 Negative image provided by developer action proportional to quantity of light-struck halides. 5 Negative image projected on to print material. 6 Developer. 7 Rinse. 8 Fixer. 9 Positive image because most light passes through least dense areas of film.

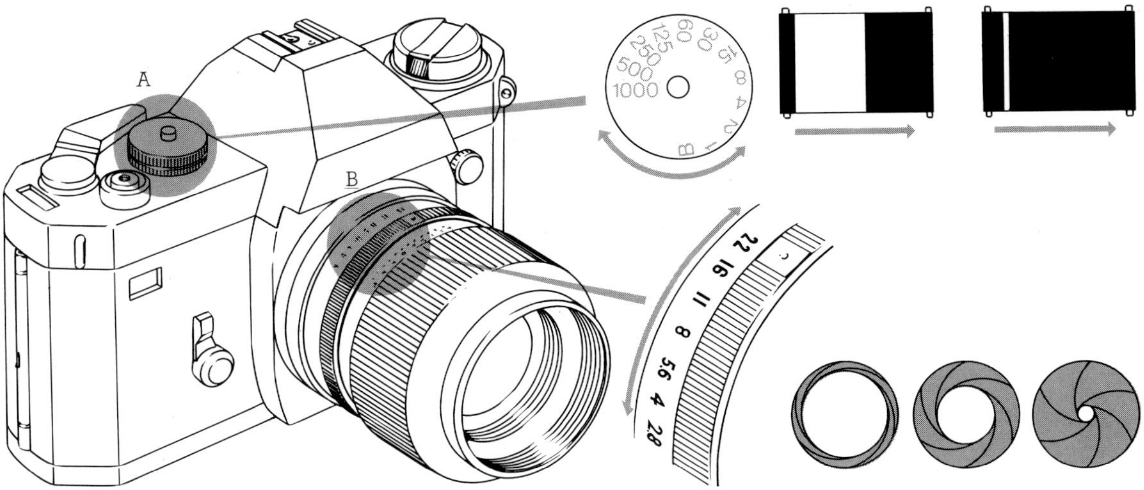

1.2 Exposure controls. A Shutter speed setting. B Lens aperture. Shutter speed and lens aperture can be varied over a wide range to control the amount of light transmitted to the film.

and in proportion to, the silver image. The silver image is then bleached out to leave only the dye image remaining.

From negative to positive

To produce a positive image of the original, you effectively repeat the development process. You put the negative in an enlarger between a lens and an illuminating lamp. The lens projects the negative image on to printing material similarly coated with light-sensitive elements. As the film image is a negative, it has the reverse effect on the printing material, compared with the effect of the subject on the film. The darker tones of the negative, representing the lighter tones of the subject, impose a barrier to the passage of light to the printing material. On development, the paper therefore shows lighter tones in those areas. Conversely, the lighter, more transparent tones of the negative produce darker tones on the print. The print is thus a negative image of the negative, ie, a positive, reproducing the tones of the original subject.

What is exposure?

Exposure is simply the act of allowing light to fall on the light-sensitive material. The action of the light is cumulative, unlike the effect on the human eye. The longer the light acts on the film, the more particles are affected and the blacker the film becomes on development. Even the darkest subject can be rendered light with sufficient exposure. The trick is to allow only sufficient light through to provide a fully detailed image of the subject. The brightest areas blacken the film very quickly. You have to stop the exposure before any of the less bright parts catch up and go equally black, but not before the darker parts have had time to produce an effect.

Exposure controls

You can control the exposure in two ways: by exposure time (shutter speed) and by the lens aperture. The first is more or less self-explanatory. The shutter is a mechanism that prevents light from reaching the film until you want it to. You open it to let light through by pressing the shutter release button. The shutter opens and then closes again after a precise interval, usually a small fraction of a second. The time for which it remains open, and during which light passes through to the film, is called the exposure time. On 35mm cameras it is usually controlled by a knob on the top of the camera with marked time settings. On larger format cameras, the shutter may be built into the lens and controlled by an external ring.

Exposure time. The figures on the exposure time (or shutter speed) control are generally arranged in the series:

1 2 4 8 15 30 60 125 250 500 1000

These figures represent fractions of a second. Thus, 1000 means 1/1000 second, 60 means 1/60 second and 1 means 1/1 or 1 second. On simpler cameras, the scale may be shorter. On many, it is extended at the slow speed end and a few have faster shutter speeds than 1/1000 second.

Aperture. The shutter allows you to control the duration of the exposure. You have a further control, based on the principle that a smaller window admits less light than a large window. The lens contains a multileaved structure forming a more or less circular adjustable hole and known as the iris diaphragm. The diameter of the central opening is controlled by a ring around the exterior of the lens. This has markings in the series:

1 1.4 2 2.8 4 5.6 8 11 16 22 32

No lens will carry the whole of that range. The standard lens for the camera generally has the lower starting number and 1.2 is not uncommon with 35mm cameras. Such intermediate figures are often used for the maximum aperture of a lens. For longer or shorter focal length lenses, the starting number, or maximum aperture is higher. On the other hand, shorter focal length lenses do not generally have aperture numbers larger than *f*22.

The numbers indicate the size of the aperture, which is the 'technical' word for the opening in the diaphragm. They are called *f*-numbers and are often expressed as *f*/4, *f*/16, etc. That means just what it says. The letter 'f' is the generally used photographic shorthand for focal length. The size of the aperture is the focal length of the lens divided by the aperture number. Thus a 50mm lens set to 8 has an aperture 6.25mm in diameter. A 100mm lens set to the same *f*-number has an aperture 12.5mm in diameter.

The longer focal length lens thus transmits more light than a shorter focal length lens set to the same *f*-number. But the light transmitted by the longer focal length lens has further to travel before it reaches the film and the difference is cancelled out. At the same *f*-number, therefore, any lens has the same exposure effect. Lens apertures are often referred to as 'stops' – a historical reference to the fact that the diaphragm stops a certain amount of light from reaching the film (these stops were originally individual metal plates with the appropriate aperture cut in each; the chosen stop was inserted into the lens through a slot in the lens barrel). This leads to the term 'stopping down' when a smaller aperture is set. 'Stopping up' could be a bit misleading, however, so we generally refer to opening up the lens when we set a larger aperture. We also use the term 'stop' to indicate the difference between one setting and another. Moving from *f*/11 to *f*/4, for instance, is opening up the lens by three stops – *f*/11, *f*/8, *f*/5.6, *f*/4. We even use the term to represent differences in shutter speed settings, because the effect on exposure is equivalent. A difference of two stops, for example, could mean a change from *f*/4 to *f*/8 or from 1/250 sec. to 1/1000 sec.

Any move from one aperture or shutter speed setting to the next results in a doubling or halving of exposure, with the likely exception of a move to or from maximum aperture, which is often an intermediate figure. So the two controls on the average 35mm camera fitted with its standard 50mm lens provide a range of at least 1/1000 sec. at *f*/16 to 1 sec. at *f*/2. That is a ratio of 1:65000.

How we use the controls

We rarely use the controls at such extremes, of course. Scenes seldom vary so much in brightness. What does happen is that, for a given scene, we may need to use a large aperture with a short exposure time or a small aperture with a long exposure time. We may need to use a short exposure time because the subject is moving. The faster the movement, the shorter the exposure time has to be in order to avoid blurred pictures. But a very short exposure time reduces the amount of light reaching the film, so we must increase its intensity by using a larger aperture.

On the other hand, we may want to use a small aperture to obtain greater depth of field. When you focus your lens on, say, an object at 3m from the camera, you get a sharp image of that object, of course; but other objects nearer to and further from the camera are equally sharply focused as far as the human eye is concerned. The distance between the nearest and farthest planes of acceptably sharp focus is called the depth of field. It varies with the lens aperture, being greater the smaller the aperture.

We might wish to use a large aperture to allow a relatively short exposure time or to restrict depth of field, so that unwanted detail in the background is thrown out of focus and thus becomes less distracting. Or we might want to use a small aperture because the background is an essential part of the subject and we want it to be sharp. That means we have to increase the exposure time to compensate for the lower light level passed by the lens. Inevitably, there are occasions when our requirements come into conflict. A moving subject in dim

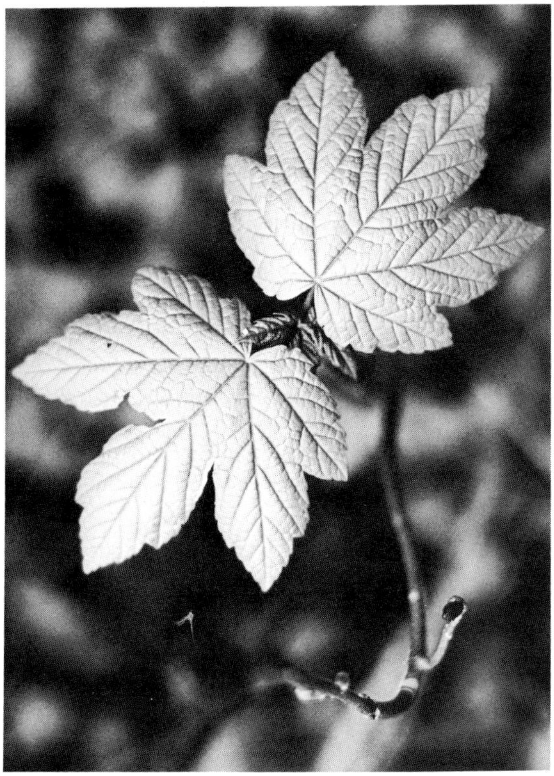

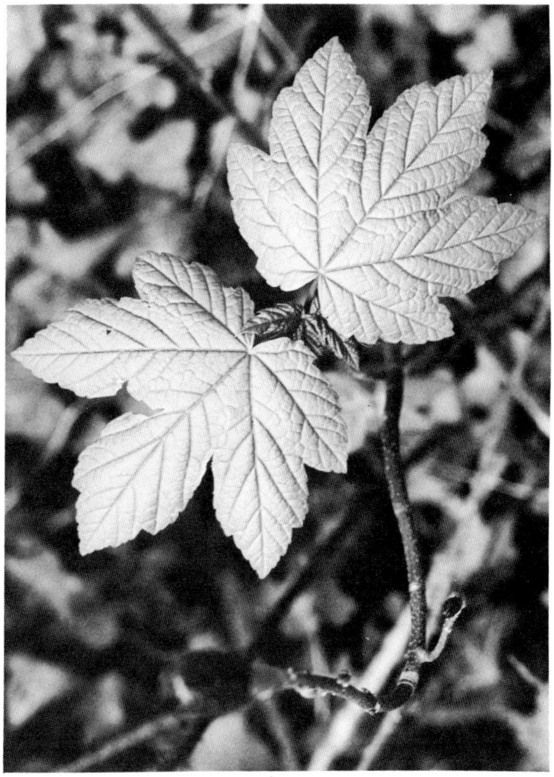

1A, 1B You can change the lens aperture to control depth of field. Changing the shutter speed in unison maintains the same effective exposure.

lighting or in conditions requiring a small aperture (and hence a longer shutter speed) is an obvious example. We may have the option of using a film with greater sensitivity to light (a faster film) or we may have to compromise.

How we arrive at the correct settings

When you buy your film, you usually find brief exposure recommendations packed with it. It might tell you, for example, to expose at 1/125 sec. at *f*/11 in bright, sunny conditions. That does not mean that no other settings are possible. A change in lens aperture can be cancelled out by a change in shutter speed. There is a so-called Law of Reciprocity which says that when the product of exposure time and intensity is the same, the effect on the film is the same. Shortening the exposure time by one step and opening up the aperture by one stop has no effect on exposure. In the bright sunny conditions of the film manufacturer's recommendation, therefore, you could change the exposure to 1/500 second at *f*/5.6 if the subject were fast-moving. The manufacturers' recommendations are a reliable guide to correct exposure in normal circumstances, but you may find that they vary from film to film. They may anticipate the most common uses of the film and bias their recommendations in that direction, knowing that their colour print film, for example, has reasonable exposure latitude.

Most camera users feel safer using an exposure meter. Indeed, they can hardly avoid it, now that most cameras have built-in meters and many of them use highly sophisticated electronic circuits. Under normal conditions, an exposure meter should give you exactly the same advice as the film manufacturer's recommendations – provided he is not one of those who anticipate common usage. It will only do so, however, if you first set the meter to the speed or sensitivity of the film in the camera. This is marked on the film container, as an ISO/ASA or DIN figure. The derivation of these figures is unimportant. They are simply comparative. An ISO 100/21° (ASA 100/21 DIN) film is twice as fast as an ISO 50/18° (ASA 50/18 DIN) film. Where you could shoot at 1/125 sec. at *f*/11 with an ISO 50/18° film, you could use 1/250 sec. at *f*/11 or 1/125 sec. at *f*/16 with an ISO 100/21°

film. The DIN system (and the second figure, quoted in degrees, in an ISO rating) uses the same principle but a different range of figures, working on a logarithmic basis. An increase of 3 in the DIN figure denotes a doubling of film speed. DIN figures, a series adopted by the German standards organisation, are normally used only in continental Europe.

The exposure meter has to be set to the appropriate film speed so that it can reflect these differences in its readings. Every external meter has a film speed setting control and so have most camera meters at present. A majority of films, however, now use an electronic coding system that allows the camera to set the film speed figure automatically. This DX coding system is dependent on contacts in the camera, which are gradually being incorporated into the new camera designs. This facility can be rather a mixed blessing when the automatic setting completely overrides any manual setting, or when the manual setting is dispensed with. As we shall see, manipulating the film speed control is often a convenient method of controlling the exposure meter.

What is an exposure meter?

An exposure meter is basically a very simple instrument. In its most elementary form, it is a light sensor connected to a microammeter which moves a needle across a scale. Modern meters (particularly those built into cameras) use electronic components to activate miniature lamps (light-emitting diodes or LEDs) or liquid crystal displays (LCDs).

The meter has a 'window' which receives light reflected from the subject. The window of a

1.3 Pre-electronic metering. TTL readings (top) are taken through the camera lens. The meter circuit is linked electrically or mechanically to shutter speed and aperture controls. The reading is generally taken at full lens aperture and translated internally to a reading at the shooting aperture.

1.4 External meters reading independently are usually fitted to non-reflexes (bottom). Control is by film speed setting only, shutter speed and aperture being set automatically.

1.5 The basic hand-held meter (right) has a sensor connected to a microammeter that moves a needle across a scale. The scale reading is translated to movable discs giving exposure settings.

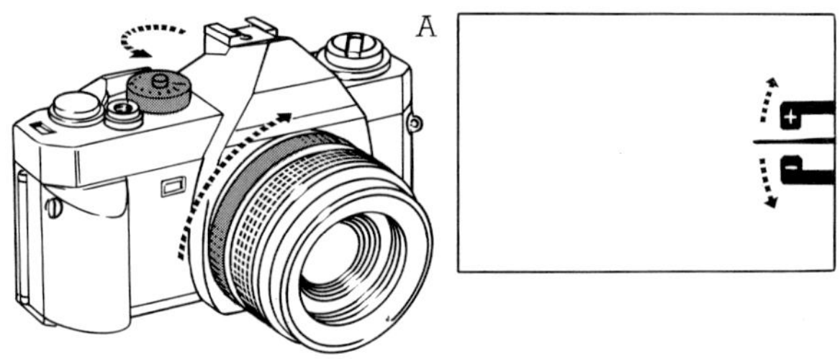

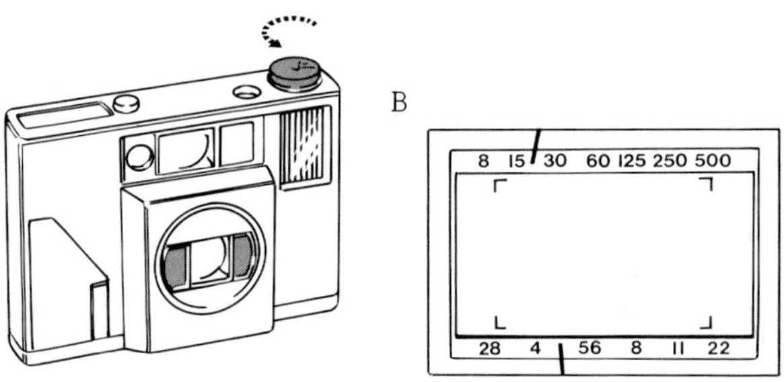

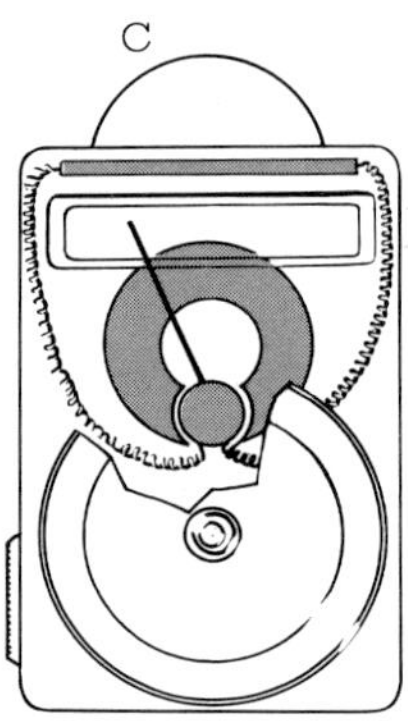

separate, hand-held meter has an 'acceptance angle' about the same as the field of view of the standard camera lens, and thus averages or integrates the light emanating from that area. The meter reading depends on the intensity of this average light level. The exposure recommendation can then be read off scales or dials on the meter. With most built-in meters, operation is automatic or semi-automatic. With 35mm single lens reflex cameras, for example, the light sensitive meter cell is within the camera body and receives light through the lens, which acts as the meter 'window'.

Automatic metering

Such a through-the-lens (TTL) metering system naturally allows the angle of acceptance to match that of the lens fitted to the camera. It also permits quite sophisticated automatic exposure metering systems to be built into the camera.

Aperture priority

The most popular form of auto exposure in 35mm SLRs is a system which couples needle movement or lamp triggering electronically with the intensity of light passing through the lens, and mechanically with movement of the shutter speed control. This is now nearly always a *full aperture* system, whereby the meter actually takes its reading with the lens set to its maximum aperture but converts the reading to what it would be if the reading were taken at the aperture set on the lens aperture control. The alternative is a *stopped down* system, when the reading is taken with the lens stopped down to the actual shooting aperture. This is the simplest system, allowing any lens to be used on the camera, together with any attachment such as bellows, tubes, close-up lenses, etc. In operation, you simply point the camera at the subject, set the aperture required and the shutter speed is set automatically by the metering circuit. As the shutter is almost invariably an electronically timed type, the meter can set it to the exact speed required steplessly (ie, at any intermediate position between the standard steps in the sequence). For this type of auto exposure, there is a special setting on the shutter speed dial, which is usually marked AUTO. If the dial is turned away from that position, the camera reverts to manual exposure control with stepped shutter speed settings.

Usually, the meter still indicates correct exposure settings however.

Shutter priority

A less popular system, and used by very few manufacturers, works in the reverse manner. The user sets the shutter speed and the meter circuit controls the lens aperture. Logically, one might have expected this to be the more popular system. It has the manufacturing drawback, however, that cameras and lenses have to be designed specifically for each individual system. The AUTO position has to be on the lens, preferably with a lock, and there needs to be some means of transmitting the value of the maximum aperture of the lens from lens to meter circuit within the camera body.

Programmed exposure

Aperture priority and shutter priority systems should, strictly, be called semi-automatic, because they require the user to set either the aperture or the shutter speed manually. A so-called programmed system makes both settings automatically. You literally point and shoot. A programmed microchip within the camera assesses the light intensity and allocates to each light level a pair of settings. The obvious drawback of a simple program is that no consideration can be given to subject content. The pairs of settings are always the same. Slow shutter speeds go with large apertures: fast shutter speeds go with small apertures. The system will never set a fast shutter speed and a large aperture or, conversely, a slow shutter speed with a small aperture.

That disadvantage has been overcome to some extent in many camera models by incorporating extra programs. The standard program acts as described. Alternative camera settings allow preference to be given to either shutter speed or aperture, depending on whether the requirement is to maintain either a high shutter speed, or a small aperture, for as long as possible.

Metering patterns

The most sophisticated metering systems are found in 35mm SLRs, where, indeed, the TTL method was first introduced. TTL metering can be operated in various ways, but the most common method is to read the illuminance of the screen image by means of sensors placed near the viewfinder eyepiece. In that position, they read the illuminance in an *equivalent focal plane*, ie, the screen image and the film are at equal distances from the lens. A very effective alternative introduced by Olympus was to place the sensors in the floor of the camera and read the reflectance of the image on shutter blind and film. That is generally known as OTF (off the film plane) metering. Many other positions for the meter cells have been tried, but those that do not read from the focal plane or an equivalent position can be complex in construction.

Integrated reading

The basic idea with this method is to meter the whole image area, averaging or *integrating* all its tones. That is where the assumption that the scene is 'average' comes in. The meter assumes this, and recommends an exposure to reproduce the scene, not necessarily as it really is, but simply as an image that integrates to a mid-tone.

Partly because it is a little difficult to read the whole image area with equal emphasis, and partly as a sales ploy, a modification of this basic method soon appeared in which the reading was biased to take more account of the centre of the image area than of the outer portions. This is known as a *centre weighted* reading and it assumes many forms, with ever more complex patterns of 'weighting' being introduced.

Spot reading

There have been many attempts over the years to introduce a pseudo-spot-reading method of exposure metering into 35mm SLRs. Instead of reading the whole image area, the meter selects only a small part of it, indicated by a 'target area' on the viewfinder screen. The value of such a method for the average photographer is somewhat limited. It tends to encourage the belief that metering a selected tone of the image will ensure correct exposure of that tone. Nothing could be further from the truth – unless that tone happens to be a mid-tone. What a spot reading does ensure is that the tone metered is reproduced as a mid-tone.

The true value of the spot method is to compare highlight and shadow readings and so assess subject contrast, or to allow an average reading to be used for exposure. Some account is taken of that by the system used in one camera, Olympus OM4, which can hold in memory up to eight separate spot readings and then provide an exposure calculated from all those readings. Again, it does not get it right automatically. You have to understand the system and you need to know more than a little about exposure in general. The more you know, the more effectively you can use this quite ingenious exposure system.

Hand-held meters

Despite the elaboration of inbuilt metering systems, particularly in 35mm SLRs, there are still plenty of photographers who prefer to keep everything under their own control by using a separate exposure meter. Users of larger format cameras are, indeed, often obliged to do so. The larger the film size, the less likely you are to find elaborate electronic aids to exposure.

Hand-held exposure meters are still available in plenty, ranging from simple, but efficient, models costing a few pounds, to those capable of operating under almost any conditions and, with all their attachments, running out at a few hundred pounds. Perhaps the best known name in the exposure meter world is still the Weston, although it has now fallen well behind the field in terms of modern technology. The Weston Euromaster is a sturdy, well-engineered, rather old-fashioned meter using a relatively simple arrangement of a needle moving across a range of adjustable scales. It is totally efficient for the majority of uses but has no pretensions to super-sensitivity.

Most of the later electronic versions, generally with digital readouts instead of scales, do claim sensitivity down to rather unrealistic levels. Indeed, they *are* sensitive down to extraordinarily low light levels, but the value of such readings is minimal. Failure of the reciprocity law comes into effect at exposure timings longer than a second or two with most films.

'Professional' meters, with wide-ranging sensitivity and accessories to adapt them to a variety of uses, come from such well-known names as Gossen (Lunasix, Profisix, Mastersix), Copal Sekonic, Minolta and Calculight. Sensitivities are usually expressed in Exposure Value (EV) terms, backed up by the exposure durations such values represent. One of these meters, for example, claims a sensitivity of EV −5 to +19. But, strictly speaking, these are light value figures and should be related to a film speed. The standard generally taken is an ISO 100/21° (ASA 100/21 DIN) film. The light value of +19, for example, represents an exposure of 1/1000 sec. at *f*/16, which is rarely a practical proposition with a slow film. Naturally, it also represents 1/10 000 sec. at *f*/4, which is out of the question with normal equipment. At the other ex-

2 A relatively fast shutter speed is necessary here, so the automatic-exposure camera must not be allowed to set a slow speed.

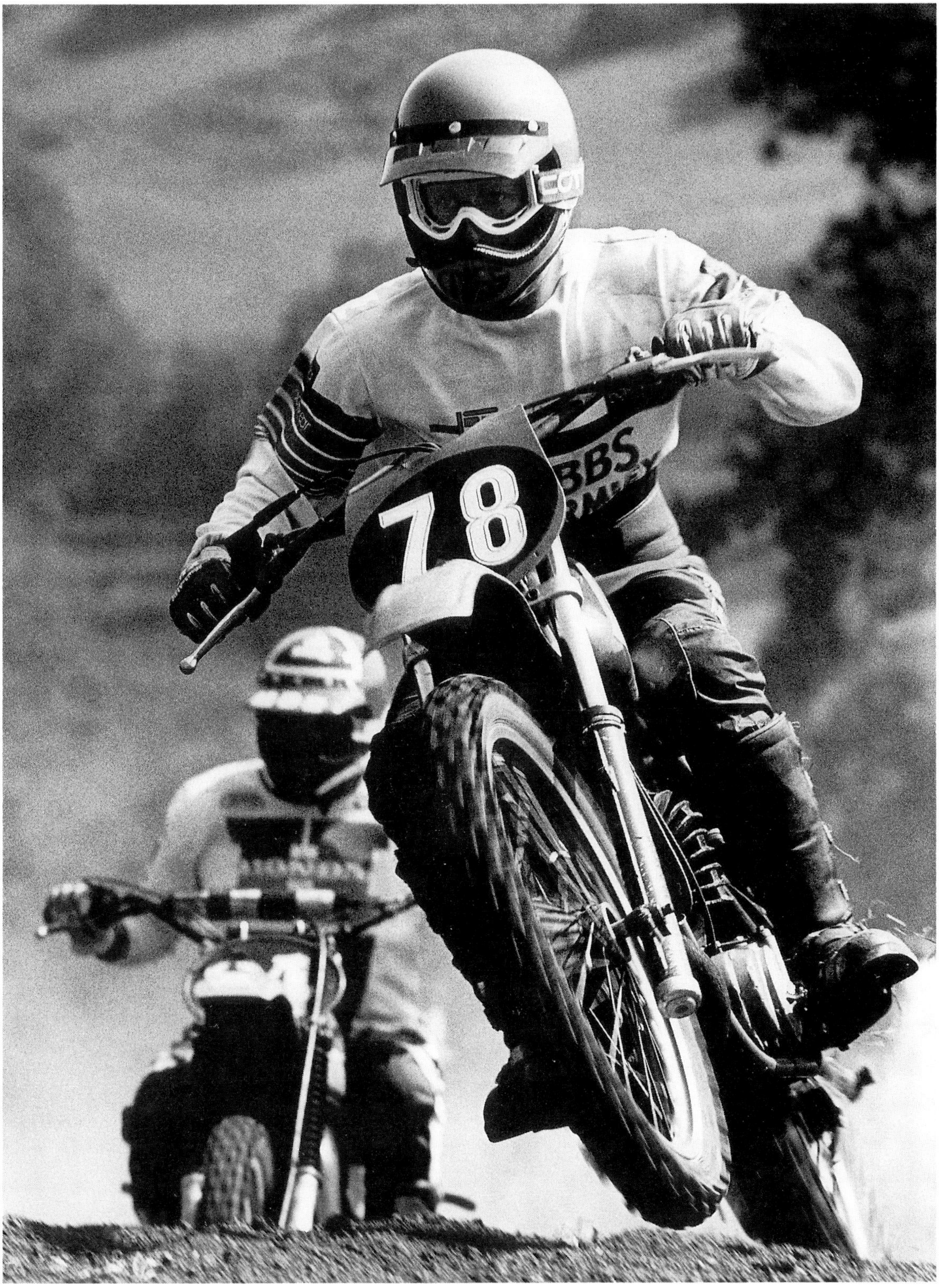
78

treme, any figure can be quoted, because there is no limit to the length of exposure you can give with any camera. So this model can claim that it meters exposures of eight hours duration. True, at a lens aperture of *f*/32. It might sound a little less impressive if expressed as 15 min. at *f*/5.6.

The real value of the hand-held meter is, of course, in its portability and ease of use. A secondary consideration is the range of attachments it can take and the uses they can be put to. Sensitivity need rarely be considered, in that all but the cheapest models have adequate sensitivity for all but the most eccentric of uses.

Incident light attachments

Most hand-held exposure meters take incident light attachments, typified by the now historic Invercone of the Weston meters. This is a shaped, translucent 'dome' or baffle covering the meter cell and allowing light to reach the cell from close to a 180-degree angle. The density of the material used is such as to reconcile the difference between reflected and incident light readings. In use, the meter is held in the subject position and pointed toward the camera. Thus, it meters the light falling on (incident upon) the subject instead of that reflected by it. The readings it gives should be accurate for all subjects, whatever the lighting, background or subject make-up, because it is influenced by none of these things. The sole criterion is the intensity of the light falling on the subject. Normally, the only adjustments necessary to an incident light reading are those dictated by the special requirements of the photographer, who may or may not want the scene to be reproduced as the eye sees it.

Spot meters

A true spot meter generally has an acceptance angle of just one degree, as opposed to the several degrees of the systems built into some 35mm SLRs and the attachments for some hand-held meters. The Minolta Spot Meter Mk II is among the more expensive models of this type, giving direct *f*-number indications with an LCD readout and a memory function. Another type (eg, the Bewi Zoom Spot) is really a semi-spot meter, providing settings to match specific ranges of long telephoto lenses, such as 250-800mm on the 35mm format.

The true spot meter is not generally used for direct exposure readings. Its particular advantage is to pick out small areas of tone in order to assess overall contrast or to assist in placing accurate lighting levels on particular areas of the subject. A single reading can provide correct exposure only if it is taken from a mid-tone. On the other hand, if the photographer wishes to vary the reproduction by raising or lowering the tonal range, it would be possible to pick out the lighter or darker tone that is to be reproduced as a mid-tone.

The fallibility of exposure meters

As pointed out in the introduction, no matter how sophisticated the design, the operation of any exposure meter is controlled by the data fed into it. In virtually all cases, that data includes the premise that everything the camera 'sees' is an average subject and that the requirement is to reproduce it as an average subject. That fact is acknowledged by the common addition of an *exposure compensation* device to inbuilt automatic exposure systems. This is frequently a dial with plus and minus settings, allowing the meter reading to be 'automatically' adjusted up to two stops either way to take account of 'non-average' subjects.

The Nikon FA and the Olympus OM4 have, admittedly, gone a little further along the road toward the 'thinking' exposure meter, with the OM4, in particular, allowing the user to do part of the thinking. But no practical electronic system can, as yet, match the well-informed human brain. Even to understand how to use the OM4 camera's metering system to full effect, the user needs to have more than a passing knowledge of exposure principles.

2 AUTOMATIC EXPOSURE SYSTEMS

There is no doubt about the value of automatic exposure systems in popularising photography. Although such systems have been with us for a great many years, the real explosion came with the 35mm compact camera. That, in turn, was the fight-back of the non-reflex camera with direct-vision viewfinder against the threatened take-over by the 35mm single-lens reflex.

Compact versus SLR

The TTL (through-the-lens) tag attached to the SLR and the consequent large, clear viewfinder image that could be focused merely by turning a ring on the lens, threatened to obliterate the traditional 35mm camera entirely. But the SLR was a rather large, clumsy apparatus at first and manufacturers of non-reflexes took to reducing the size of their cameras in self-defence. The fixed lens of the non-reflex also made it an easy matter to build in fully automatic exposure systems that made the cameras extremely reliable, even for the most inexperienced photographer. When automatic focusing devices were added, the cameras became literally 'point and shoot' instruments of very high quality. The SLR had to find a way back.

The advent of the microchip pointed the direction. SLRs had already overcome the metering disadvantage of their interchangeable lenses by fitting mechanical or electric links between lens and camera body. Tiny light-sensitive cells could be placed inside the camera to read the light passing through the lens, giving reasonably accurate readings no matter what lens or other attachment was actually fitted to the camera. For a while, the auto-exposure SLR offered more or less the same facilities as the compact, without automatic focusing. The problem with any kind of automatic exposure system, however, is that it relies on generalisations – primarily the generalisation that every subject consists of a mixture of tones averaging out to a mid-tone of a specific value.

Programmed exposure systems

As most subjects do so average out, and particularly the subjects chosen by the average hobby photographer, the relatively simple systems of both the compact and the SLR achieved a high rate of success. A development of this success was the totally auto-exposure camera, in which the meter circuit set both shutter speed and lens aperture in response to its reading of the light value and the information transmitted to it concerning the speed (or, sensitivity) of the film in the camera. Even that has now also been automated to eliminate mistakes or omissions in manual setting.

The automatic setting of both shutter speed and lens aperture is carried out according to a rigid 'program' and, not surprisingly, has become known as programmed exposure. The program links shutter speeds and apertures in the only practical way: high shutter speeds are always accompanied by small lens apertures and slower shutter speeds by larger apertures. There is an obvious disadvantage in that system if either subject movement or depth of field are important factors in the picture. It is an even greater disadvantage in those cameras that provide no information of the settings made in programmed mode.

Various ingenious devices were introduced to offset these disadvantages, but it needed the advent of the microchip and the adaptation of its

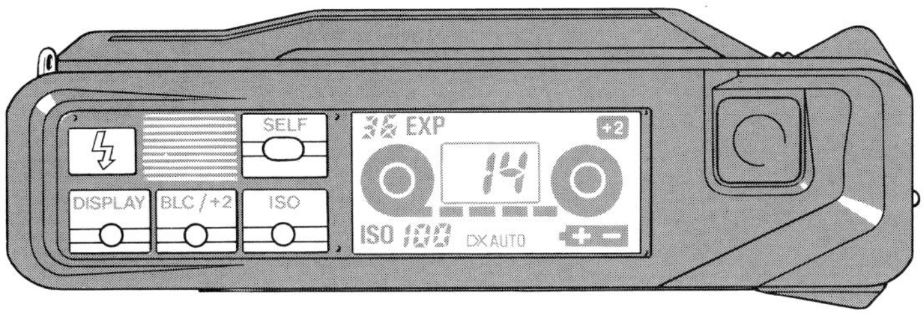

2.1 The modern 35mm compact camera commonly uses liquid crystal display (LCD) information panels and push button controls. Film transport and rewind are often motorised.

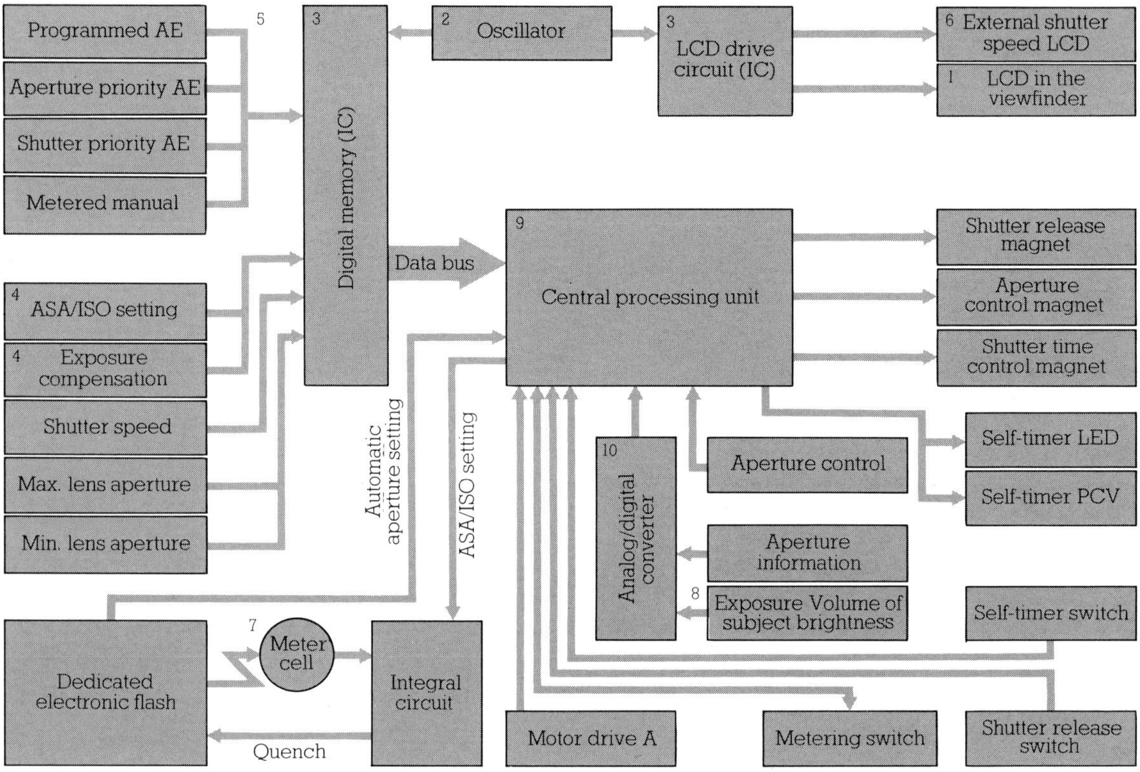

2.2 Typical circuitry of a 35mm multimode SLR camera with fully automatic control of exposure in four modes (including flash), plus manual override.

memory capacity to photographic uses to produce really workable systems. In the current state of the art, the most sophisticated cameras use not just one program but two or three or more. The simplest expansion has two settings allowing the user to select programs which maintain either a fast shutter speed (for action) or a small lens aperture (for depth of field) for as long as the light conditions and film speed allow.

Weighted meter readings

The point-and-shoot capability of programmed exposure cameras has proved useful for many types of photographer and has been by no means confined to the hobby or so-called amateur photographer. The increasing exposure latitude of all types of film (but particularly print films) has considerably reduced the effect of minor, and sometimes even major, inaccuracies. Nevertheless, no matter how sophisticated the exposure system, it has, until recently, depended entirely on the concept of an average subject, whereas users of sophisticated cameras, and those with pretensions to 'creative' (imaginative would be a better word) work, frequently encounter non-average subjects. Then, auto-exposure systems can achieve spectacular failures. The SLR had a slight advantage in this respect in that it could influence the reading by 'weighting', ie. attaching more importance to the centre parts of the picture than the outer edges. Primarily, this countered the possible undue influence on the meter reading of a large bright sky area.

In fact, the value of such weighting systems is doubtful, and they certainly do nothing to solve the problems of subjects that are totally over-light or over-dark. It seemed that nothing much could be done about that. The exposure meter is a completely brainless entity. It cannot interpret the actual nature of the subject. All it can do is follow the instructions fed into it. It is a programmed robot.

We all know, however, what robots can do, and how they can, in fact, possess a certain rudimentary 'intelligence'.

Using computer technology

This intelligence is imparted by the extensive programming carried out by a computer and, in recent years, incredibly powerful computers have been crammed into extraordinarily small 'boxes'. A 'thinking' exposure system needs only a tiny fraction of that computing power and it is possible to build it into a camera. One of the things a computer does best is to carry out conditional commands. It can be told to proceed with a given task if stated conditions apply. This is the IF . . . THEN action of the computer. It is told that IF so and so is true THEN do such and such. Another vital computer function is its ability to store masses of information, or data, in an unbelievably small space. This data is available for immediate recall and the computer is capable of comparing it or parts of it with other data and coming up with a 'true' or 'false' answer.

Thus, if the computer memory holds a store of data relating to exposure meter readings and the types of picture they represent, it can compare any new reading with its store, find a match and recommend an appropriate exposure. That is how one modern sophisticated metering system works, with the important proviso, of course, that it does not operate on a single meter reading from the whole subject area. It takes advantage of the ability of a metering system to take 'spot' readings from various different parts of the scene. It is this multiple reading that is compared with the data in the memory bank to produce an exposure recommendation. Alternatively, of course, the meter circuit can simply average out the multiple readings to arrive at its decision.

Nikon's AMP system

Both methods are used in modern SLR cameras – notably in the Nikon FA and the Olympus OM4. The Nikon FA can probably lay claim to being the nearest approach to a truly automatic exposure camera so far. It uses the computer store and comparison principle by dividing the image area into five portions – one in the centre and one occupying each large corner. Nikon call this an automatic multi-pattern (AMP) system. Metering is automatically carried out in each portion and the results are compared with similar patterns in the camera computer's memory. When a match is found, the nature of the picture is established. The overall

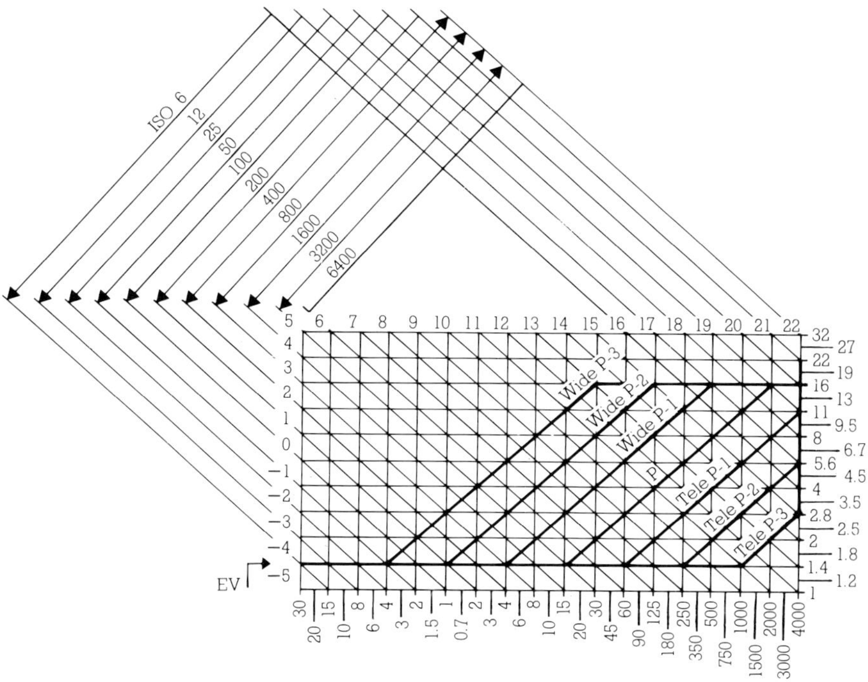

2.3 Programmed exposure. The graph illustrates the structure of a multiple program. The first rising line is a 'depth' or wide angle program, reaching the smallest aperture at the lowest possible light value. Subsequent lines, representing alternative programs, progressively maintain larger apertures and faster shutter speeds as long as possible to cope with camera or subject movement.

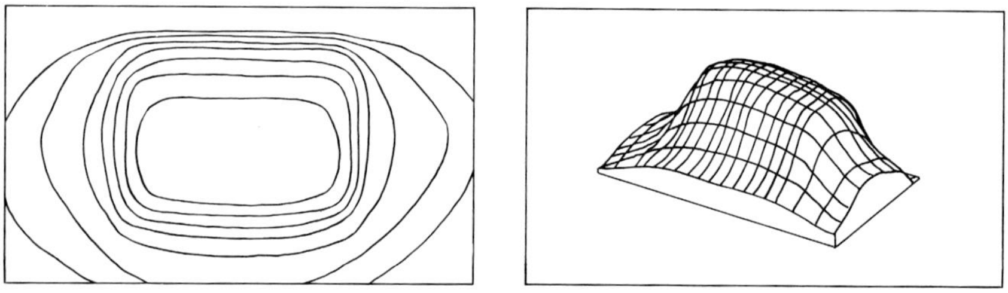

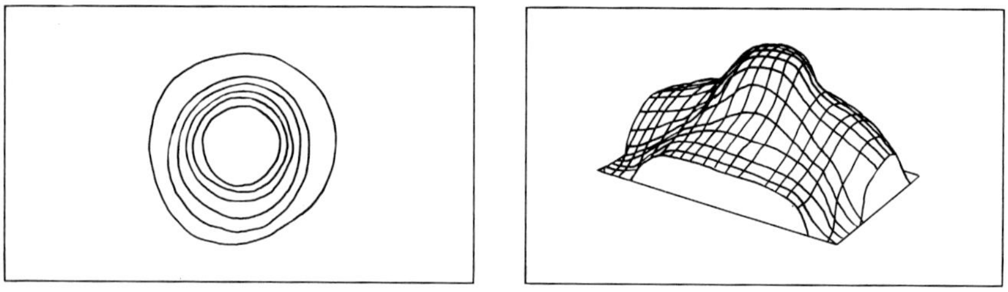

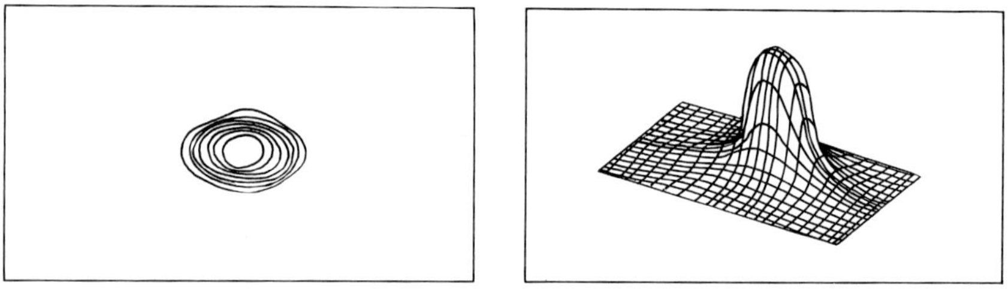

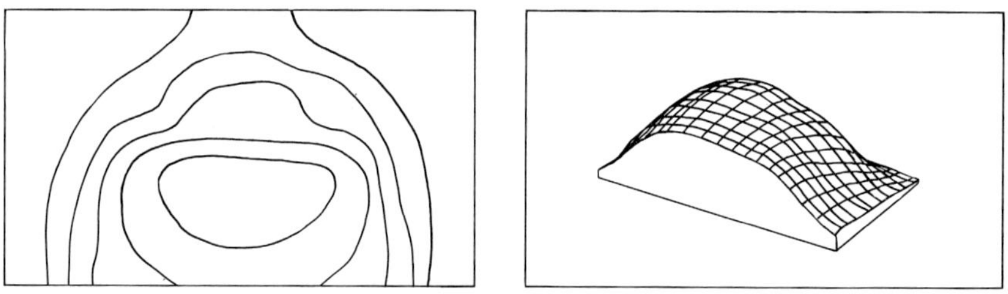

2.4 Metering patterns and three-dimensional representation. Normal centre-weighted.

2.5 Partial metering from central area.

2.6 'Spot' metering.

2.7 Metering from film surface.

3 A scene containing several elements that may be greatly affected by exposure choices: strong backlighting, moving and stationary subject, wide range of subject distances. Selecting different exposure variations or combinations of settings would result in entirely different pictorial effects in each case.

light intensity and the film speed are then taken into account to set the 'correct' exposure. It is an ingenious system and it works extremely well – in most cases. It doesn't particularly like extremes such as silhouettes and it works best in the horizontal format, carrying the same disadvantage as any centre-weighting system.

The camera is a multimode type, which means that it has several automatic exposure options. It can use 'shutter priority' metering, in which the user sets the shutter speed and the meter sets the aperture, or the more popular alternative on single mode cameras of 'aperture priority', where the user sets the aperture and the meter selects and sets a suitable shutter speed. In addition, it has two programmed exposure modes, changing automatically when suitable lenses are fitted. With lenses of longer focal length, the bias is toward faster shutter speeds. There is, of course, also a fully manual mode, which does not use the AMP system but reverts to a normal full-field centre-weighted pattern. Centre-weighted metering can also be selected for the automatic modes if required.

Multi-spot readings

The strength of the Nikon system for most subjects is that the AMP circuits are brought into play automatically: the user needs no particular knowledge of exposure principles. The Olympus OM4, on the other hand, demands more than a passing knowledge of such principles to be used to full advantage. When first switched to automatic metering, the OM4 uses normal centre-weighted metering. A separate button switch is provided to allow the change to spot metering. In this mode, the meter reading is confined to the central two per cent of the image area. Pressing a 'spot read-

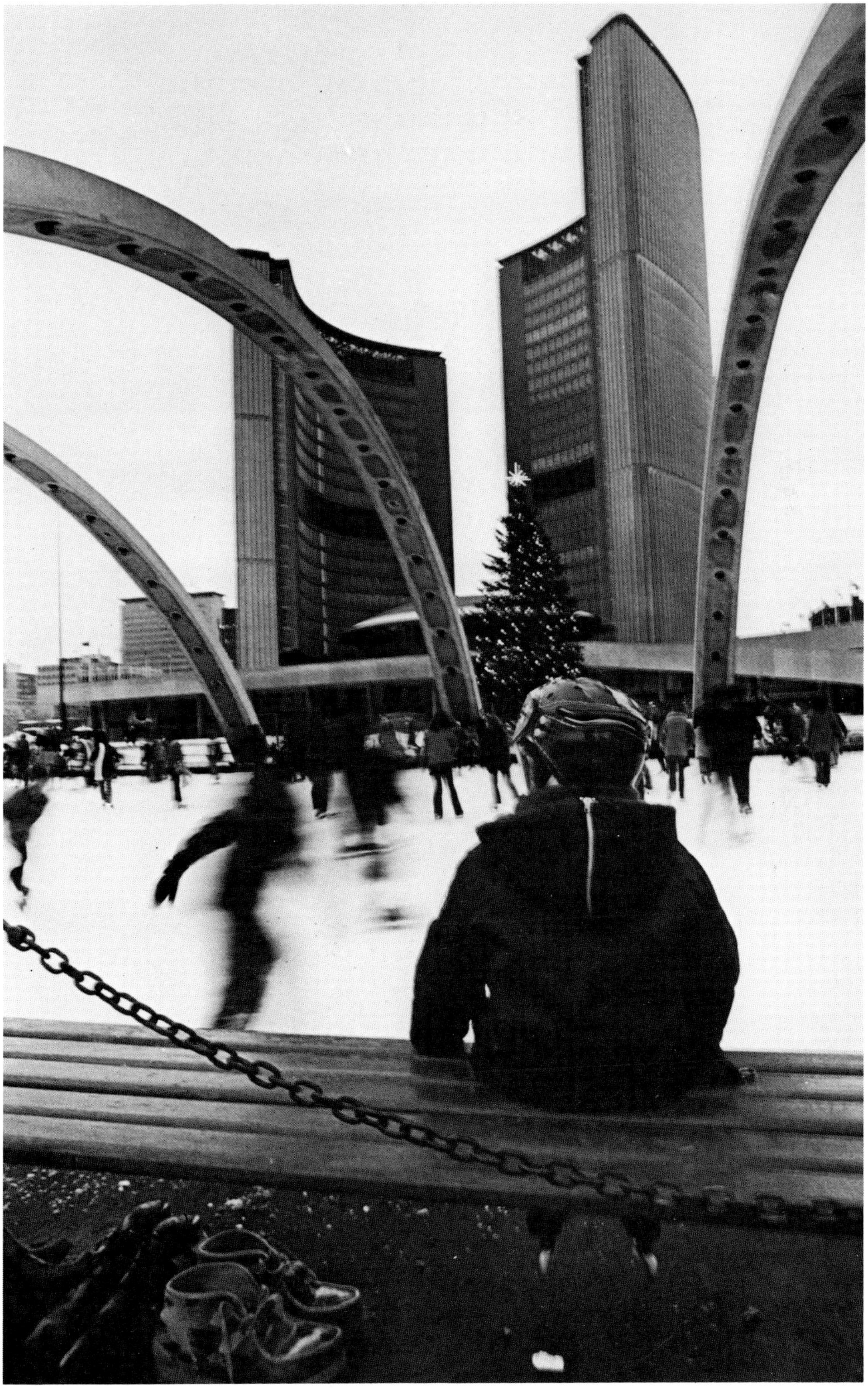

ing button' takes a reading from the area that central portion covers and stores it for about two minutes. Further readings, up to a maximum of eight, can then be taken from other areas. As each reading is taken so the metering circuit combines it with any previous readings to arrive at an exposure recommendation. Thus, the user with sufficient knowledge of exposure principles can use a series of readings to bias the exposure in any required direction.

Again, the system is ingenious but there is at least a suggestion of technological overkill. It cannot be denied that a reasonable knowledge of exposure principles is needed to use any kind of spot reading exposure meter. The amount of knowledge needed to combine several separate readings meaningfully is possessed by few people brought up on normal auto exposure systems – which is virtually anybody aged under 40 or so, depending on when they first used a camera seriously. Oddly, this ultra-modern camera and others like it should appeal far more to unprejudiced 'old-timers', who *had* to learn how to use hand-held exposure meters.

Another technological miracle camera that has found favour with knowledgeable photographers is the quite extraordinary Canon T90. With an unbelievable number of exposure modes, including seven programs, it also uses a spot metering mode that will average out up to eight readings.

So, as every year passes and as microchip technology is increasingly adapted to photographic use, exposure systems in cameras come nearer to the ideal of accurate automatic exposure. With the exception of the Nikon FA, however, and any other camera that might adopt a similar system, such cameras are demanding more and more knowledge of basic principles from the user. In truth, automatic is an odd word to apply to systems that require an ever greater manual input before they can come up with their 'automatic readings. You simply cannot use the full potential of these cameras without already knowing or subsequently acquiring much more than a passing knowledge of what exposure really means.

Battery power

Virtually all exposure metering systems built into cameras require battery power because the rather weak signals generated by their light-sensitive elements have to be passed through an amplifier circuit. Beyond that, however, the more complicated systems use electronic circuits that also need power. Many cameras also have electrical or electro-magnetic shutter release mechanisms and there is an increasing tendency to build automatic film advance and rewinding into the camera. In fact, the majority of 35mm SLRs are now totally inoperative without their batteries, even if only because their shutter releases are electric.

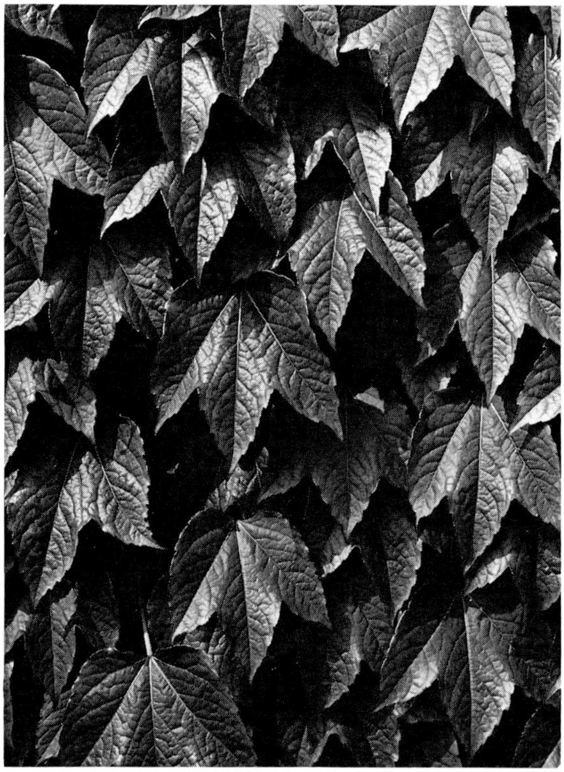

4 Subjects that fill the picture area with evenly distributed tones are ideally suited to all forms of automatic metering. The amount of shadow detail recorded on the negative or slide may be varied with exposure override adjustments.

Whether this is a desirable development or not is immaterial. The sophisticated circuitry cannot work without a source of power.

What does give cause for concern is the voracious appetite for batteries of badly designed circuits and the inability of circuits designed down to a price to survive variations in current. Fortunately, most cameras are now conceived with economic power consumption in mind and battery design has simultaneously improved to allow greater capacity in a given size.

On the other hand, such are the marketing ar-

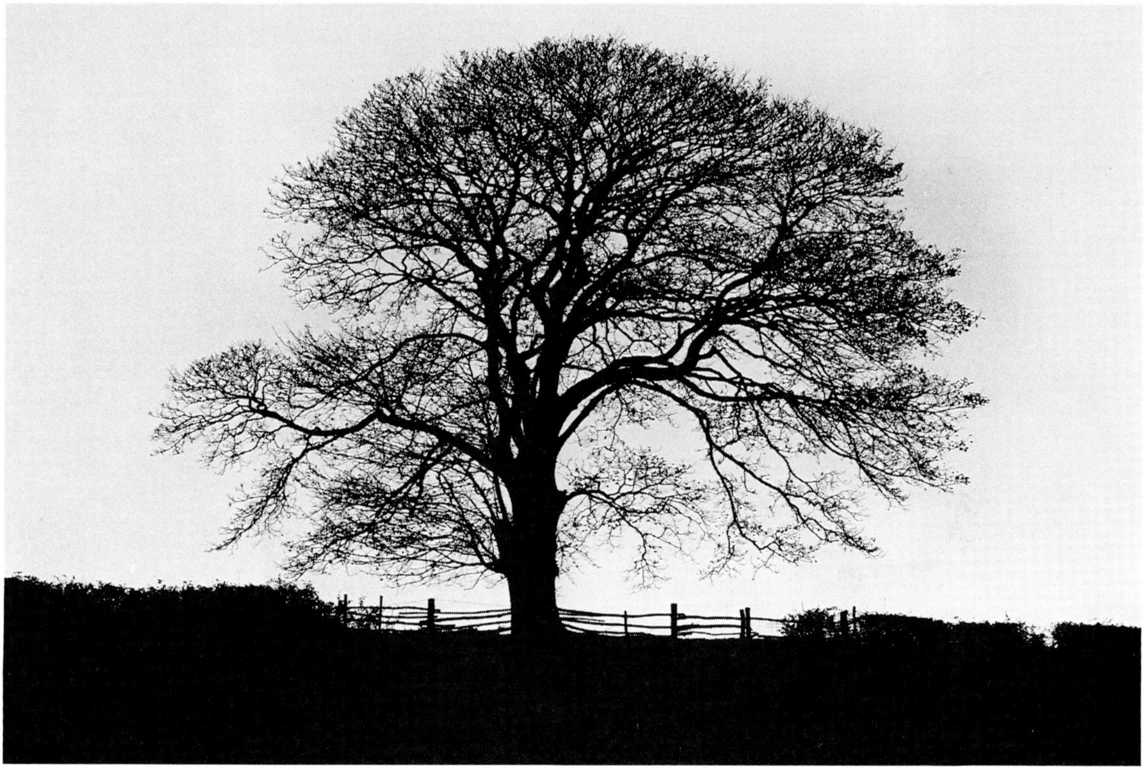

5 The opposite extreme is a subject with a bright, though detailless background. The auto meter cannot differentiate between the components and simply sets the average brightness, in this case rendering the subject itself simply as a silhouette.

rangements for many types of battery that the purchaser has little idea how old the battery is when he purchases it. The 'Best Before' inscription now used for so many other products has not been received favourably by the battery trade, almost certainly because many of their products do not reach the shops for many months after production. It is vital, therefore, that camera users buy their batteries from a reliable source known to have a reasonably rapid turnover.

These strictures apply particularly to the small silver oxide button cells and the increasingly used manganese alkaline long life AAA and AA types. Ordinary zinc-carbon batteries should never be used in photographic equipment. Their life is short and they are prone to leakage on exhaustion, which could irreparably damage the electrical contacts.

There is an increasing tendency in some types of camera – particularly 35mm compacts – to use the newer lithium batteries, which are claimed to have a shelf life of about five years and can give very rapid recycling times for small, built-in flash units. Nevertheless, it is wise to consult the manufacturer's instructions before using lithium batteries because, with some circuits, they can produce a current surge that may prevent the metering system working correctly and may even damage it.

Much the same sort of thing is said about rechargeable nickel cadmium (nicad) batteries. These are often used as replacements for manganese alkaline AA and AAA batteries. They give only an output of 1.2 volts per cell against the 1.5 volts of the alkaline types but that is no real problem. Alkaline batteries soon drop to near that level in use.

The problem with nicads is that they can deliver quite a surge of current if the components used have a low tolerance.

It is always wise to use only the batteries specified by the equipment manufacturer. Recommended alternatives are normally quoted. If the type of battery you propose to use is not on the list, check first with the manufacturer or distributor of the equipment.

3 EXPOSURE AND TONAL RANGE

The process of exposure consists of exposing the film to light. Correct exposure requires something more particular than that. The idea is to reproduce on the film as many of the tones of the subject as possible with the correct spacing or gradations between them. The generally accepted basis for assessing correct exposure is to allow just enough light on to the film to reproduce a mid-tone in the subject as a mid-tone on the film.

That seems reasonable enough, but what is a mid-tone? There again, the convention has been established that a mid-tone is a tone that reflects 18 per cent of the light falling on it. Accordingly, there are commercially produced 'grey cards' that do just that. A reading taken from such a grey card, placed in the same light as the subject, will recommend camera settings to reproduce that mid-tone correctly. Normal photographic films are made in such a way that, if the mid-tone reproduces correctly, all other tones in the subject will fall into place and also be reproduced correctly. There is the proviso that the tonal range of the subject must be within the capability of the film, but we shall come to that later.

Ansel Adams' Zone System

Exposure (and, indeed, photography itself) is all about tones and brightnesses – and colours, too, with the right type of film. Around 40 years ago, Ansel Adams translated tones into zones and introduced his Zone System. The system is based on the recognition of a range of tones in the subject, followed by the calculation of an exposure level that will reproduce the tones 'correctly' or, quite frequently, in the way that the photographer wants them to reproduce. By assigning numbers to each individual tone, Adams could identify a particular tone in his subject, take a meter reading from it and assess the exposure he required from that reading.

The method relies on the fact that an exposure meter reading of any tone will recommend an exposure to reproduce that tone as a mid-tone. If it is not to reproduce as a mid-tone, then the exposure is adjusted by the required number of steps to bring it to the tone required. Adams' system went much further than that. It also encompassed the processing of the film, to allow the tonal range to be extended or compressed. Essentially, it dealt with each subject separately and demanded the use of sheet film. It cannot be operated satisfactorily with rollfilm. It also demanded a rather leisurely approach to photography and meticulous note-taking. As this book is principally for those who treat photography as a pleasurable hobby, few readers will be prepared to make the exhaustive tests or keep the extensive records that Adams' system demands.

Nevertheless, it is possible for any photographer to use part of Adams' system, and much of this book is based on his ideas of tone visualisation. He was not alone, of course, in pointing out that both the subject and the photograph consist of a collection of tones. How many discrete tones there are in the original and how many can be reproduced in the photographic image is largely irrelevant. For normal pictorial work, the idea is to reproduce as exactly as possible the tones of the original. The fact that we can usually appear to record them all is a tribute to the photographic process, despite all its well-publicised limitations.

Limitations of the photographic process

Perhaps the most often quoted limitation is that a black-and-white paper print has a tonal range of only 1:50 or 1:60 (less for non-glossy prints). This is considered very restrictive, yet how many of us can say that we have been frustrated by the fact that the paper is incapable of bringing out the full quality of our perfectly-exposed negative? Many may well find it difficult to make a good print from a given negative, but the fault generally lies in the original camera exposure, not the paper.

Most photographic subjects have a tonal range no greater than about 1:100. If you do not believe this, try it! Take your hand-held meter to your favourite subject and measure the darkest shadow area and the brightest highlight in which you would want to see detail in the print. (If you do not have a hand-held meter, you would be well advised to get one. There are so many occasions when a through the lens (TTL) meter is just too clumsy to use. There is no need to spend the earth on a separate meter: a good selenium type is perfectly adequate and needs no battery.)

A typical 'amateur' film can handle a range of

6 Extremes of tonal range: Sun in the picture. This exposure 'problem' does, however, allow scope for creative variations – altering the effect by changing the exposure given.

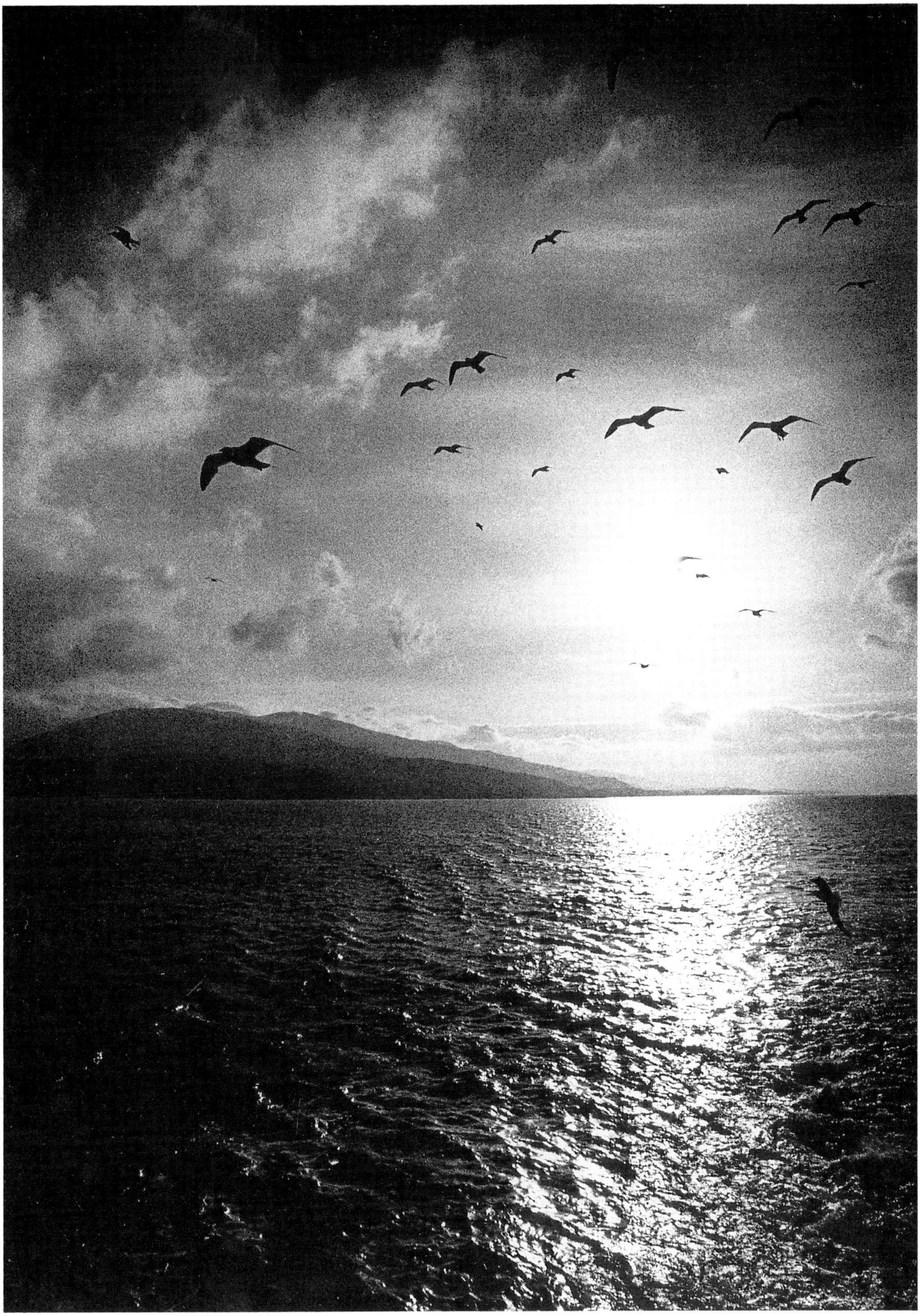

tones in the subject of 1:200 or more. Of course, a subject can have a much greater tonal range than this, but such subjects are by no means as common as you might think. When they do occur, there are special treatments that can help cope with them. Of all the problems facing the photographer, the unlikeliest is that of running across a subject that his film cannot handle. His real problem is to learn how to get those tones on to the film. In most cases, this is a question of getting the camera exposure right.

Tonal representation

A very useful way to approach this problem is to follow Ansel Adams' idea of envisaging the tones of the subject in ten steps. Those given here are not Adams' precise groupings, but they are broadly similar, and are more appropriate to the aims of this book:

1 *Total black.* Openings into dark areas (windows, doorways, arches, etc.) shot from brilliantly lit areas. Deepest shadows. Any dark area in which no detail is expected to show.
2 *Darkest tone.* Deep shadow with some tone but no detail. Some distortion (errors in hues) likely with colour film.
3 *Darkest detail.* First sign of detail in dark area. Black fur texture. Detail in black ironwork, clothing, wood, etc.

7 Few prints achieve the darkest black or the emptiest white. The numbered tones on the grey scale correspond approximately with the numbered tones on the print and in the text.

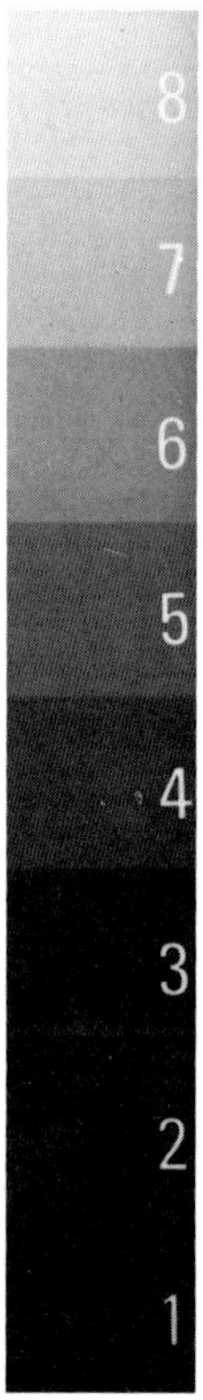

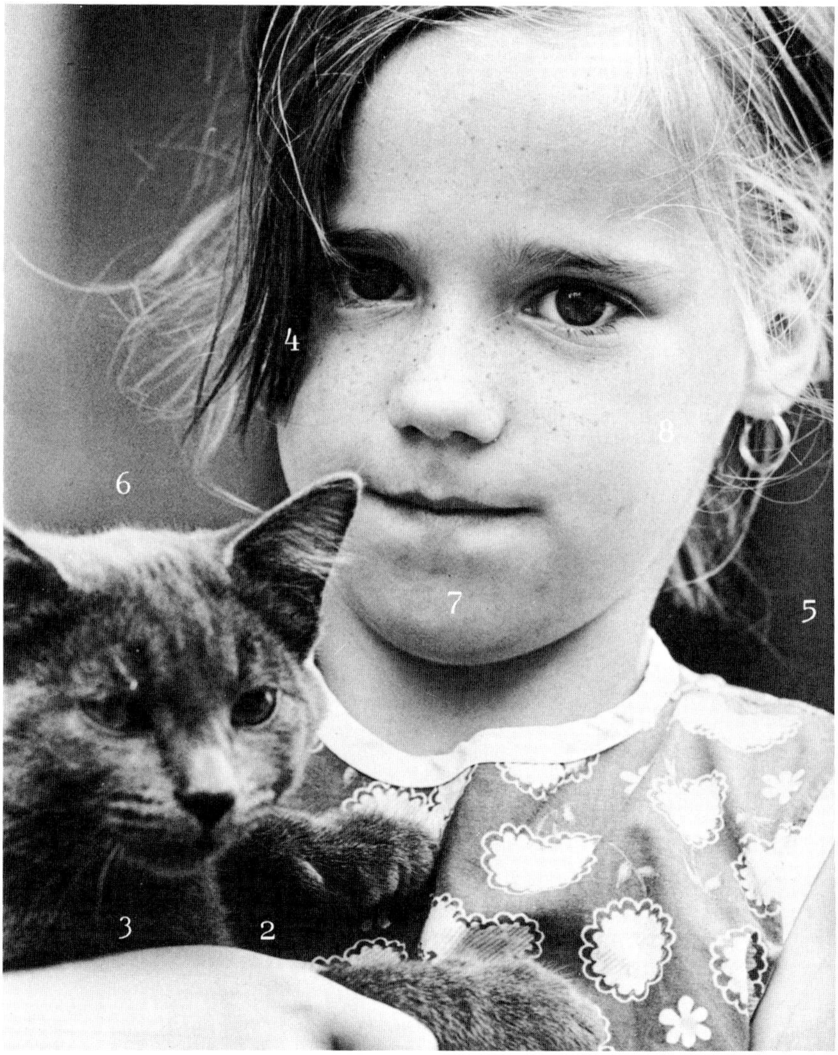

4 *Less than black.* Average dark tones of clothing, hair, tree bark, etc. Dark foliage.
5 *Normal shadow.* Average depth of shadow from sun in clear sky. Normal foliage. Very sunburnt or dark skin. Green grass in wet conditions.
6 *Mid-tone.* Standard tone of 18 per cent reflectance. Average shadow value in sun plus cloud. Average sunburnt or darkish skin. Red brick. Green grass in dry conditions.
7 *Flesh tone.* Normal Caucasian skin tone. Deep blue sky. Stone or light brick buildings.
8 *Lightest grey.* Silvery, pale yellow, green and cream tones. Last sign of colour for colour films. Very pale skin. Snow in shade. Typescript on white paper.
9 *Highlight detail.* White with slight detail. Embroidered table linen, bridal dress, etc.
10 *Blank highlight.* Strong light sources or specular reflections. Fully lit white backgrounds.

These are, approximately, the tones that should appear in the final image, representing recognizable tones in the subject. Check them for yourself, using a reliable meter and a standard grey card (obtainable from photographic dealers) for comparison. You can, of course, add to this list and even extend it to half-steps if you feel you can work that way. Ten steps such as these, however, are reasonably easy to remember. In a difficult situation, you will be able to recall that, on the average sunny day, ground shadows in open areas should be about equal to a mid-tone reading. Alternatively, direct measurement of a deep blue sky should give you about one stop less than a mid-tone reading.

The principle of this listing is that each tone is approximately one exposure step (or stop) from its neighbour. Within this range, the average film can reproduce these tones proportionately. In other words, if one of these tones is reproduced correctly, all the other tones will fall naturally into place. To explain this, we need to go briefly (and with the minimum of technicalities) into the real meaning of exposure and the nature of the characteristic curve.

Exposure as a multiple action

The subject is recorded on the film by the action of light passing through a lens. The lens forms an image of the subject on the film surface, and as that image consists of various intensities of light reflected from myriad points in the subject, it produces different effects in the various areas of the film. Thus, an exposure of, say, 1/125 sec at *f*/8 does not mean that the entire surface of the film receives one specific dose of light. It receives a whole range of exposures (in terms of light) varying over the image area according to the amount of light reflected by each point in the subject. This is the root of the exposure problem. Look at it like that and things become clearer.

The characteristic curve

The camera does not react in the same way as the eye. Unlike the eye, the lens diaphragm does not vary its aperture as it scans dark and light areas – at least, not in a single photograph. The various intensities of light transmitted by the lens are in a fixed proportion that cannot be varied during the fixed time of exposure. A tone corresponding to Tone 6 in our list has just about twice the intensity of Tone 5. If the tonal range of the subject is within the tonal recording capability of the film, and if you give the correct exposure, the relationships between the tones of the photo-

3.1 Simplified representation of characteristic curve. In the toe and shoulder areas, additional increments of exposure build density slowly. In the straight-line area, density is proportional to exposure. The ideal general purpose film has a long straight line portion.

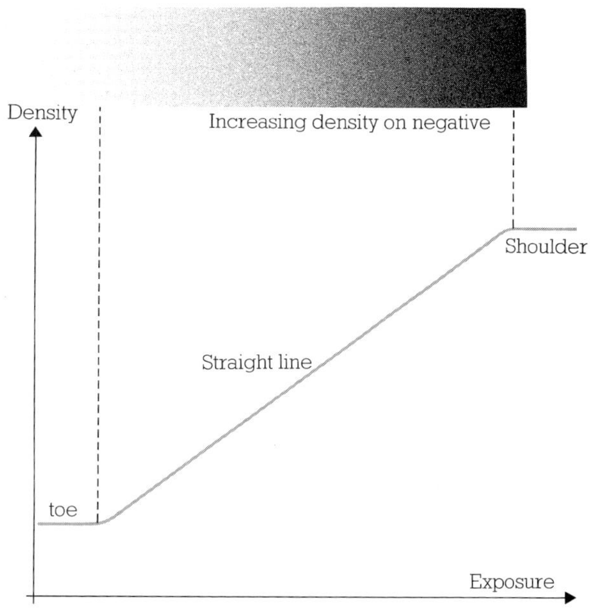

graphic image will be consistent with those between the tones of the subject.

The immutability of this composite exposure is imposed by the nature of the film material. The light-sensitive coating on the film reacts to light in a certain way. A given intensity and duration of light produces a given blackening of the film. If you vary either the intensity (lens aperture) or duration (shutter speed) of the exposure, the extent of the blackening will vary in proportion. The relationship is so predictable that a graph can be constructed, plotting the degree of blackening against the exposure. Such a graph is called the characteristic curve of the film. It is a curve and not a straight line because the proportional relationship between blackening and exposure does not extend to the lowest or the highest light intensities. It flattens out into a *shoulder* region at the top and levels off into a *toe* region at the bottom. Between these two limits, however, most films have a reasonably linear (*straight line*) portion.

Thus, the characteristic curve is basically a line progressing diagonally across the graph, low exposures on the left giving low densities on the film and high exposures on the right giving high densities on the film. The shallower the slope of the *straight line portion* of the curve the longer the range of different tones that can be accommodated on the film. The steeper the slope, the shorter the range of tones. A short range means high contrast, as the middle tones are compressed. A long range means lower contrast, with a full range of middle tones. So the slope of the line indicates the contrast characteristics of the film. As already implied, the average film has relatively low contrast and can produce densities corresponding to about 1:200 or so in the subject tones.

How exposure calculations are made

Now we begin to see why automatic-exposure cameras are so successful. The average subject fits easily into a 1:200 ratio. It might have a longer range of tones if you were to measure the extreme highlights and deepest shadows, but you do not usually expect to see detail in those areas, especially when they are relatively small. So variations of exposure simply produce greater or lesser density in each tone. The relationship between the tones is preserved and the negative is quite printable. That applies equally to black and white and to colour negatives and, to a limited extent, to colour slides. As there is no printing stage with colour slides, variations in colour rendering may occur if the middle tone exposure is moved too far from its correct position on the characteristic curve. The ability of a film to cope with variations in exposure is known as its *exposure latitude*. It is

3.2 The image is formed by innumerable focused beams carrying different intensities of light to different areas of the film.

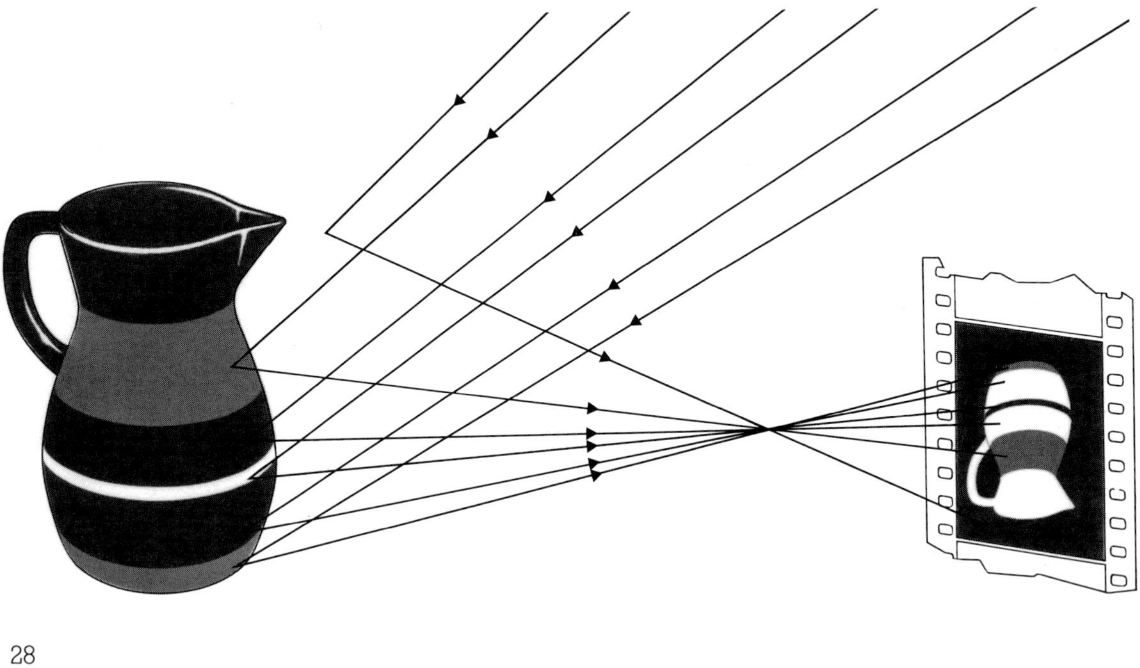

this characteristic that allows auto-exposure cameras to work so successfully. Even quite drastic errors in exposure can still produce printable negatives. The simplest models of these cameras, however, are not well suited to the production of good quality colour slides.

Principle of the exposure meter

The essence of exposure calculation now begins to emerge. All you have to do is to ensure that one important tone is reproduced correctly on your film. Provided that the film has a reasonable exposure latitude (and all popular films do), all other tones then fall naturally into place. Exposure meters work on the principle that the important tone is a mid-tone of about 18 per cent reflectance. You can point the meter at such a tone in the subject, or at an artificial one such as a standard grey card, or at a reasonable approximation such as the back of your hand (check this, though: not all skin colours are the same), or you can point the meter more generally at the subject.

The principle by which a general reading is taken from the whole subject area is that nearly all subjects average out, or *integrate* to a mid-tone. If all the various intensities of light reflected from the average subject were scrambled, the resulting tone would be a mid-tone with 18 per cent reflectance. So a straightforward general reading gives you camera settings that will place the mid-tone in its correct position on the characteristic curve, leaving all other tones to fall into place of their own accord.

For most ordinary day-to-day photography, it really is as easy as that. If it were not, exposure meters, not to mention auto-exposure cameras, would be useless. An overall reading of an 'average' subject will always give a satisfactory exposure. In such cases, you can forget about exposure problems and concentrate on the focusing, framing, composition and impact of your pictures. That is the true value of the auto-exposure camera for any user.

Exposure for effect

Sooner or later, however, many photographers feel that they would like to put just a little bit more into their pictures. A child swinging high makes a pleasant picture with the sun coming from behind the camera or a little to one side. But suppose you shot straight into the sun, waiting until the child's body passed across it? What kind of exposure does that need? Obviously, a 'straight' reading will not do. It would indicate a rather short exposure because of the high intensity of light from the bright sky. The result would probably be a very thin negative with little or no density in the figure and only average density in the sky area. It would be unprintable, because the exposure for the child himself would be so far down the characteristic curve as to be within the toe region, where different exposure levels produce only slight variations in density.

You have to decide how you want a particular tone in the subject to reproduce. Let us suppose that you want a reasonable amount of tone in the sky so that the sun's rays can be seen creeping around the figure. You might meter the sky away from the sun and decide that a mid-tone was about the best compromise. The meter is calibrated to reproduce any tone it sees as a mid-tone, so you would then give the exposure recommended by the sky reading.

In effect, this places the sky tone lower on the characteristic curve than it would be in a normal picture, so, accordingly, all other tones are placed correspondingly lower. The child's face and clothing, the swing supports and all other parts of the picture appear much darker than normal on the print, some areas probably approaching solid, detailless black. There would be some tone in the sky, however, and the exposure should be short enough to prevent the sun and sky from burning out to a blank white, which they might well do if you had taken your meter reading from a mid-tone, or had used an auto-exposure camera.

That is just one example of how you might want to vary your exposure to take a different picture. At the other extreme, you might wish to shoot at night by street lighting, moonlight or even floodlights. There, you could have great extremes of contrast. Indeed, any two photographers might have diametrically opposed ideas about how the final image should look. One might want the moonlight shot to look brilliant, the other to produce a substantially dark image with highlights here and there. Another again might well wish to change the whole tonal representation of the subject to produce a composition of lines and masses. There are as many possibilities as there are individuals.

There are also opportunities in other directions. You do not have to work with natural light. You can modify it with filters and thus change its effect on the film. You can vary the film processing. All we have said so far on the reaction of film to light, its contrast characteristics, etc., depend on standard processing conditions. Vary the processing conditions and those characteristics vary too. Having processed the film, further possibilities arise when you make the print.

Whatever your aim, however, the first thing is to get the exposure right on the film. Ansel Adams' tone visualisation ideas are a useful starting point; but you must couple them with a clear idea of what you are aiming at. You not only want to recognize the tones in the subject but to know how you want them to reproduce on the print. And you have to consider whether this will mean adjusting film processing, printing on a different grade of paper, using specialised printing techniques, or otherwise modifying normal procedure. All those have to be taken into consideration in assessing the camera exposure.

Colour film limitations

If you work with colour slide film, the opportunities for departing from the 'norm' are much more limited. Generally speaking, your exposure has to be very accurate for a truly representational image. There is very little adjustment you can make after the camera exposure. Slight variations in contrast and apparent film sensitivity can be made by adjusting the first development time. The faster colour films can be uprated for low light work, but there may be unpredictable changes in both colour balance and contrast.

Colour print film is more tolerant. It has extraordinarily wide exposure latitude, provided that the tonal range of the subject is not excessive. Here again, however, opportunities for manipulation after the camera exposure are limited. Overall colour casts can be removed by filtration at the printing stage, but little can be done about contrast. Uprating is rarely successful.

8 Exposure based on backlight. This causes loss of shadow detail and produces a silhouette effect.

9 Two stops more exposure gives more detail in shadow areas.

10 Deliberate underexposure for effect. The background could be pegged on tone 1 or 2 to ensure isolation of the chair and development increased to maintain contrast.

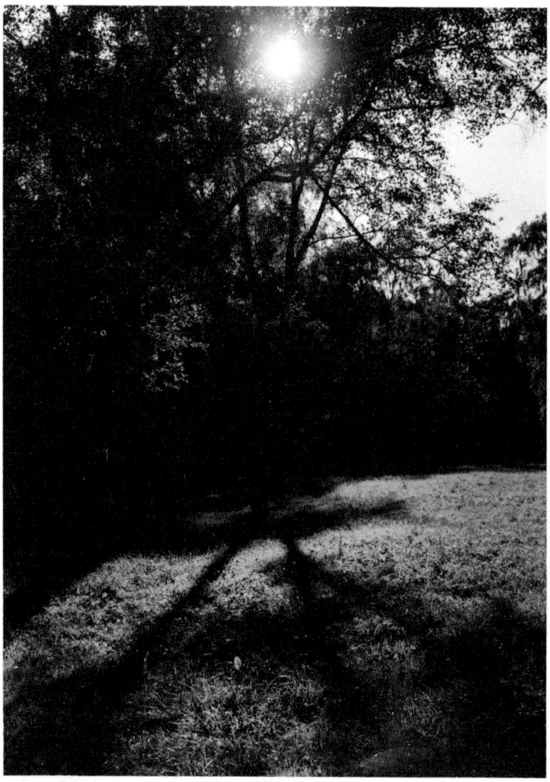

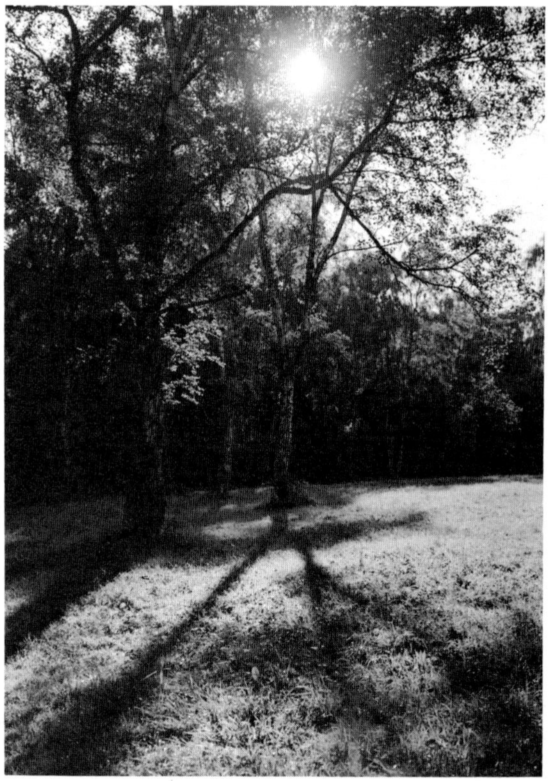

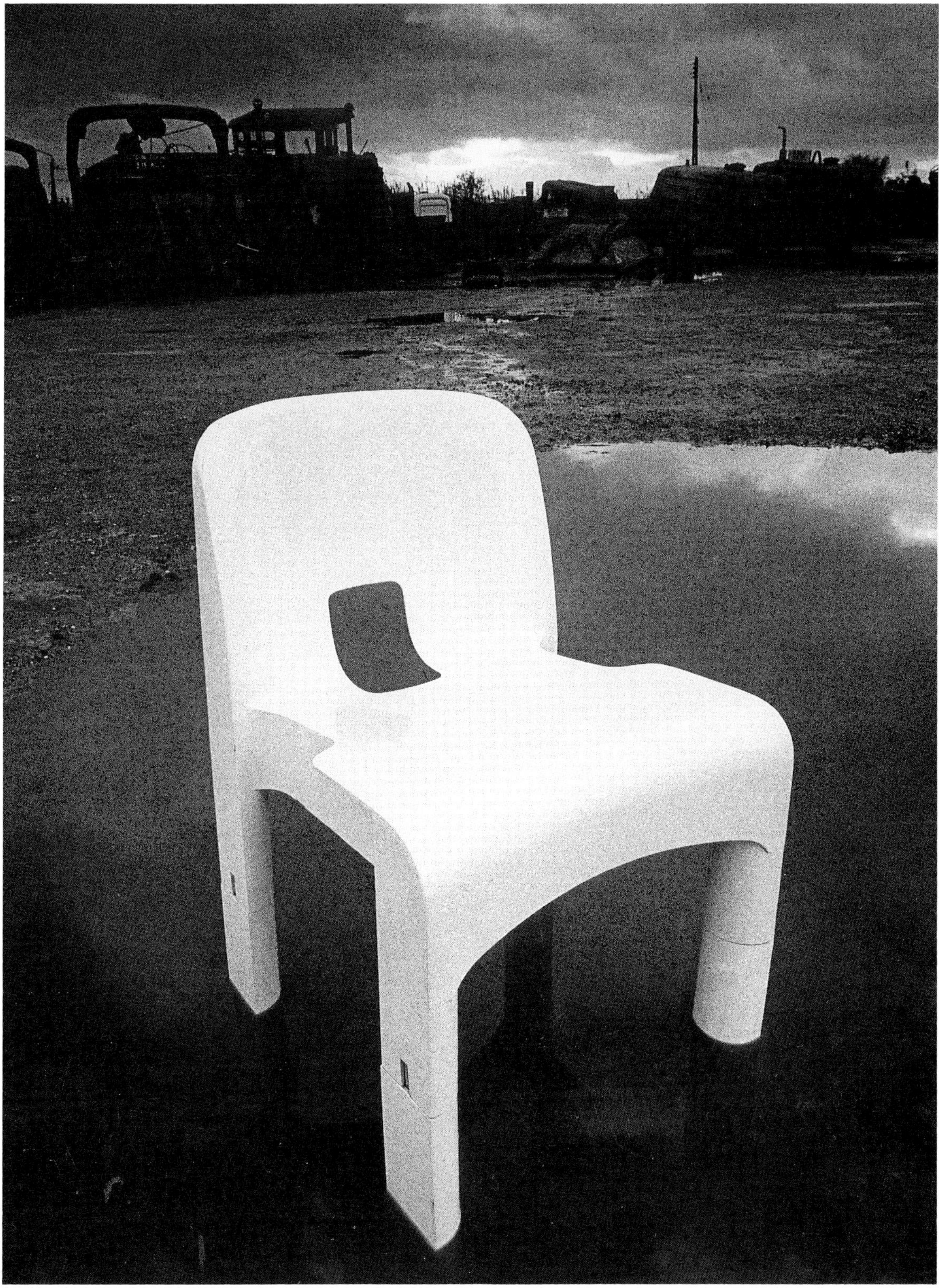

4 NON-AVERAGE SUBJECTS

Exposure is no problem with the majority of photographic subjects. An exposure meter or an auto-exposure camera provides camera settings that reproduce most scenes to perfection. It is only the unusual, or non-average subject that could run you into trouble. 'Subject', in this case, means not just the actual landscape, figure, street scene, etc., but its lighting, tonal range, surroundings and, most important, the representation of it that you want your image to convey.

Integration to grey

Most photographic subjects fall into the 'average' category. Large quantities of film are expended every summer on photographs of buildings, monuments, country cottages, ploughed and unploughed fields, mountains, beach scenes, fairgrounds, faces and figures. As we have seen, such subjects are generally perfectly suited to auto-exposure cameras or straightforward exposure meter readings of the whole scene. They consist of a variety of tones which, if they were scrambled together, would integrate to a mid-tone very close to the generally accepted standard.

Every material reflects some light, however little – nothing but a black hole is totally non-reflecting – though no material reflects 100 per cent of the light falling on it. White matt paper approaches the maximum, reflecting some 90 per cent of the incident light. We say matt paper, because we are concerned with diffuse reflection as opposed to specular (direct) reflection from the surfaces of shiny materials such as glass, water, coatings of polish or varnish, which are too unpredictable to handle as a standard. Few materials in nature, however, reflect as much light as white paper. The average reflectance is taken as about 18 per cent.

A standard mid-tone is provided by a grey card produced specifically for the purpose and available from photographic dealers. You can, of course, make up your own from substitute materials, provided you check it against a standard card but be sure that it has a matt surface. Glossy surfaces cause the specular reflections just referred to and these are totally unrelated to the tone of the card. The standard grey card is normally supplied in packs of two, each measuring 20 x 25cm (8 x 10in). One side is grey and reflects 18 per cent of the light falling on it while the other is white and reflects 90 per cent. The white side can be used when the light is too low to give a reading from the grey side. The reading should then be multiplied by a factor of 5 for correct exposure. Usually, an increase of two stops is adequate.

An average subject should give approximately the same reading as a standard grey card in the same lighting conditions. A subject can 'integrate

4.1 The standard grey card has a grey side reflecting about 18% of the light falling on it. The white side reflects about 90%. The white side can be used in low light and the indicated exposure multiplied by 5.

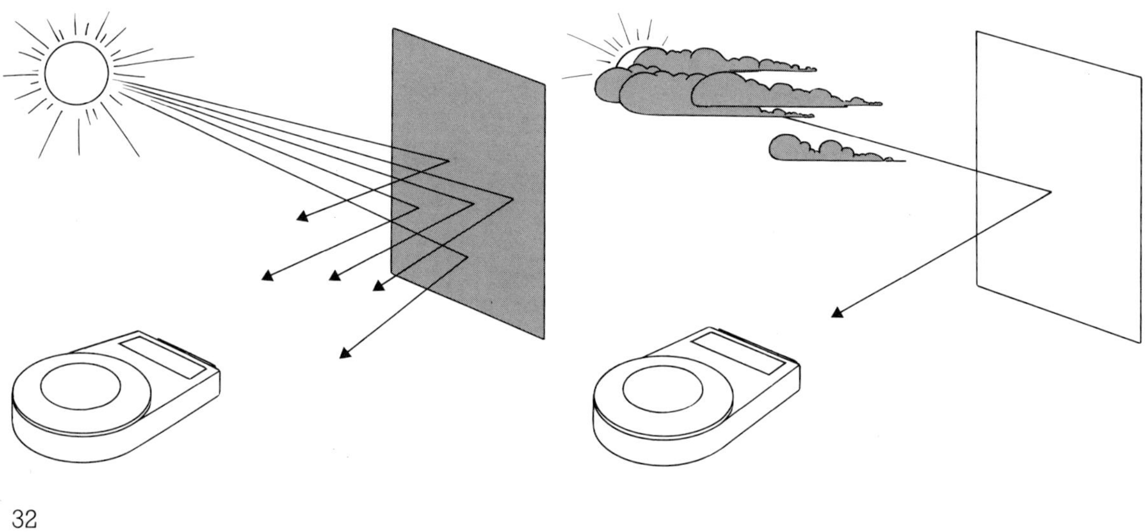

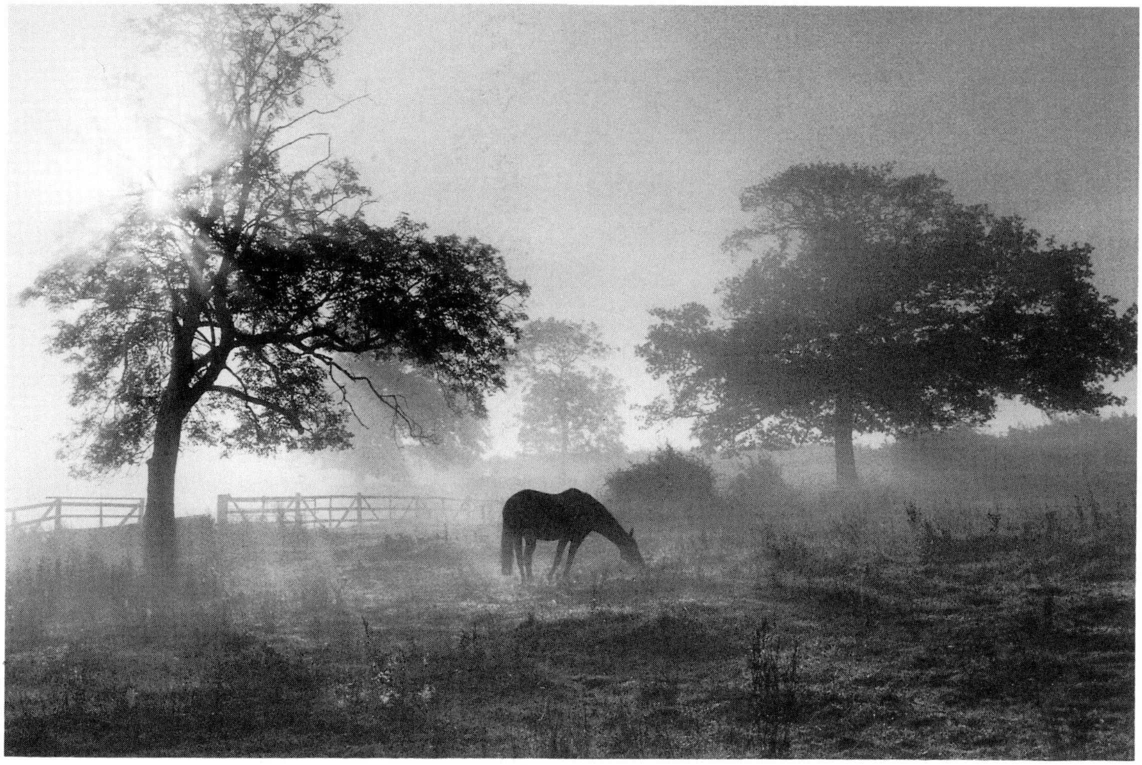

11 One of the most difficult exposure problems. Shooting into the sun and avoiding a total silhouette. A grey-card reading of 2 to 3 stops more than the meter indicates is a likely solution.

to grey', however, without being average. A pure black and white chessboard should integrate to grey. So should a landscape with dark foliage, bright cornfields, green grass, a few small white buildings and a bright, slightly cloudy sky. Likewise, a well-lit portrait of a model with fair skin, mid-brown hair and moderately dark clothing against a light background that does not occupy more than about a third of the picture area.

Contrast and tonal range

The chessboard is a high contrast subject. In the sense that it has a wide spacing between its lightest and darkest tones, so is the landscape. The portrait would seem to have a short range of tones, ie, relatively low contrast, certainly when compared with the chessboard. The portrait also seems to have a shorter scale than the landscape. But has it? If you look at the portrait, you see the darkest part as the hair or perhaps some part of the clothing. The lightest part is, perhaps, the face or the background. But what about the eyes, teeth, even the inside of the mouth if the lips are parted? There should be both deep black and almost pure white in those features. These areas might be very small, but they are important.

A long-scale subject needs careful exposure calculation. You cannot afford to stray far from the optimum, mid-tone based exposure, without losing detail in either the shadow or highlight areas. If you treat the portrait as a short-scale subject and calculate that you can therefore reduce the exposure to keep the graininess down or to produce more saturated colour, you may well show your model with a lack of sparkle in the eyes or with dingy looking teeth.

The true short-scale subject has virtually no highlights or deep shadows. A misty or foggy scene is an example: so are some industrial subjects, such as hardware, machinery, textiles, etc. illuminated specifically to show every feature in

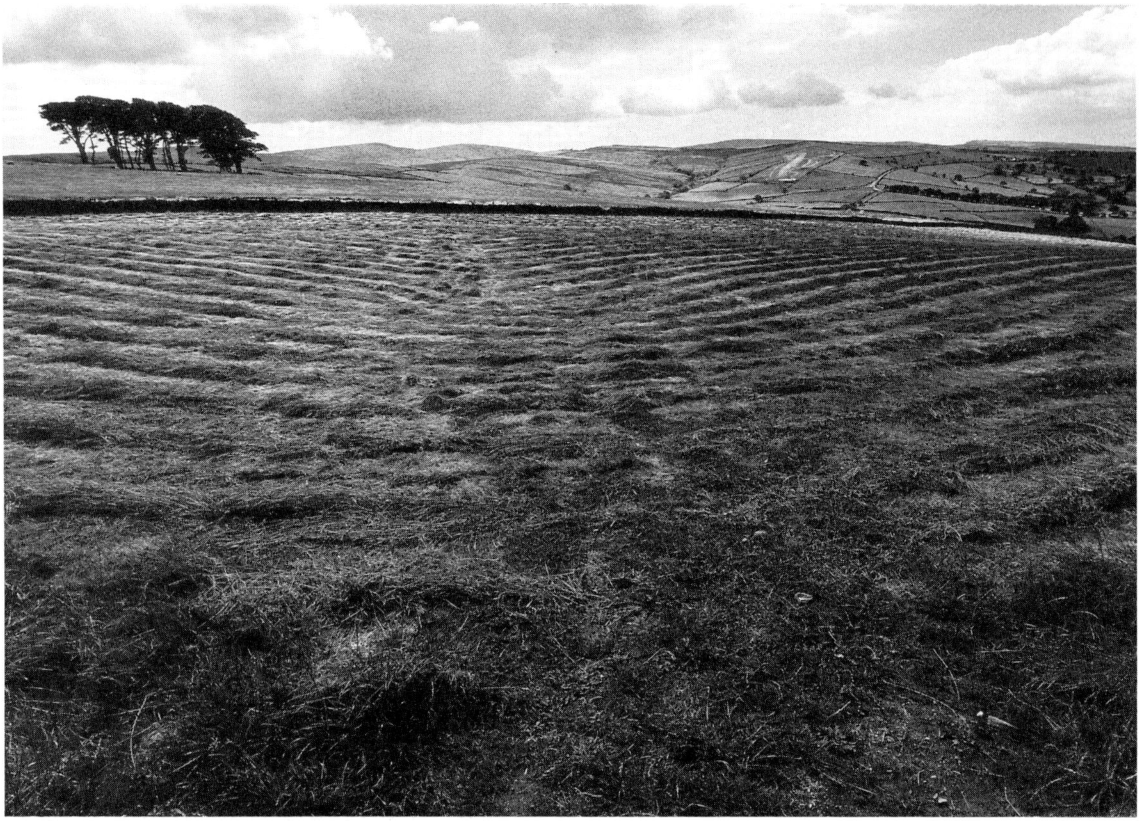

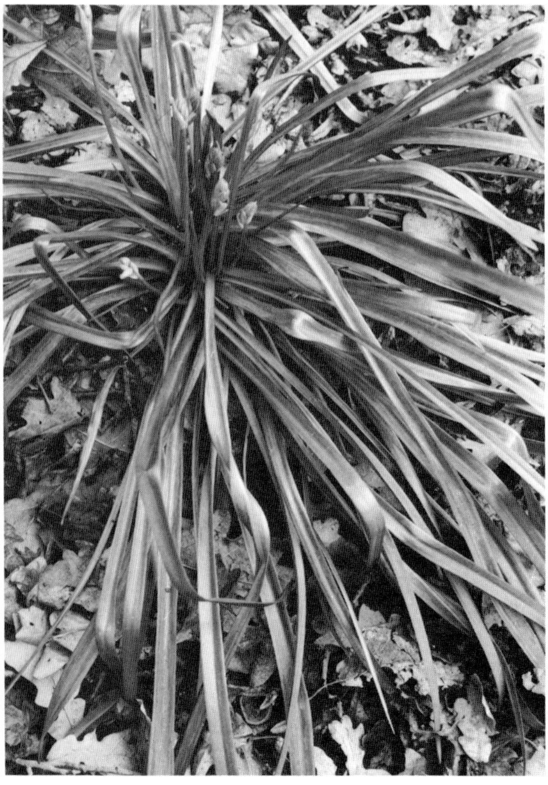

12 (Above) A relatively short-scale subject because there are no brilliant highlights. Exposure can be quite short to allow the trees to be printed in silhouette.

13 (Left) A short-scale subject? Not really. Careful exposure assessment is necessary to preserve detail in both highlight and shadow areas.

detail. For general photography, however, it is as well to forget the concept of short-scale subjects as far as exposure is concerned. You cannot go wrong with an exposure based on a mid-tone; you can go sadly astray if you misjudge the nature of the scene and decide for other, less valid reasons, to give a shorter or longer exposure.

High contrast in the subject is a much more difficult characteristic to handle. The chessboard, for example, might seem perfectly simple; but it is not. If it must be reproduced as genuinely stark black and white, you would do best to photograph it on high-contrast film. You then simply have to expose and process it to get maximum density in the white square portions, and print for contrast.

If, as is more likely, both black and white are less than absolute, and you want a 'correct' result, you have a bit of a problem. In a normal subject,

14 A medium-scale subject. The figures, though light in tone, are not particularly strongly illuminated. Contrast has been exaggerated by high contrast printing.

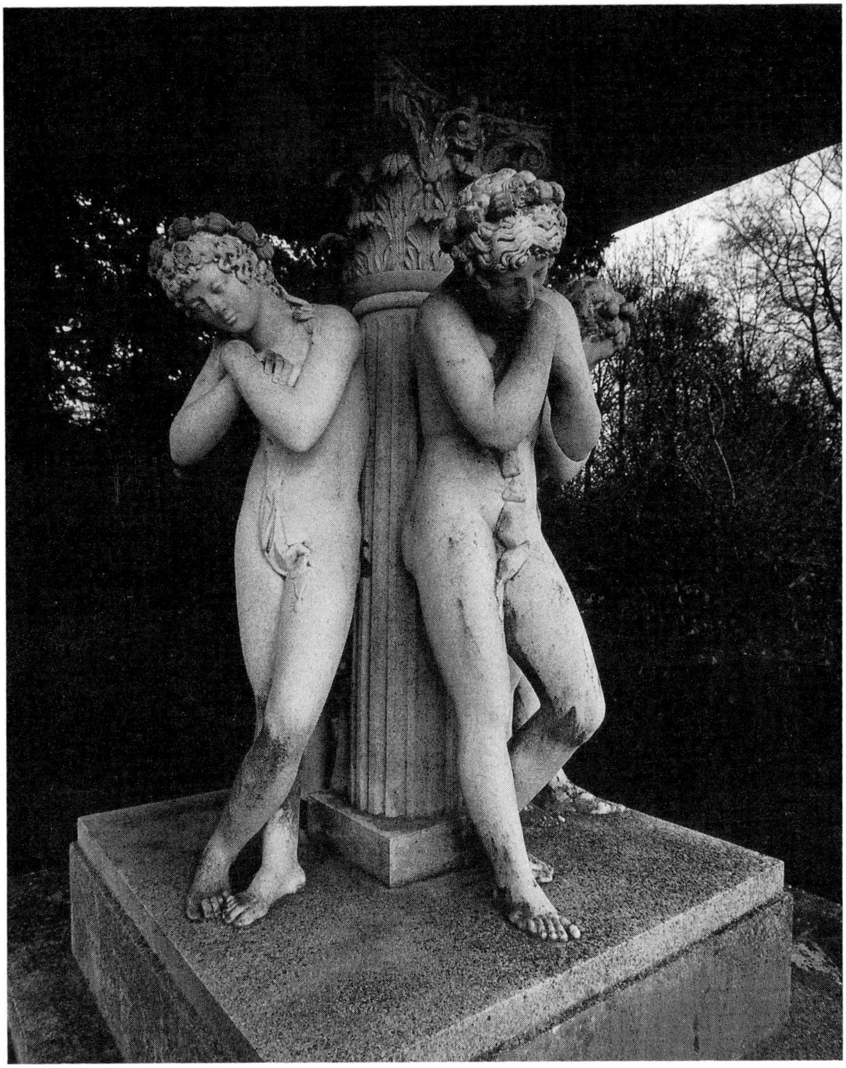

you do not often have to handle such extremes of tone and still produce detail. You can generally sacrifice detail in at least one of the extremes to get the other and the middle tones right. This time, there are no real middle tones and a normal exposure would leave you with a too-light black and a too-grey white. If it does, there is not a lot you can do about it. You can bias the exposure slightly one way to avoid loss of detail at one end or the other, probably the white squares. You might be able to improve matters a little by varying the film processing but, generally speaking, very high contrast raises severe problems if you aim at a totally faithful reproduction.

Dealing with high contrast

The chessboard example is rather hypothetical; but similar problems arise in wedding photography, low light shooting with light sources in the picture area, brilliant sunlight on white clothes, white buildings with prominent features, strong backlighting, and in combinations of indoor and outdoor scenes.

A common example is a view of light-coloured buildings with an archway, recessed door, alley or similar heavily shaded area in which you want to show some detail. Take such a building, well lit by a relatively high sun but with a door, in which you wish to show at least a little detail, thrown into shadow by an arch. A mid-tone exposure should give fine modelling in the main part of the building, but the door could disappear into total shadow. Increased exposure to show detail in the door makes the building look white and lightens its natural shadows too much. What do you do?

The obvious answer is that you go home and

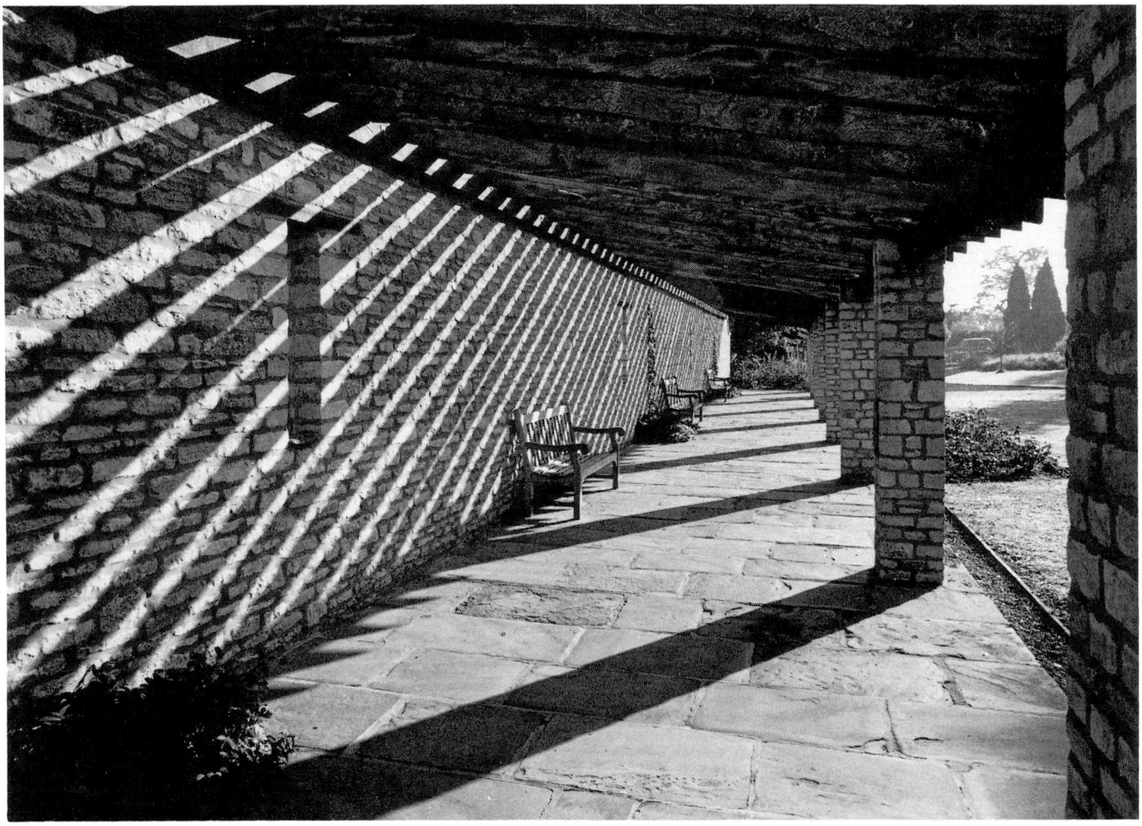

come back again when the lighting is more suitable – sensible, but often impracticable and sometimes impossible. Approaching this problem by the method advocated in the previous chapter, we can recognise the tone in the archway as Tone 3. We cannot hope to reproduce it lighter than that. So we meter it and then meter the brightest part of the building in which we wish to retain detail. Provided there is no more than six stops difference between the two readings, taking us to Tone 9, we can reasonably expect to get some detail at both ends of the scale. But the highlight area we measure will reproduce as brilliant white with just faintly discernible detail. It could be suitable for whitewash, white painted pebbledash or some other rough rendering. If that is too light for the actual subject, the problem is insoluble unless you can find a method of throwing more light into the doorway.

15 Provided that there is no more than a 6-stop difference between readings from the sunlit areas of wall and the deep shadow in other parts the full range of tones can be reproduced.

Texture and background

Apart from tonal scale and contrast, there are other characteristics of the subject which raise problems in exposure. One important feature is the texture of the subject. A furry animal, for example, has a certain overall tone; but within that tone there are innumerable tiny areas of different reflectances too small to be distinguishable to a meter, if the subject is lit correctly. Flat lighting, from a cloud-filled sky or frontal floods, kills texture; the fur is reproduced as a lifeless even tone. Sidelighting from sun, spotlight or a directional floodlamp can bring the fur to life as the light is reflected differentially from individual hairs and slight variations in tone.

Lighting emphasises texture; exposure either preserves or destroys it. Underexpose and the differences are minimised or lost; overexpose and the higher lights are spread, coarsening the texture and raising the overall tone value. Exposure is not easy to assess in such a case. You have to decide what overall value the fur tone has in relation to a mid-tone. It might be, say, two stops darker. This would mean giving two stops less exposure than that indicated by a close-up reading. But, in general, the fur needs to be reproduced fractionally lighter in order to show the texture to advantage, so 1-1½ stops might be more nearly correct. You should get the same result by adding one half to one stop to a grey card or incident light reading. (As previously explained, incident light readings require a special translucent cover over the light cell, and are made by holding the meter at the subject position and pointing it toward the camera position. Most hand-held exposure meters provide such a facility.)

Background tones can also have a significant effect on exposure calculations. You may assess your subject as having a reasonably normal distribution of tones that integrates to grey; but you might overlook an excessively light or dark background. A general reading could be heavily influenced by the background tone and indicate an exposure that is wrong by at least one stop. Close-up readings of the subject are often recommended as a solution to such problems, but this advice too often overlooks the fact that true mid-tones can be difficult to find at close range. You can read from another identifiable tone and adjust the reading accordingly, but you are then in the realms of guesswork. The sensible solution is a grey card or incident light reading.

Recognising the problem

There are many types of 'subject failure' as it is called (somewhat unfairly, because it is the meter that fails); we shall deal with them more fully as they arise. For the moment, it is necessary to learn to recognise the 'non-average' subject. The simplest way to do this is to obtain a good hand-held exposure meter and use it frequently. Take general readings from as many subjects as possible and compare them with grey card or incident light readings for the same subject under the same lighting conditions.

While you are about it, take close-up readings of as many different objects and types of material as you can and compare them with grey card readings in the same position. Remember that the grey card reading gives the correct exposure for representational reproduction of almost any subject. Learn how to adjust a reading from various other tones and try to remember the relationship of the various tones to a mid-tone.

Get used to metering the lightest and the darkest tone in the subject (discounting specular reflections). Count the number of stops between them. Your film can handle at least seven. See how often you find a greater range than this, and learn to recognise such subjects.

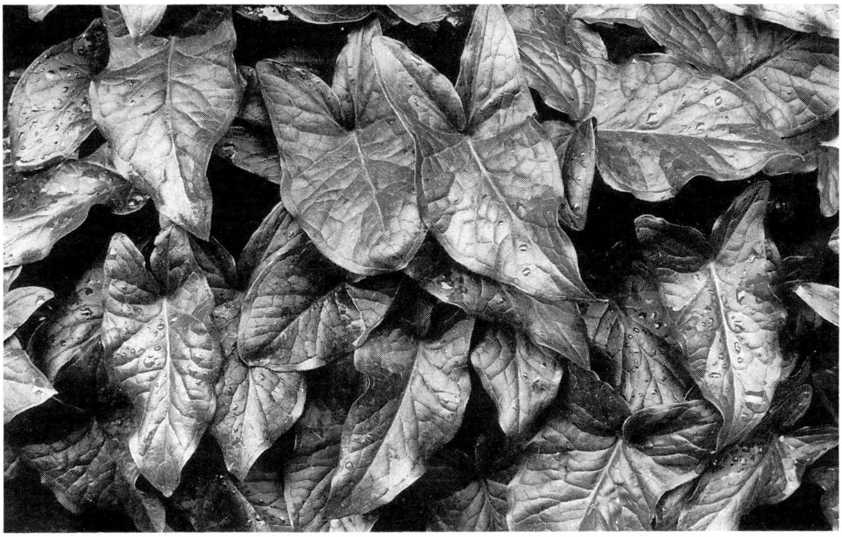

16 Contrast between leaves and background and tonal range in the leaves themselves needs to be at least maintained, so normal or a little less exposure could be accompanied by slightly extended development.

The quickest way to learn how to handle exposure problems is to recognise their nature as they arise. The more you try to put your own ideas into photography, the more likely you are to be shooting non-average subjects. You need to know when a general reading is not good enough; when you may have to sacrifice detail at one end of the scale or the other; and what is likely to happen if

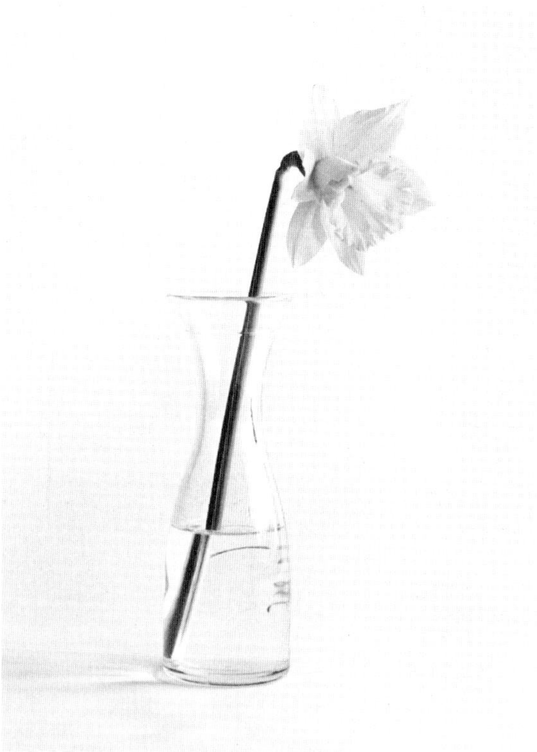

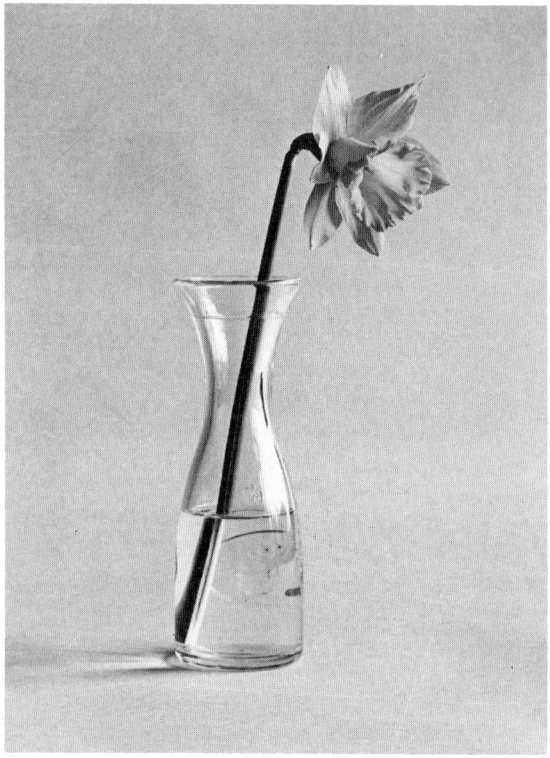

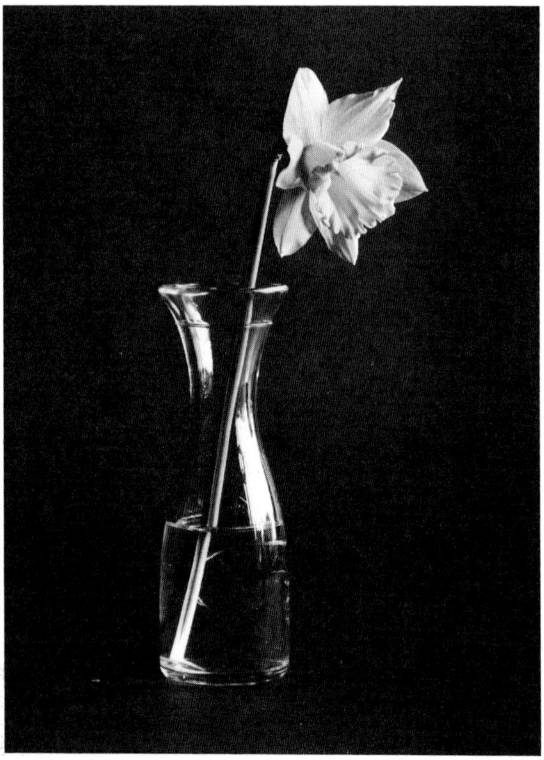

17-19 Direct readings would recommend different exposures but the main subject needs the same exposure each time. Accordingly, a grey card reading is the best solution. Rendering of the glassware naturally varies with the amount of light reflected from the background.

you want to reproduce a particular tone in a lighter or darker shade.

Post exposure controls

The relationship between the various tones in a subject, and the capability of the film to demonstrate it, is best shown with colour slide film. Modern monochrome films have enormous exposure latitude (for acceptable results) and the image they provide can be further modified by adjustments to the film developing and subsequent printing procedures. Very little control of this kind can be exercised with colour slide film. There is no printing process and any variation in film development can have undesirable effects on colour fidelity.

The variations you might use in monochrome to falsify tones and put across your own particular

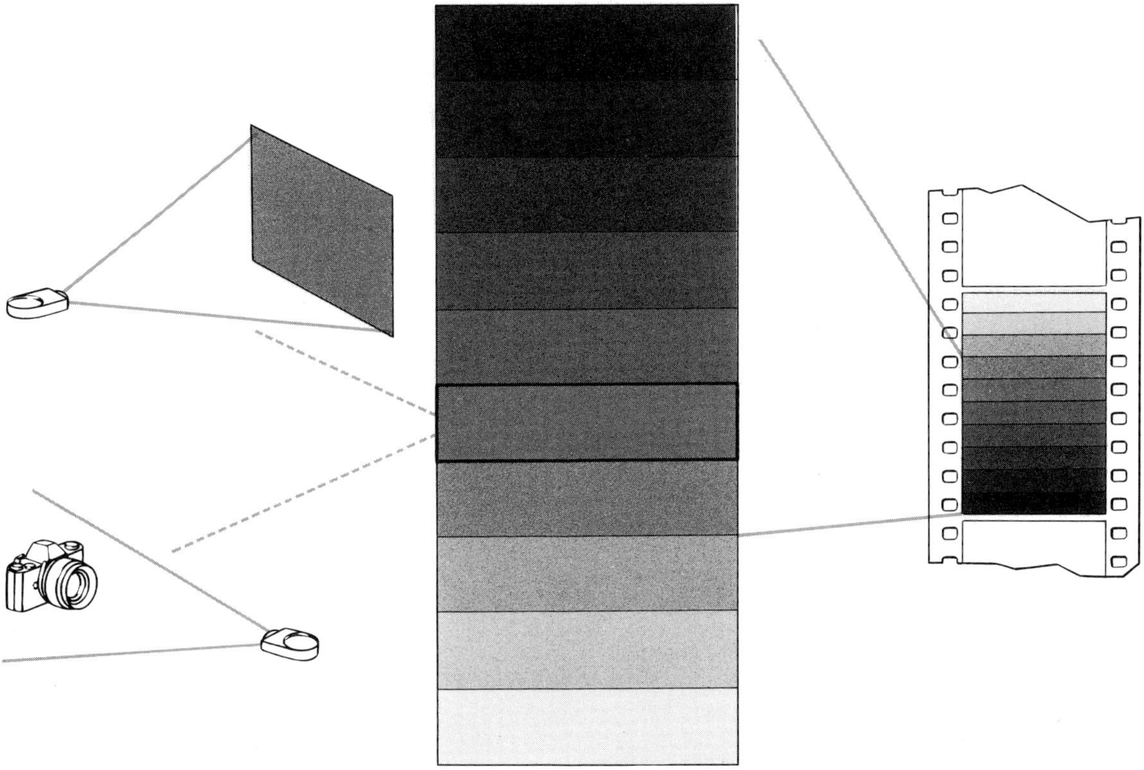

rendering of a subject are virtually impossible in colour without significant changes in hue, too. You may be able to accept this, particularly in low light or night-time shooting. You may even welcome it, but you will not be able to predict it without having a good deal of experience with that particular film. Not all colour films react in the same way to variations in exposure.

4.2 The film has a restricted tonal range capacity and has to compress the tones of a long-scale subject. For an average subject, the same exposure should be indicated by reflected light, incident light or grey card readings.

5 THE IMAGE AND THE FILM

In photography, your raw materials are the subject and the film. Depending on the type of image you want, you have to match the subject or the image to the characteristics of the film. Although there are many different types of film, you are not likely to run into trouble matching the subject to them. Modern films can handle a wide range of tones, and there are few subjects that fall outside their capabilities. There are some subjects that are best handled by special high contrast film, but these are exceptions. With suitably adjusted processing and printing, the average film can give you all the contrast you are likely to want.

To learn how you can adjust exposure, processing and printing to suit the image required, you need to know something about the characteristics of the film.

Colour sensitivity

All general purpose monochrome films are panchromatic. This means that they are sensitive to light of all colours – a sensitivity imparted by the incorporation of dye substances in the film coatings. Thus, even on a monochrome film, a coloured subject is reproduced in a range of tones corresponding reasonably closely to the different brightnesses (strictly, luminances) of the coloured surfaces of the subject. This assumes, among other things, that the subject is photographed in daylight or light of similar colour content.

If you photograph in monochrome light (such as yellow sodium street lighting), the tonal differences in the print are not representative of the brightnesses of the various colours of the subject as seen in daylight. Even by the light of a domestic tungsten filament lamp, the result is different from that given by daylight. This is because there is proportionally more red and yellow in the light from filament lamps, and less blue, than in daylight. Blues tend to reproduce darker than you might expect and reds and yellows lighter.

The effect is not as pronounced as it was in former times, when it was necessary to use purple rather than red lipstick in female portraiture. However, it cannot be ignored. Similarly, if you put a coloured filter over the camera lens, you alter the colour of the light reaching the film and consequently alter the tonal values. This can be useful in photography. Most people are aware that a yellow filter absorbs blue light and renders blue sky darker, so that white clouds stand out prominently.

The principle can be extended to other applications, which will be dealt with later.

The colour sensitivity of monochrome films is not identical with that of either the eye or exposure meter photocells. Even between one type of photocell and another, there is a difference. The selenium cell approximates most closely in sensitivity to the film. Generally, all films are rather more sensitive to blue than is the eye, so that blue sky tends to reproduce paler than might be expected. Cadmium sulphide (CdS) and silicon photosensors are more sensitive to red than either the film or the eye, and need to be blue filtered to provide a closer match.

Films are also sensitive to infrared (IR) and ultraviolet (UV) radiation, both of which are invisible to the human eye. UV sensitivity is partly responsible for the excess blueness of distant scenes in clear air photographed in colour (as at high altitude), and also causes a hazy, low contrast effect on black and white film (an effect also partly due to the tendency for visible blue light to be scattered by solid atmospheric particles). Unwanted sensitivity to IR radiation would cause some kinds of green vegetation to reproduce rather lighter than they appear to the eye.

Specialised films

Some films have restricted colour sensitivity. They are generally available only in sheet form for the larger format cameras, but there are one or two in roll and 35mm sizes. The most common types are orthochromatic, blue-sensitive and infrared-sensitive.

Orthochromatic films. Orthochromatic (which means correct colour) is an unfortunate description nowadays. Originally, films were blue-sensitive only. When the colour sensitising process was first introduced, the films were called orthochromatic because they gave improved tonal rendering with most colours. They were still largely insensitive to red and orange, which thus recorded black. Even the first panchromatic films were somewhat insensitive to red.

Orthochromatic films are still used in some applications because they give some colour sensitivity but can be handled under red safelighting.

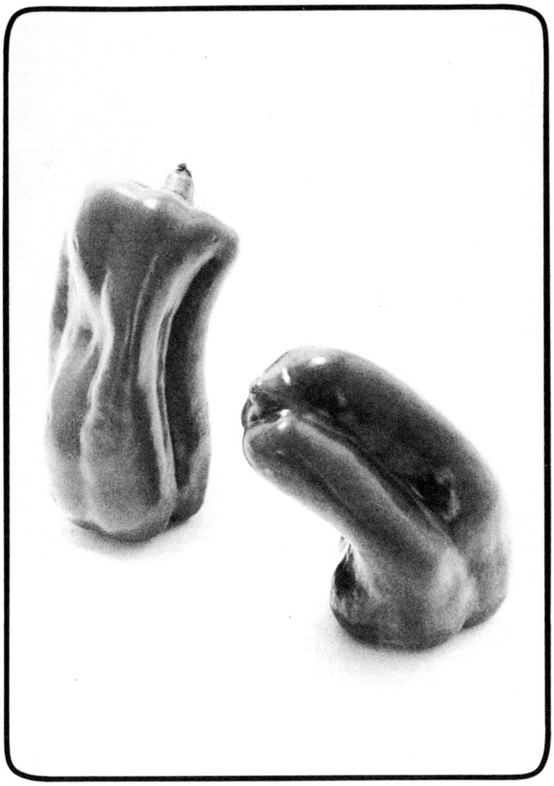

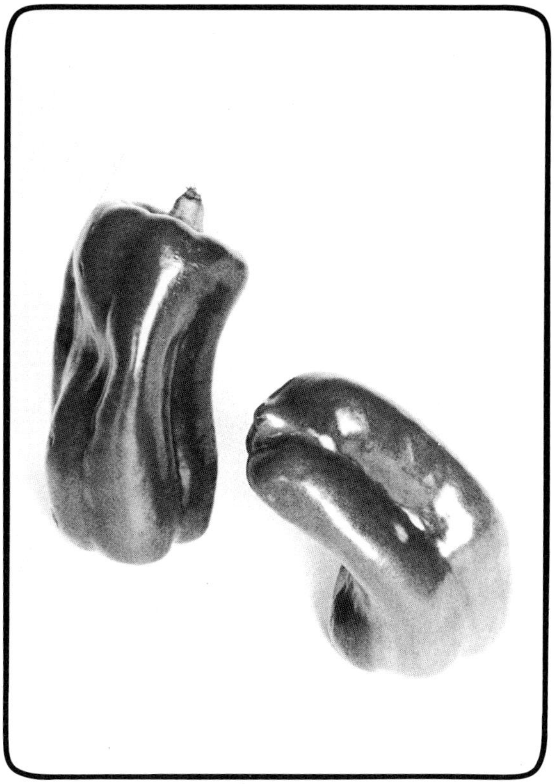

20-21 The lefthand pepper is red, the other green. The lefthand picture was taken by tungsten light, the other by daylight. The predominantly reddish tungsten light makes the red pepper noticeably lighter.

Blue-sensitive films. Blue-sensitive films are commonly used for high-contrast black and white work, such as diagrams, printed matter, charts, etc. They can be handled in ordinary darkroom safelighting and have the additional advantage that instructions can be marked on the original in blue. The high sensitivity to blue reproduces it as white, ie, maximum density on the film.

Infrared films. Infrared films are basically blue-sensitive but also have high sensitivity to a limited region beyond the red end of the visible spectrum. Used in conjunction with deep red filters, they produce images of IR radiation only or of IR plus a little visible red. With a suitable filter over the light source, photography can be carried out almost without visible light.

General sensitivity (speed)

Films differ in their overall sensitivity to light. The amount of light necessary to produce a given degree of blackening is less or greater according to the film's sensitivity to light, commonly called *film speed.*

Film speed is indicated by a rating on the ISO (International Standards Organisation) scale. The first figure is arithmetical, a doubling of the figure indicating doubled sensitivity. The second is logarithmic, an increase of the figure by three indicating doubled sensitivity. These two types of figure were formerly known as ASA and DIN speeds respectively, the initials of the US and German standards organisations.

General purpose black and white films are loosely classified as slow, medium or fast, typical speed figures being ISO 50/18° (ASA 50/18 DIN), ISO 100/21° (ASA 100/21 DIN) and ISO 400/27° (ASA 400/27 DIN). The degree sign was once used in the DIN figures to indicate its logarithmic nature. Although it was subsequently dropped as being rather pointless, it was reintroduced with the ISO standard.

There are many other film speeds, of course, and the definitions of both medium speed and high speed are becoming blurred. An ISO 200/24°

film would now be classified as medium speed and, although ISO 400/27° is still regarded as fast, there are much faster films up to ISO 1000/31° and beyond. The figures have no real meaning in themselves. They simply provide a basis for comparison and a means of calibrating exposure meters and compiling exposure tables. Naturally, they also depend on processing methods. The recommendations given by an exposure meter for a given film speed are accurate only when processing is standardised according to the procedure in the relevant International Standard.

They depend, too, on the accuracy of the camera shutter speed markings and lens aperture designations. It is not unknown for two lenses set to the same *f*-number to transmit different amounts of light. As a perfectionist, you should conduct tests with all your lenses and every batch of film you buy, and certainly with different cameras. You could rate a film as marked and a friend could rate it twice as fast; yet you both might get identical results owing to shutter speed or aperture variations.

Many film characteristics are related to film speed. Generally speaking, the easiest way to make a faster film is to increase the size of the silver halide particles that provide its sensitivity to light. This can lead to their clumping or overlapping at different depths in the light-sensitive layer or layers (known, erroneously, as the emulsion: it is actually a suspension). Development of the film increases the clumping effect of the particles, making the 'granular' structure of the image visible on enlargement. The picture is then said to be grainy, generally regarded as an unsatisfactory condition and sometimes so prominent as to prevent the rendering of fine detail. The effect is less noticeable than it was in the products of some years ago, but it is still true that a faster film tends to produce a more grainy image.

Contrast and exposure latitude are similarly affected by the different emulsion structures. Slow, fine-grain films produce rather higher contrast images, the quality of which also greatly depends on the level of exposure and development. High-speed films tend to produce images of lower contrast and to have greater exposure latitude.

Speed, grain and contrast also depend on the developing procedure. The effect may vary with different films and differing degrees of development but, in general, development increased beyond the recommended level increases both contrast and grain size. Prolonged development increases the effect of the developer by reducing more of the light-sensitive particles and possibly by penetrating the film to a greater depth – so increasing individual grain size, the tendency to clump, and the general blackening effect. As the developer can work only on particles that have received sufficient exposure, however, over-development has a greater effect on highlights and mid-tones than on shadow areas.

The effect of development on film speed is less clear cut. The minimal effect that prolonged development can have on shadow areas means that those areas can rarely be persuaded to show more detail – the true criterion of increased film speed. When there are no very low tonal values in the subject, density in the film may be increased throughout its tonal range. An increase in film speed then appears to have been achieved by prolonged development.

Similar effects may be provided by different developer formulations; there are several such products on the market for which increased film speed is claimed. There could be some justification for those that claim an increase of up to half a stop. Beyond that, any significant increase in apparent speed will inevitably be accompanied by a deterioration of image quality.

Colour film characteristics

In basic characteristics, colour films are very little different from monochrome films. They are primarily monochrome emulsions with other materials incorporated to release dyes in proportion to the silver image when treated with a specific type of developer. They consist of three emulsion layers separately sensitised to red, green and blue light. All other colours can be synthesised by appropriate mixtures of these three. As the light has to pass through one layer to reach the second and through two to reach the bottom layer, each must be of different sensitivity. Overall sensitivity therefore depends on that of the bottom layer.

Although the three emulsion layers are microscopically thin, they inevitably have an effect on image sharpness as compared with the single layer of a monochrome film. The emulsion layers are also especially sensitive to the colour of the exposing light. Quite wide variations may have little effect on the tonal range, but comparatively small variations can affect the reproduction of colours significantly. Most colour films are in-

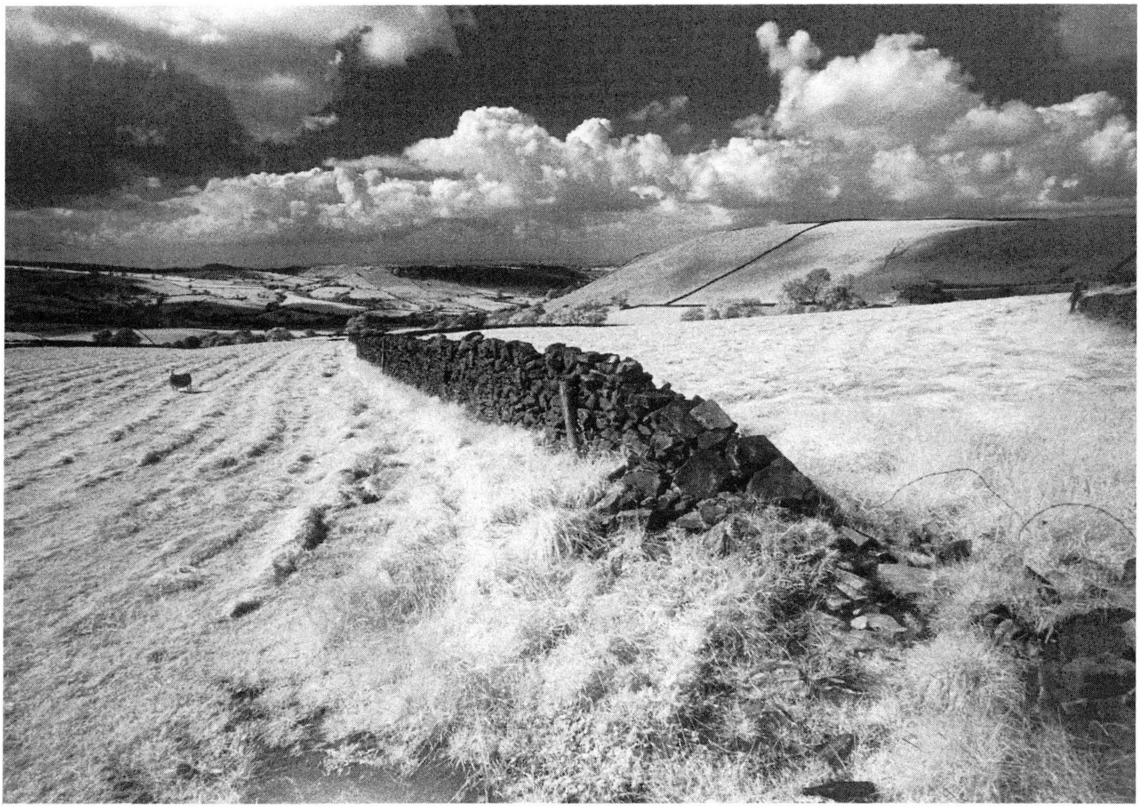

22 The dramatic effect provided by infra-red film and a red filter. Exposure cannot be accurately measured by ordinary metering. Set the guide ISO number given for the film and bracket exposures one stop either side of the meter reading.

tended for use in daylight – ideally daylight from direct sun with some white cloud in the sky. Early morning or late afternoon light can be different in hue and its effect on colour film is noticeable. The greater proportion of red and yellow in artificial (tungsten-filament) light produces a strong orange-yellow cast.

Matching the image to the film

If you have a reasonable knowledge of the characteristics of your film, you can match the image to it without too much difficulty. In technical terms this amounts to placing a particular tone correctly (for your purpose) on the characteristic curve of the film. As mentioned in Chapter 3, the characteristic curve is basically a straight line indicating that density in the negative is proportional to the exposure that each part of the negative receives. At the highest and lowest levels (the shoulder and the toe of the curve), this proportional relationship fails. If your exposure is too short, the darker tones and shadow areas run together as almost clear film. If it is too long, the lighter tones and extreme highlights all reach maximum density and fine detail is lost.

The first simplified graph shows the straight line portion of an imaginary characteristic curve. Each additional increment of exposure marked on the base line produces additional density on the film, as indicated by the height of the line above the base line at that point. Assuming correct exposure of all the tones in a subject, as listed in Chapter 3, each tone would, in effect, be 'placed' on the curve as shown. Assuming an average subject integrating to a mid-tone, a reflected light meter reading would have given an exposure that placed Tone 6 correctly in position 6 on the curve. All the other tones must fall naturally into place and reproduce correctly – or as near correctly as the film can manage.

The second graph shows the characteristic curve of a high-contrast film. The steepness of the line indicates that only a few exposure steps are required for the film to progress from virtually clear to maximum density. The long-scale subject of the previous graph, indicated this time by the dotted line, needs a 1:10 exposure ratio to accommodate all its tones. They cannot all be compressed on to this film. The fourth exposure increment should not even reach the density required for a mid-tone but, in fact, it puts maximum density on the film.

Thus, if you give the minimum exposure, so that Tone 1 is placed in position 1, all tones in the subject brighter than Tone 4 are rendered as maximum density on the film. If Tone 6 is placed correctly, all tones above 7 and below 4 are lost in maximum and minimum density. This can be a useful characteristic when you undertake 'posterisation' work and need to produce negatives with only two tones – completely transparent and completely opaque – but that is beyond the scope of this book.

Although the characteristic curve will be mentioned again, we do not need to go into it more fully. Our simplified description is all that is necessary to understand the relationship between the luminances of the subject and the corresponding densities on the film. By placing a particular subject luminance higher or lower on the characteristic curve, you can dictate the tone in which it will be reproduced in the final image, but only by similarly altering all other tones. The principle can generally be applied to both monochrome and colour films, although any drastic shift is likely to bring about some colour distortion, particularly with colour slide films. With monochrome films, the film processing can also be adjusted to alter the slope of the curve. Then, although a tone may be 'misplaced', it can be reproduced correctly with some compression or expansion of the overall tone range.

For all practical purposes, placing a tone higher or lower on the curve simply means giving more or less exposure than that recommended by a grey-card or incident-light exposure meter reading.

5.1 Correct exposure (lower strip) can accommodate all tones from virtually clear to virtually opaque film. Overexposure (upper strip) moves all tones along the 'curve', creating additional density in all areas. The lighter tones (black areas) may block up.

Variable speed films

The concept of 'correct' exposure is somewhat obscured by the fact that modern negative films, both monochrome and colour, have quite extraordinary exposure latitude. This has been exaggerated by the advent of monochrome films that owe their origin to colour film technology and which are, indeed, processed in colour negative film chemistry or in their own special solutions of similar composition. These are the so-called *chromogenic films* – Ilford XP1 and Agfa Vario-XL. The two films differ slightly in detail, but the basic idea is the same.

The Agfa film, for example, has two emulsion layers, one high speed and the other low speed. Both layers incorporate colour couplers with *development inhibitors* – the special treatment borrowed from colour negative technology to combat the effects of overexposure. Processing in a colour developer, followed by a combined bleach and fix bath (exactly as in colour negative processing), gives a single-coloured dye image.

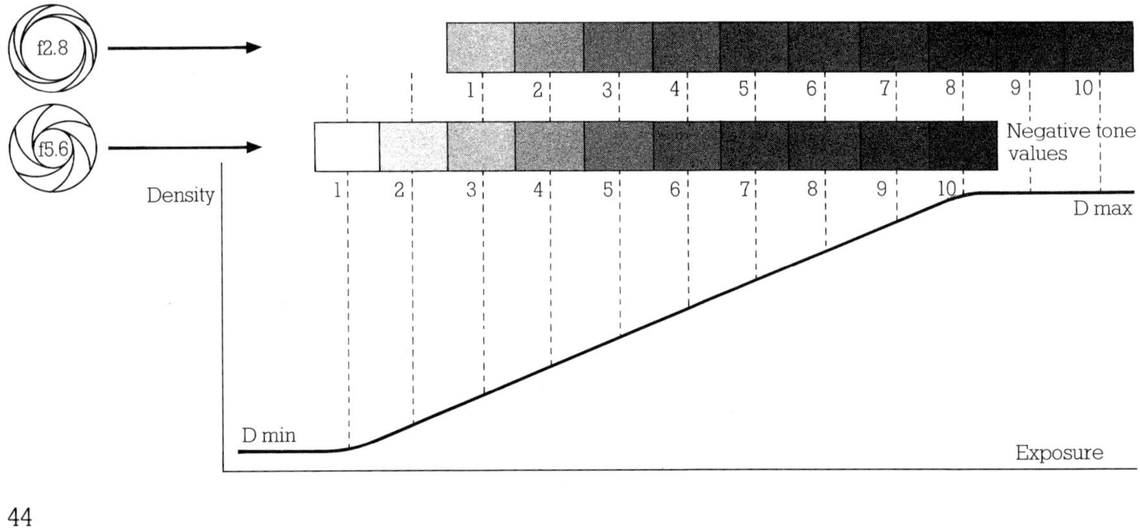

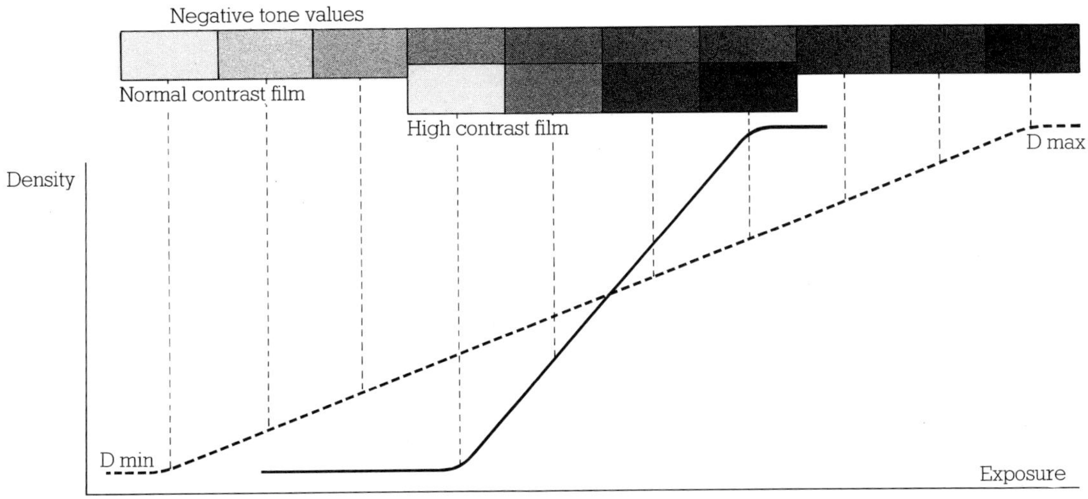

5.2 A normal general-purpose film has a long straight-line portion to its characteristic curve, with a moderate slope. A high contrast film has a steeper slope and thus accommodates fewer steps in its tonal range. The gradient of the slope is an index of contrast and can be affected to some extent by development.

As the colour is relatively unimportant, exposure latitude is independent of colour balance problems. The image components are dye instead of solid silver grains, so there are no problems with irradiation, which can produce light scatter between solid particles. Nor is there any base development fog – the slight overall density caused by the action of developer on silver halides, even those that have not been exposed to light. The image has better acutance (edge contrast) and a smaller, more compact grain structure, even with considerable overexposure.

In practice, the immense advantage of these films is that they can be regarded as having a variable speed or sensitivity. There is likely to be some overlap between the manufacturers' recommendations and actual practice, but the general principle is that XP1, for example, can be treated as an ISO 400/27° (ASA 400/27 DIN) film for most purposes. The fact that such a film generally needs an exposure of about 1/1000 sec at *f*/11 in strong sunlight need not bother you. You can give XP1 1/1000 sec at *f*/4 or any equivalent exposure between those limits in such lighting conditions and still process the film in the same solutions for the same time.

Overexposure gives finer grain. With a normal film, three stops overexposure would give a noticeable increase in grain size and contrast. With XP1, the negative is denser but the grain is *finer*. So the film can be rated anywhere between ISO 50/18° (ASA 50/18 DIN) and ISO 400/27° *on the same roll* and processed normally. The results vary in density but are comparable in image quality to those obtained from a conventional ISO 125/22° (ASA 125/22 DIN) film.

There is more. The film can be push-processed up to ISO 1600/33° (ASA 1600/33 DIN) by the usual method of increasing development time. Not only that, but the three stops overexposure latitude is still available. In other words, the same roll can be exposed as if it had a speed or sensitivity variable from ISO 400/27° to ISO 1600/33°. In this case, however, the extended development does result in a noticeable increase in grain size.

Agfa's recommendations are slightly different. They do not assign an actual speed figure to their film but say that it can be exposed for any speed from ISO 125/22° to ISO 1600/33°. They say that it achieves the same standard of quality as an ISO 125/22° film if overexposed by up to four stops. Processing is the same at all speeds.

6 FILM PROCESSING CONTROLS

If the raw materials of photography are the subject and the film, the final product depends on processing the film and making the print. The aim should be to make the printing a straightforward process. You cannot avoid the necessity for occasionally introducing some control, but you should not need to rely on doing so. All the real work should be done in the production of the negative, ie, exposure and development plus, in the case of colour films, ensuring that the right type of light source is used.

How the image is formed

The camera lens forms an optical image of varying intensities at the film surface. These intensities of light affect the light-sensitive particles in the film differentially, as already mentioned. At this stage, however, there is no measurable darkening of the film. We have an invisible, or *latent* image.

To make the latent image visible, the effect of light energy is amplified by a chemical solution which acts only on the light-sensitive particles (which are silver halides) that have actually been exposed, ie, affected by light. This is accomplished by a *developer* solution containing chemical compounds which reduce the exposed halides to metallic silver.

There is an optimum time and temperature for the development of a film. The developer could continue to act until there were no exposed halide particles to develop. That is *development to finality,* which would be used only if the film speed were being vastly uprated. It would produce a very dense, grainy negative incapable of showing fine detail. Printing papers, on the other hand, are commonly developed to finality, because their grain structure is extremely fine and they undergo no further enlargement. Full development can therefore be used to enable the paper to produce its 'maximum black' where appropriate.

Varying the development time

The development time of a monochrome film can be varied to some extent to assist with exposure problems, as moderate changes affect tonal values without having a drastic effect on grain size. The same control is available only to a very limited extent with colour films, where tonal values are linked to colour rendering.

Reducing contrast. It is possible, for example, to increase the exposure and shorten the development time with a monochrome film to reduce contrast. You may run across a subject with great extremes of tone, such as a wet night scene with brilliant reflections on road or pavement surfaces. You probably do not want stark white reflections; they should have some tonal gradation. So should some of the darker areas. Normal exposure and development might give a 'soot and whitewash' effect of very high contrast. You can tackle such a problem by pegging the highlights one stop higher than the tonal value required – say at Tone 10. Meter this tone and peg the exposure at four stops more than the meter reading, which recommends an exposure to give Tone 6 in that area.

Alternatively, you can meter a grey card in the highlight position and give one stop more than the reading. As a further alternative, meter the white reverse of the grey card in the highlight position if the light is very low and give 3 ½ stops more than indicated. All of these methods should give a similar result. What you are aiming at is one stop more than a 'normal' exposure. You then shorten development time to approximately three-quarters of the normal time.

The principle is that the increased exposure tends to increase density by raising all tones except the very deepest shadows. With normal development, the highlights would become blocked and devoid of detail. Curtailed development has a greater effect on the higher densities (representing the highlights) than the lower. Tones 7, 8 and 9 are brought back to normal, with lower tones progressively less affected.

Increasing contrast. To increase contrast in a low-contrast subject, the opposite treatment can be used, placing the required tone lower than normal and increasing development by about 30 per cent to bring it up again. In practice, the results of such treatment depend largely on the characteristics of the particular film and developer used. Modern films do not always respond as well as those of some years back. Moderate changes in contrast are possible, but the results are not completely predictable without preliminary tests.

Increasing speed. With modern films, variations in exposure and development are more com-

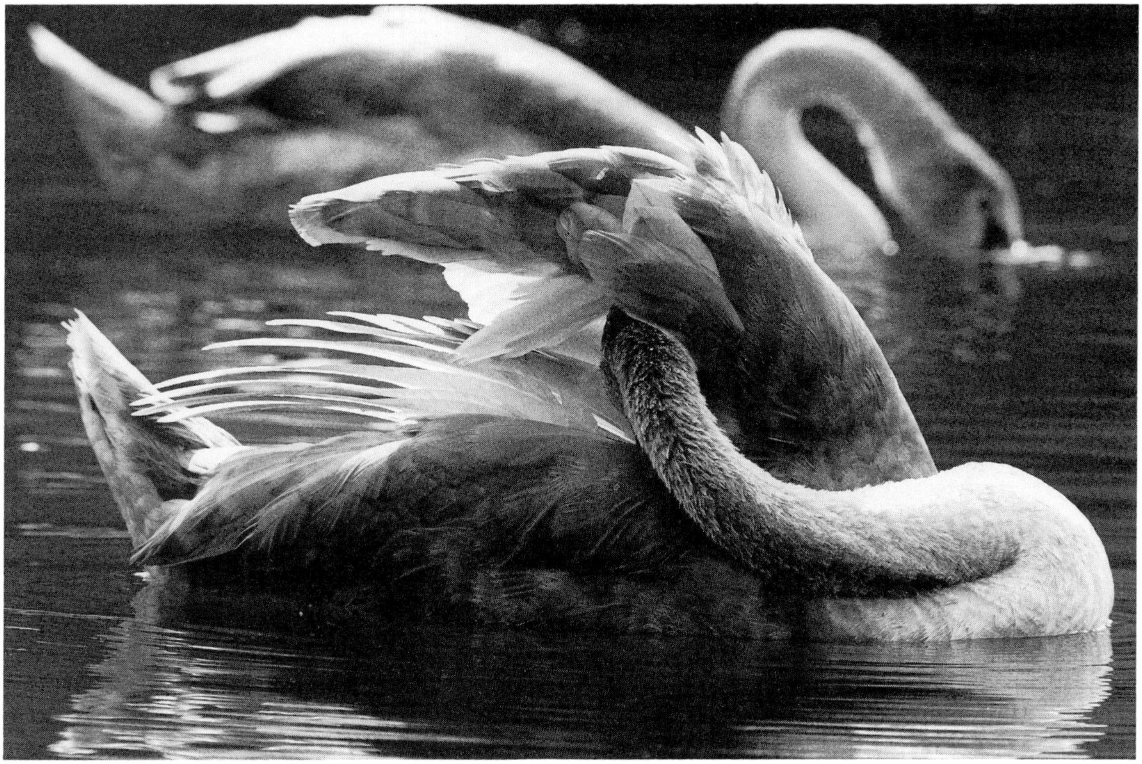

23 Strong backlight and large shadow areas make a difficult metering problem. A full exposure and curtailed development is the usual answer.

monly confined to attempts to increase the film speed. Sometimes the film manufacturers suggest reducing exposure and prolonging development to achieve this. The aim is to permit photography in exceptionally low light conditions, or to allow fast shutter speeds or small apertures to be used in unfavourable lighting. The introduction of extremely fast films is making this practice less necessary, but it is still quite widely used for photography in 'impossible' conditions.

Push processing (forced development)
Forced development is now most commonly known as *push processing* and is associated with uprating a film, or exposing it as if it were faster than the manufacturer's recommended speed rating. The resulting underexposure is compensated for by increasing development time. The technique can be applied to fast monochrome or slide films, but is not particularly recommended for colour negative film, where colour and density are controlled by the same developer. With colour slide film, the extension of development time is applied only to the first developer, which is a monochrome type.

Extended development inevitably results in increased grain size, some distortion of tones and, in colour slide film, loss of contrast and colour saturation. Clearly, this type of treatment must involve sacrificing one thing for another. The manufacturers have set their exposure and processing levels to give optimum image quality in resolution of detail as well as in contrast; if you force the development, both will be altered. If you can tolerate the graininess and loss of detail, push processing is acceptable. You might, for example, use it in fog and mist on the grounds that the effect suits the subject. You would certainly use it in low-light conditions where it is more important to get the picture than to produce a photographic masterpiece.

Some manufacturers publish details of push-processing timings. More often, the practitioner is obliged to make his own experiments. There can be no standard recommendations for all films, but

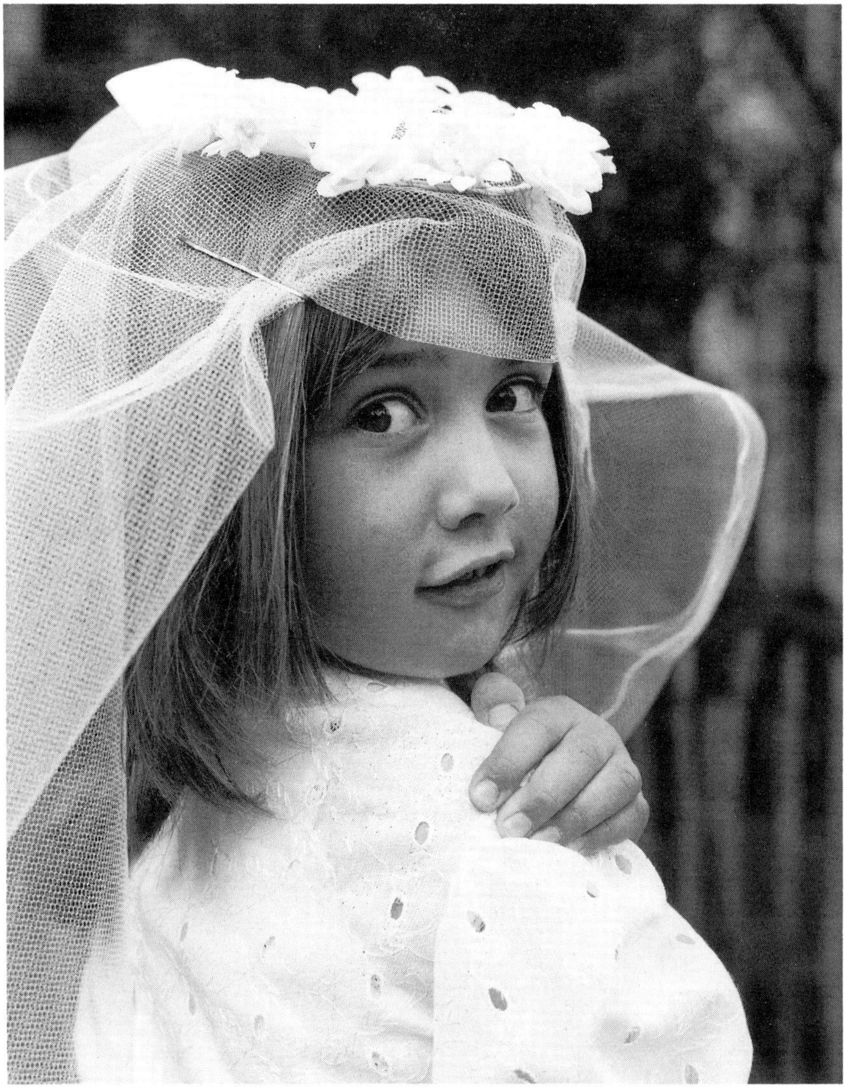

24 In poor light a high contrast subject may not require special exposure/development treatment, but with average subjects one stop underexposure and 50% increased development time would help.

25 (Pages 50-51) The deliberate use of a grainy image and pushed processing reinforces atmospheric effects.

a good starting point is 1.5 x the normal development time for a one stop push, 2.5 x for two stops and 4.5 x for three stops. Thus, if you meter a given tone so that it is pegged at three stops below its normal position on the characteristic curve (ie, taking a direct reading of a Tone 9 in the subject and giving the exposure the meter recommends), you are effectively rating the film three stops faster than its recommended speed. A 4.5x increase in development time should then give you reasonable separation of the mid-tones and possibly some detail in the lower highlights. Depending on film and developer, the grain size in the middle tones will vary from intrusive to objectionable, so you should use this technique only as a last resort, or for effect, as in the picture overleaf.

For up to one stop or so (a claimed doubling of film speed) the process was a standby long before the term 'push-processing' entered photographic jargon. It worked reasonably well for subjects with no marked shadow areas and, with the so much improved modern films, is still a useful standby. Beyond the one stop range, the loss of image quality is generally too high a price to pay.

Colour slide film can be successfully uprated in the same way but, again, anything more than a one-stop uprating is more likely to be used for effect rather than to achieve greater speed. Colour slide films of ISO 1000/31 (ASA 1000/31

DIN) are now available and will generally provide better quality than an uprated slower film. Some photographers, however, may push process a slower film with preferred colour rendering to the speed they need in preference to choosing another film that is normally rated at that speed.

Fine-grain developers
Most film developers are standard formulations designed to suit the majority of negatives. Within reasonable limits, the formulae can be varied to give different results. The current variations are those which increase speed, improve acutance, or give extra fine grain.

This last attribute is now of little importance. At one time, it was almost mandatory for 35mm work, but the quality of modern films is such that graininess has long ceased to be a problem, and special developers are now justified only for the very smallest formats. True fine-grain developers lower effective film speed and, as slow, very fine-grain films are available, there seems to be little point in processing faster, less fine-grain types in this manner at the expense of film speed.

High-definition developers
The principle of high-definition type developers is often poorly understood. They have been around for a very long time, but have received rather more publicity in recent years as the relationship between resolution, contrast and *visual sharpness* has been better realised.

High-definition developers (also known as acutance developers) produce sharp images not by fineness of grain, but by sharper definition of the boundary between adjacent tones – a sort of stepped formation of tones rather than the tendency for one tone to 'bleed' into another. This makes most images look sharper than those produced by conventional processing, although they may not, in fact, have higher resolution of fine detail. High-definition images of this type are best produced by the modern breed of camera lenses, which are also designed with greater attention to contrast characteristics than in the past.

Speed-increasing developers
Speed-increasing developers are also a mixed blessing. The manufacturer produces what he considers the most generally acceptable formula, but sometimes offers an alternative that has a minimal effect on the film speed rating that can be satisfactorily used. Independent manufacturers produce their own speed-increasing developers and frequently claim much greater benefits. Depending on the particular film, and your image quality requirements, genuine increases in sensitivity (in as much as that there is some improvement in shadow detail) can be obtained up to about 50 per cent, or half a stop. An ISO 400/27° film may be able to be rated at ISO 650/29°, with little discernible loss of quality. Beyond this, an increase in grain size is inevitable and various other undesirable features may emerge. The resulting picture may be perfectly acceptable for its intended purpose, particularly if only minimal enlargement is required. Nevertheless, we delude ourselves if we think we are getting something for nothing.

Two-bath methods. There are older formulae and special processes which formerly worked well, but they are less suitable for modern films. Two-bath processes were once very popular and still have their enthusiastic adherents among those whose avowed aim is the ultimate in image quality. There were two main types, one using plain water as the second bath and the other using a strong alkali such as potassium hydroxide.

Water-bath method. The principle of water bath development is that the developer continues to work for a longer time where it has the least work to do. The film is first saturated with almost any kind of developer and next it is transferred to plain water, where it lies undisturbed for several minutes. It is then transferred back to the developer for another saturation, and so on until development is judged to be complete. In the water bath, the developer in the highlight areas is rapidly exhausted, and development in these areas is retarded. In the shadow areas, the developer takes much longer to become exhausted because it has little to work on. So the intensity of the shadow areas builds up with no effect on the highlights.

The result of such treatment is claimed to be a genuine increase in effective film speed without the usual accompaniment of high contrast and empty highlights. The immersion in water needs to be fairly prolonged, because the longer the developer continues to work in the shadow areas, the more pronounced is the disproportionate shadow and highlight development, and the greater the shadow detail. There is always the proviso, however, that shadow detail cannot be

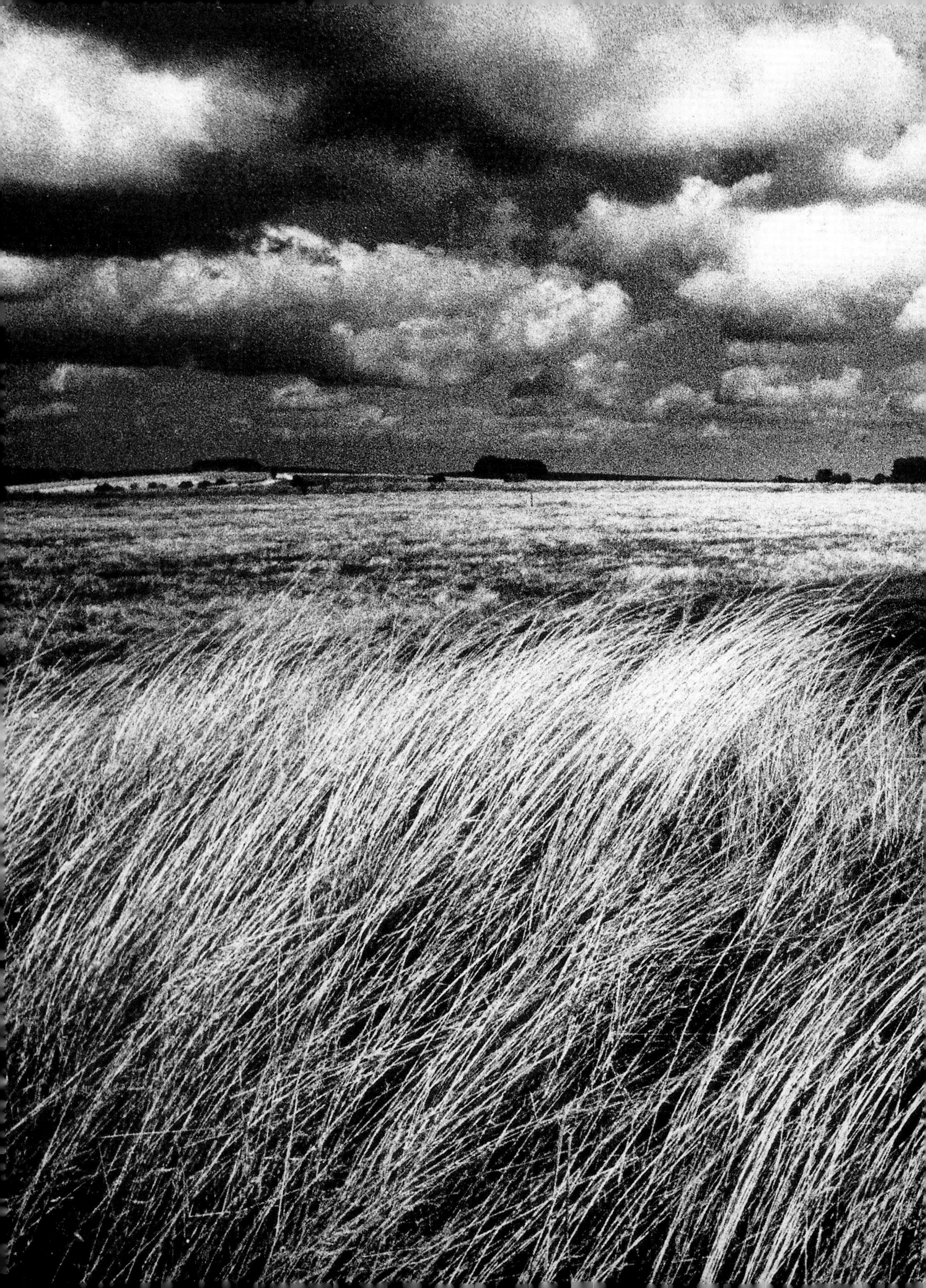

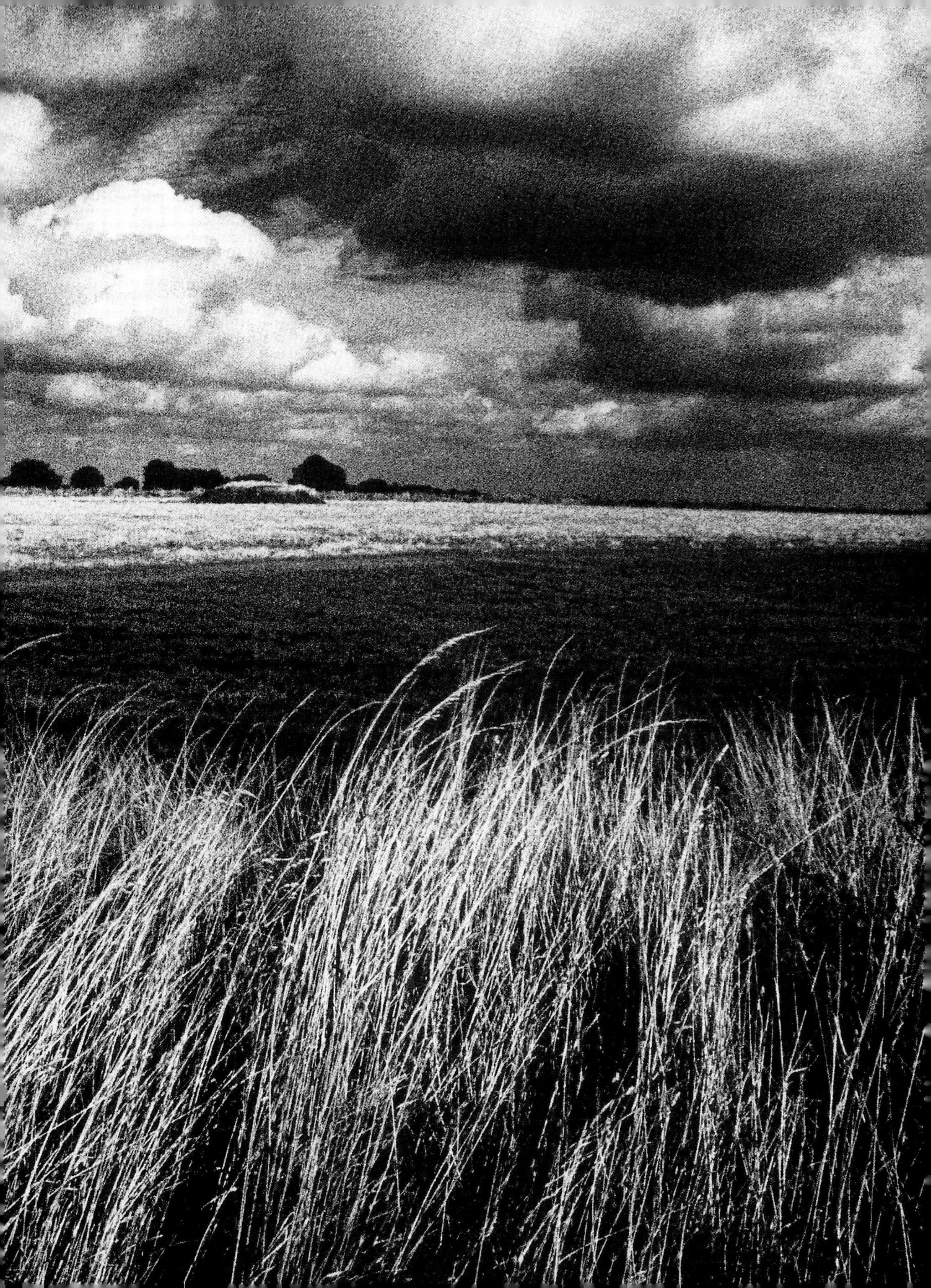

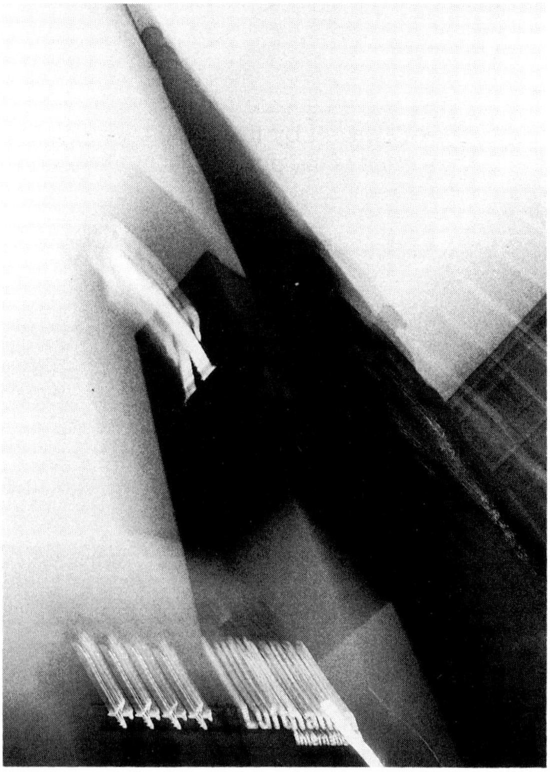

26 An interesting effect created by deliberate movement of the camera during the half-second exposure.

increased unless the film was given a certain minimum exposure. No amount of trickery can produce a usable density unless the film has had sufficient exposure to produce a latent image.

The obvious drawback of the technique is that it really needs development by inspection. You have to know what is happening at each step. With panchromatic films, that would demand a previous immersion in a desensitising bath. Moreover, it is not easy to handle rollfilms in open dishes, so the technique is nowadays of limited use.

Alkali-bath method. The alkali-bath method is somewhat similar in principle. You first saturate the film in a developing solution that does not contain any alkali. As an alkaline substance is used as the 'accelerator' in most developers, the film develops only very slowly without it. You then transfer the film to a solution of a strong alkali to accelerate the developer action. On a similar principle to the water-bath method, the developing agent becomes rapidly exhausted in the highlight areas and less so in the shadows, which are therefore brought up more strongly. Again, the assumption is made that the original exposure was sufficient to give the developer something to work on.

The great advantage of this method compared with water-bath treatment is that it saves a great deal of time and can be carried out in a normal spiral developing tank. Experiments can also determine the effect to be obtained from varying times of immersion in the alkali bath.

Conclusion

It is inevitable that control of image quality during film processing is of limited value with modern equipment and roll and 35mm film. A great deal of control can however, be exercised usefully by those working with sheet film for single images. Nevertheless, film processing is vitally important, and we shall be returning to it later.

It is quite permissible to depart from manufacturers' instructions for film speed and for time and temperature of processing. These instructions depend on various 'norms' that are not always applicable to individual cases. Not all lenses pass the same amount of light at the same aperture settings, and not all shutter speeds are accurate. Exposure meters vary in their efficiency and accuracy. Prolonged development can be accompanied by a significant fall in solution temperature if you work in a cold darkroom. And so on. Above all, there is no single overall density of negative that is ideal for all individual preferences and different types of enlarger. The density of colour slides may need variation to suit the view apparatus.

Photography itself is by no means an exact science and, although exposure and processing can be automated to a high degree, perfection is an individual goal and the roads leading to it are many and varied.

7 CONTROLS IN THE PRINTING PROCESS

The controls available in printing from monochrome negatives are almost limitless. The best printers will also tell you that some control is nearly always needed. That is true enough for those striving for perfection or for a particular effect to suit the end use of the print. The first steps are simple enough. Producing an acceptable print from a good negative is not a dauntingly skilful task. It is the production of a first-class print that calls for more than a little skill.

The printing process is, in principle, the same as that for film processing. In practice, it differs, however, because print materials are much slower than films and are not usually panchromatic. They are usually developed singly and the progressing development can be watched under a safelight. Whereas in shooting a picture a lens is used to form an image of the subject on the film, in printing, a lens serves to project that image on to 'paper' (usually called printing paper but, in fact, nowadays often consisting of a sandwich of paper between layers of polyethylene). In effect, the negative takes the place of the subject and the paper replaces the film. When you develop a film, you get a negative image of a positive subject. When you develop the print, you get a positive image of a negative 'subject' photographed by the enlarger lens.

The developers are essentially the same, too, with the proportions of the constituents varied to provide a more vigorous action for the print developer. There are no grain problems with printing paper, because the speed of the paper is slow enough for the grains to be infinitesimally small – and they are in any case not enlarged. The only grain of significance is that in the negative image, and there is little that can be done about that at the printing stage.

Charcteristics of printing paper

Like the film, printing paper is coated with an 'emulsion' of silver halide particles suspended in gelatin. There are further layers which do not concern us here. The negative image projected on to the paper contains a range of tones representing (inversely) the tones of the original subject. Just as with the film, when the enlarger lamp is switched on the paper receives varying degrees of exposure to light according to the densities of the various parts of the 'subject' (the negative). This time, the proportions are reversed, so that the greatest exposure is received by the areas representing the darkest parts of the original subject, because they have the least density in the negative.

Development of the paper is a process similar to that of developing the film. The exposed silver halide particles are reduced to metallic silver grains, and a positive image appears, reproducing the original subject in all, or almost all, its tones. The contrast range of the tones that the paper can reproduce is limited to a ratio of about 1:50 or 1:60, compared with the 1:500 or so of the film (ie, maximum to minimum light transmission, not usable tones). That is because the film densities are measured by transmitted light and those of the paper by reflected light. Photographic papers are never totally non-reflecting in the black areas and the amount that can be reflected by the white areas is less than that which can be transmitted by clear film.

So the wide range of tones in the original scene has to be compressed to a 1:60 range. This, as it happens, is not nearly as drastic as it sounds. It simply means that the 10 tones in the subject that we have listed at one-stop intervals have to be represented in the print at about three-quarter stop intervals. Progressing by one stop each time from 1 to 10 gives 1:512, whereas progressing by only three-quarters of a stop each time gives about 1:60.

The effect is that the whole range of tones is compressed and in the print we cannot see as many intermediate tones as were present in the subject. But do we really see all those tones in the original? What we actually see is conditioned by the nature of perception, which is influenced by the way the eye works and by past experience. When we look at a scene, we do not analyse all the various tones in it, and worry if some are missing. We are used to seeing our friends and relations in a variety of lighting conditions. We are accustomed to looking at newspaper pictures, television images, glossy magazine reproductions and photographic prints. Good, original photographs are by far the best quality images, but we accept each for what it is. Only in the most exceptional cases are we ever aware that the images lack some of the finer tones of the original. Even if we saw the original, we probably did not perceive those tones. Also, we seldom compare a

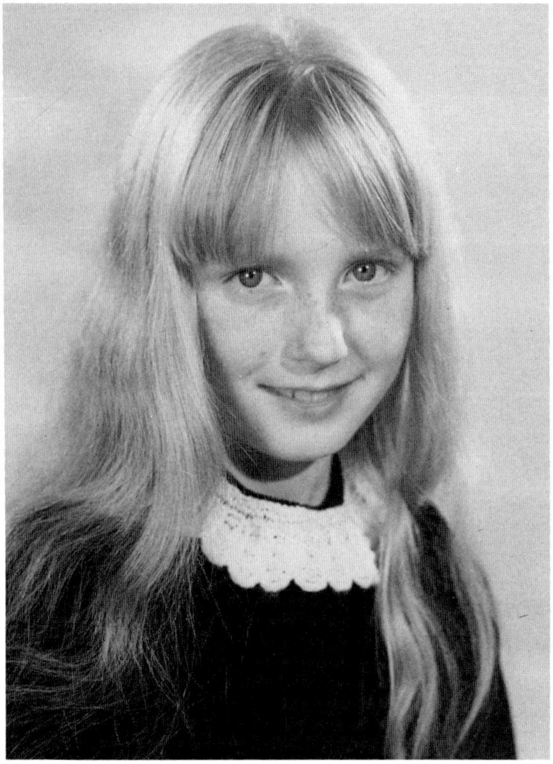

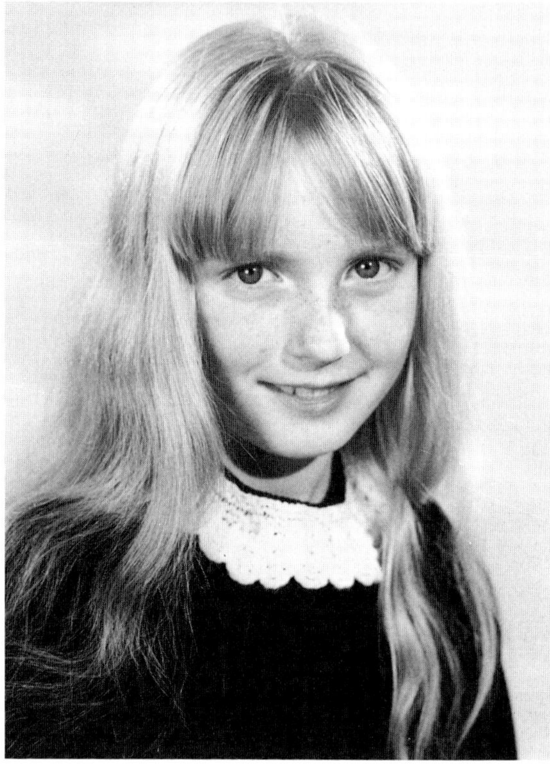

photograph directly with the original scene.

It is as well to realise that there are differences between the subject, the negative and the print, but there is no need to feel any sense of frustration about it. A good printer can even manipulate the photographic process to show more in the image than we perceive in the subject.

The photographer's aim should be to produce a negative that reduces to a minimum the need for manipulation in printing. With most subjects, it should be possible to eliminate manipulation altogether. Where some control at the printing stage is likely to be necessary, the camera exposure must be made with that fact in mind.

In most cases, the need for control of the printing process concerns contrast. The negative is either a little too 'flat' or, conversely, has too much contrast to give the best print on the normal grade of photographic paper. Most papers are supplied in a variety of contrast grades. Emulsions are manufactured to give low, medium or high contrast results with a normal negative. A negative with contrast that is too low, therefore, can be printed on a harder (higher contrast) grade of paper – and vice versa. Nevertheless, the aim should be to make the negative do most of the work. If you photograph printed matter on white paper, black-and-white drawings, etc., use a slow, higher contrast film for preference. The highest contrast paper grades should be reserved for emergency use.

There are special high-contrast films and developers available for pure black and white subjects. It makes little sense to use ordinary, relatively low contrast film when you are aiming for the greatest contrast in the print. If you cannot avoid such a situation, it is best to copy the resulting negative on to a high contrast film (and recopy it if necessary) before making the final print.

Using contrast grades

If, in spite of all your efforts, the negative does not fit the paper characteristics, you may find that the print cannot produce a real black without adding too much density to the highlights, or can produce both black and white, but not much detail in between. In the first instance, the negative is too flat; there is not enough contrast between the low and high densities. The obvious answer is a higher contrast grade of paper. In the second

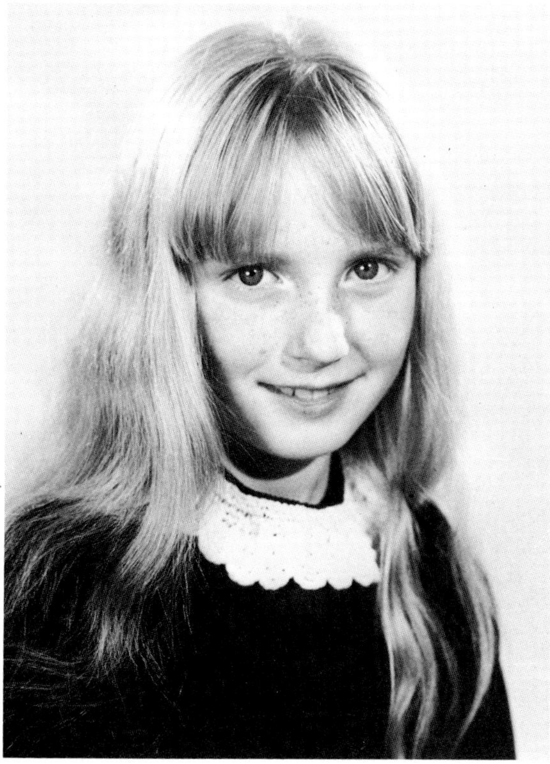

27-29 The effect of printing, from left to right, on soft, normal and hard grades of paper.

30 (Overleaf) The aim should be to get the contrast in the negative. When that is not possible, a hard grade of paper can produce the desired effect.

case, the reverse applies, but there is somewhat less chance of success. It is likely that the subject itself was too high in contrast. Printing on a soft grade of paper is rarely successful with such a negative, because it is difficult to produce a good, strong black. Soft (low-contrast) papers are best confined to deliberately produced low-contrast subjects.

A range of paper contrast grades is indispensable for roll and 35mm film users: the film cannot always receive optimum processing for every image. Paper grades are a legitimate part of the photographic image if used intelligently, but they should not be relied on to get you out of trouble arising from careless camera exposure.

Paper contrast grades are available only for monochrome work. Papers for colour printing are supplied only in the one grade and the control of contrast must be dealt with in the camera exposure, either by avoiding the high-contrast subject as much as possible, or by varying the lighting. Although a limited amount of control can be exercised with colour slides (because colour development is a separate step), the single developer used for colour negatives and colour prints gives no scope for manipulation.

Also for monochrome use, there are papers that allow various degrees of contrast to be obtained on the one paper. These multiple-grade papers have mixed emulsions of differently sensitised silver halide particles. When the colour of the exposing light is varied by the use of special filters, the effect on the emulsion varies to produce higher or lower contrast. The principle is no different from that of employing different grades of paper, but there is an obvious advantage in needing to stock only one 'grade'.

Localised printing control

Contrast grades are used to influence the overall contrast of a print. Sometimes, it is more satisfactory to vary the exposure given to different parts of the image. In printing, this is relatively easy, because you can see the image during the exposure – even in colour.

The simplest case is where moderate overexposure of the film has caused faint cloud traces in the sky to disappear in the print. An exposure that produces the required tones in the rest of the print is too short to get the additional density into the sky area, which accordingly prints dead white. Careful shading of the landscape or other area, while giving extra exposure to the sky area, can effect a marked improvement. Slightly more difficult is the case where a small part of the picture area, away from the edge, has been similarly overexposed. Then the whole image has to be shaded, apart from that small area.

These techniques are called 'burning in' or 'printing up'. The opposite treatment is 'shading' or 'dodging'. You could regard printing up the sky as the same as shading the landscape, but the terms 'dodging' and 'burning in' are generally applied to localised treatment of small areas within the borders of the print.

When all else fails, there is the ultimate control of tone separation (not to be confused with 'posterisation'). Tone separation involves the preparation of two copy negatives from the original, one to record shadow detail, the other, highlight detail. These are prepared on ordinary camera film and

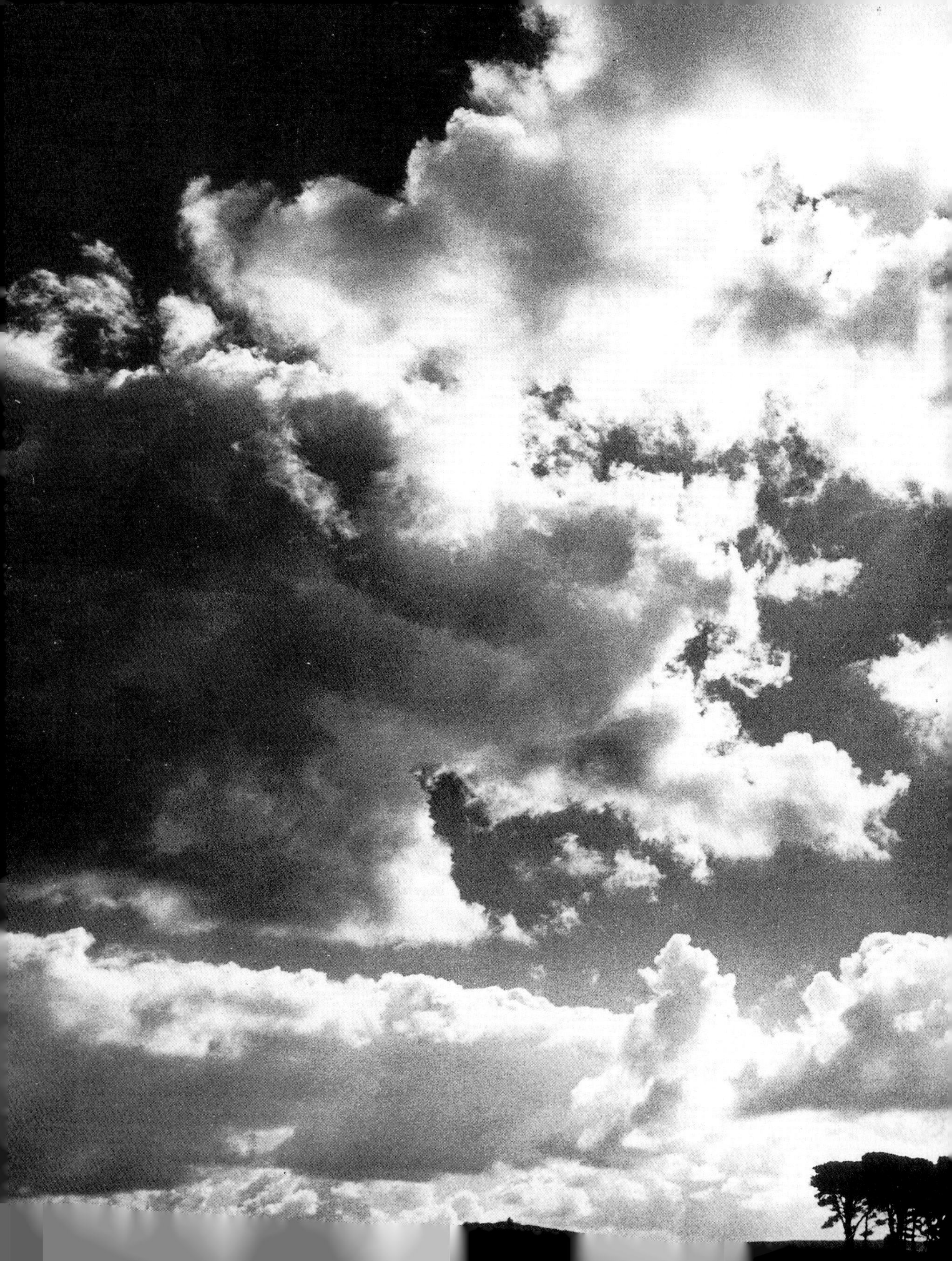

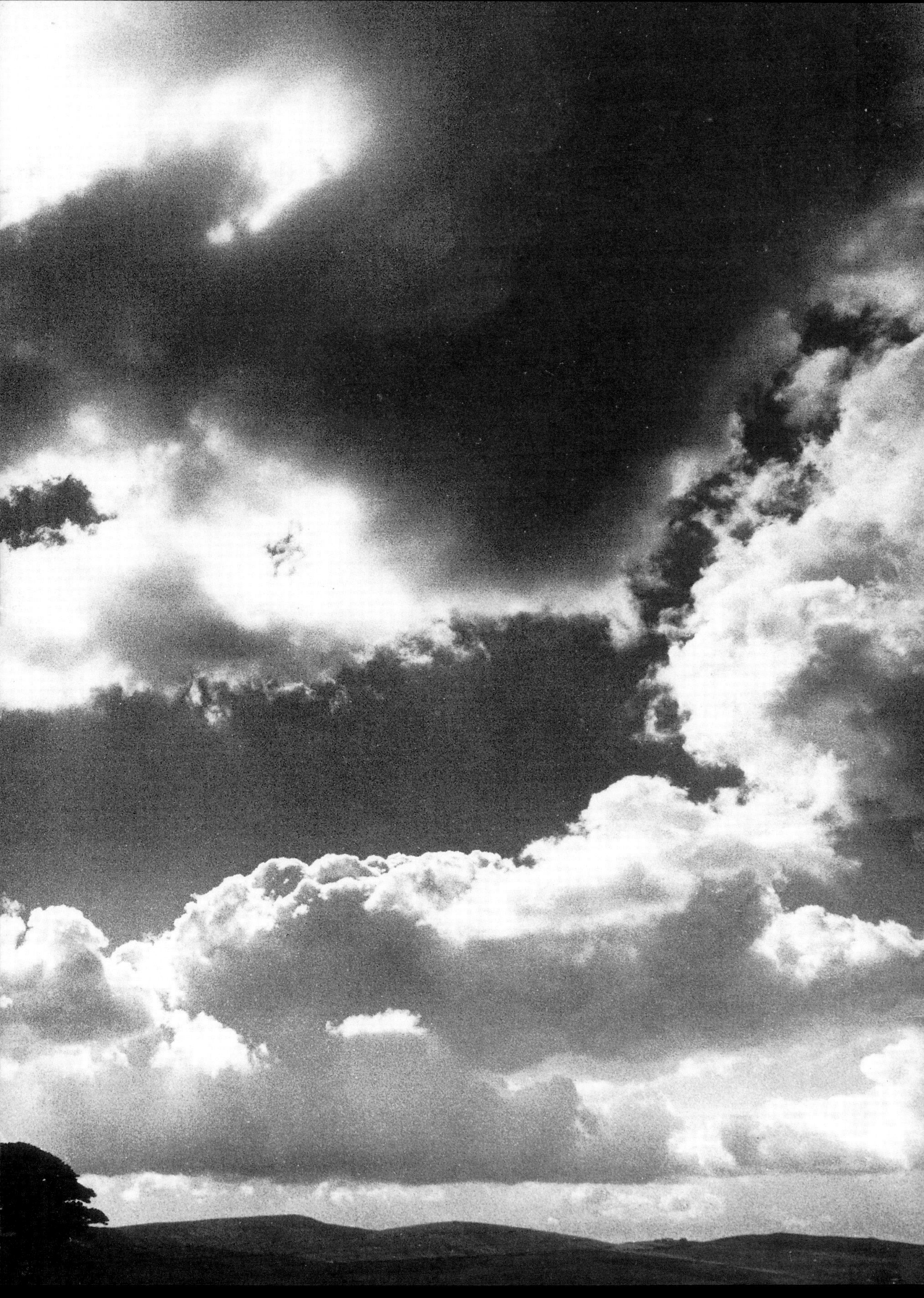

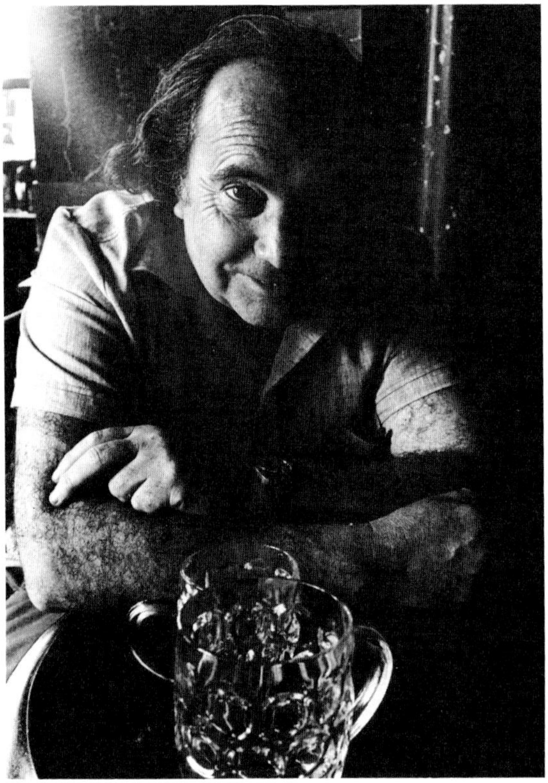

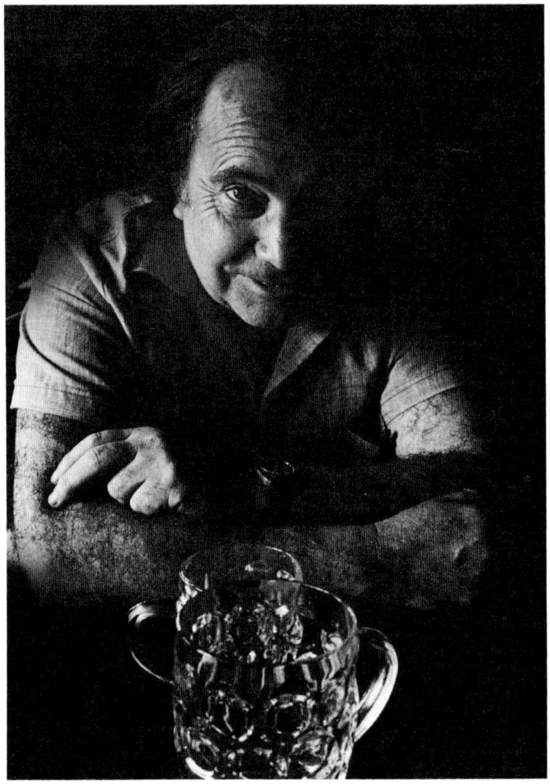

31-32 An extreme case of printing-up to obscure unwanted detail. A small torch (flashlight) was used to blacken the bottom lefthand corner.

are printed separately on the same sheet of paper. This is a specialised process not recommended for 35mm work, except by working from enlarged copy negatives. There are many other specialised darkroom techniques to change the nature of the image, rather than to correct faults in the negative, but their detailed discussion is outside the scope of this book.

Print processing control

As a print is processed by exactly the same principle as a film, similar controls are available. On the other hand, as printing paper is supplied in various grades, it is not necessary to try to handle contrast by varying exposure and development time or by changing the developer.

Full development. Although the procedure and chemicals are more or less the same, there is one significant difference between film and print processing. The print, with its invisible grain construction, can be developed to finality, ie, until there are no more exposed silver halide particles left to develop. Full development is, in fact, one way of avoiding the combination of overexposure and underdevelopment that the tyro printer is often guilty of. It produces flattish prints with weak blacks.

There is a school of thought which maintains that every print should contain a maximum black and a pure white. This assertion is not as silly as it might at first seem. Even the most offbeat subjects do, in fact, contain at least tiny areas where such tones should appear. You cannot obtain both tones, however, except by correct exposure and development of the print, ie, with the minimum exposure that will produce a maximum black at the recommended development time. The advantage of full development is that, provided the exposure is correct, development can be extended considerably beyond the recommended minimum time with little change in tonal values.

Nothing but the best

You must be able to recognise a good print when you see one – that is one of the values of photographic exhibitions. Very few reproduction processes can approach the quality of a photographic print. If you have never seen the best that photo-

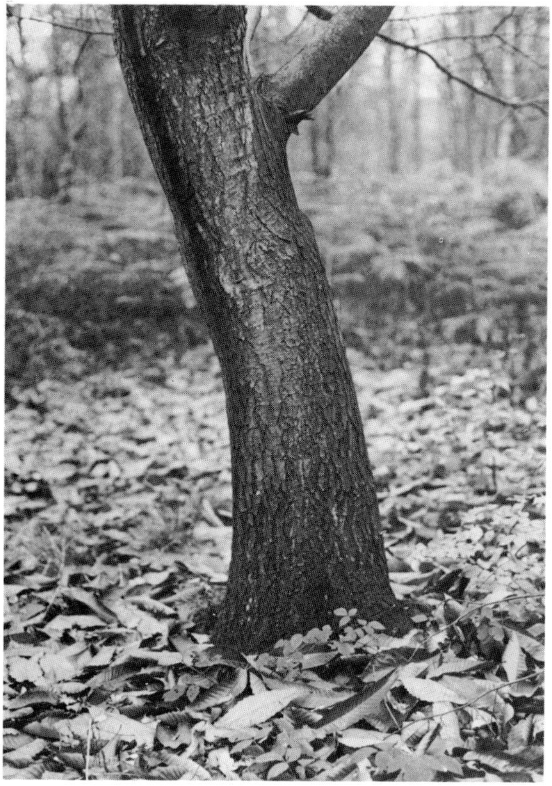

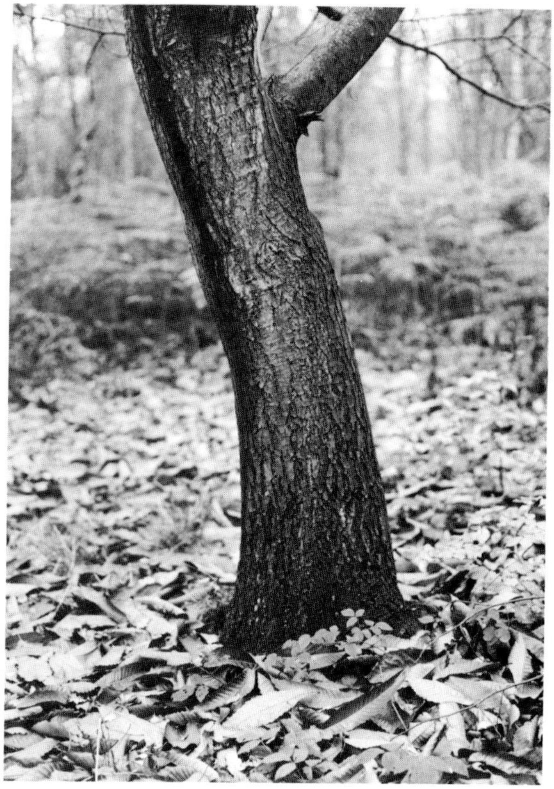

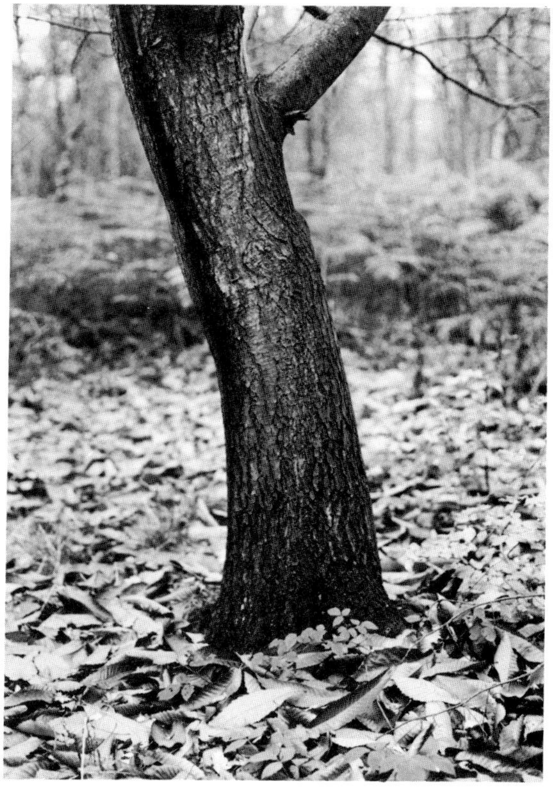

33-35 The effect of print exposure and development time. Left to right: long exposure, short development; normal treatment; short exposure, long development.

graphy can do, you are in no position to judge your own work. Correct exposure in the camera is the first vital step in the photographic process. Without it, you cannot get the best possible image in the print. On the other hand, indifferent printing technique can nullify all the work you put into producing the negative.

The basic technique is the same as that for the film – correct exposure related to the paper characteristics and the developer used. Papers vary; the normal types used with the recommended developers generally require a minimum of two minutes development at about 20°C (68°F). Chlorobromide papers (special versions designed to give warmer tones) may be restricted to 90 sec to produce their best 'colour'. Many resin-coated papers, as most of them now are, develop fully in 60 sec. In general, time and temperature are not as critical as with film processing. Development can be extended with little loss of quality if the temperature falls slightly.

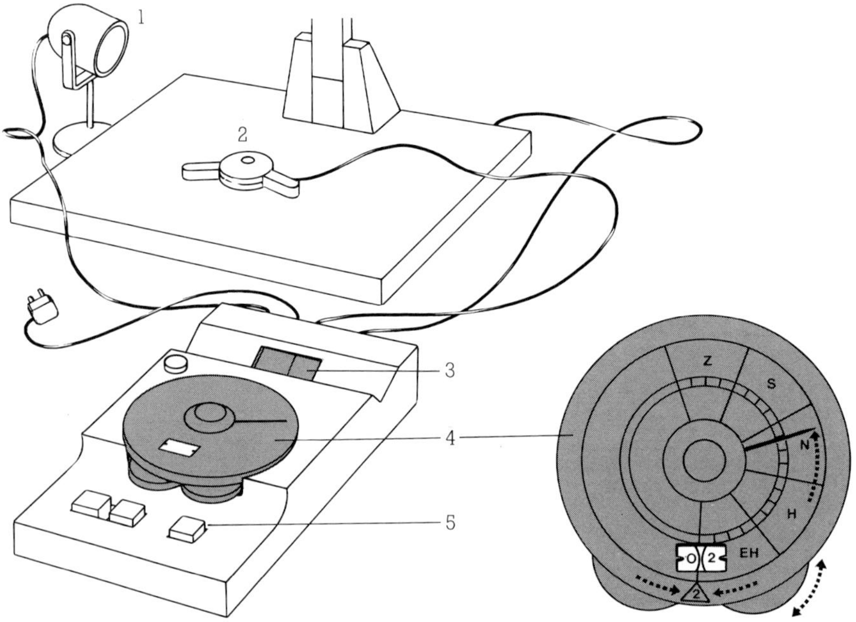

7.1 Enlarging exposure meter. 1 Safelight. 2 Meter probe. 3 Indicator lights. 4 Calculator discs. 5 Control switches. This type uses readings from highlight and shadow areas to indicate both exposure and paper grade.

Exposure *is* critical. It is possible to make what might seem to be a tolerable print by over-exposing and pulling the print out of the developer before the minimum time, when it appears under the safelighting to have reached the density required. Invariably, the resulting print will not be the best possible. It will not have a maximum black and will lack contrast throughout the rest of the tones. Similarly, if you under-expose, no amount of extended development will bring up the highlight detail that did not receive sufficient exposure.

For the best possible results, adhere closely to the manufacturer's instructions and to the findings of your own tests. Standardise your paper, chemicals, time and temperature. You will then always know exactly what you are doing and will be able to reproduce previous results exactly.

8 PUTTING THEM TOGETHER IN PRACTICE

The controls available for use in planning and producing the final image add up to a formidable list, especially for monochrome work. Now we come to using them in practice.

Average and non-average subjects

TTL meters are now almost universal in 35mm single lens reflex cameras and the general method of assessing exposure manually with these cameras is to point the camera at the subject and adjust the lens aperture and/or the exposure time until a readout in the viewfinder indicates that the controls are set for correct exposure. For most subjects, that is enough. What you are doing is taking a general integrated-light reading of the whole subject. The meter receives a value of the average light of the subject. If the subject has a reasonably even distribution of tones (ie, it is an average subject), the reading should be the same as a direct reading from a standard grey card.

Whatever the reading is, the meter interprets it as if it were taken from a single standard tone and gives the exposure recommended to reproduce that tone. If the subject does not have an even distribution of tones, the meter is misinformed. The subject may, for example, have a preponderance of light tones, making its average tone about Tone 7 or 8. The meter then reads Tone 7 or 8, but believes that it is reading Tone 6. So it recommends an exposure to average the subject out to Tone 6 – amounting to one or two stops underexposure. If the subject is largely dark-toned, the meter might read what is, in fact, an average of Tone 4 or 5, translate it as Tone 6 and so recommend one or two stops overexposure.

In other words, a straight reflected light reading of a predominantly light subject will always recommend underexposure. A predominantly dark subject on the other hand causes the meter to recommend overexposure. To avoid this problem, learn to assess the overall tonal value of your subject. Most subjects do average out to a mid-tone. Many others may be near enough to avoid any gross error in exposure. Some subjects may be obviously nowhere near average. It is those that fall between these extremes that can raise problems.

We have already indicated the most reliable method of learning to recognise non-average subjects. Equip yourself with a separate meter and a grey card or incident light attachment, and take a direct reflected-light reading of all types of scene and subject, comparing the direct reading either with an incident light reading or with a reading from a grey card held in front of the subject. Be careful not to throw your own shadow or that of the meter over the grey card, but make sure that the meter is close enough to read the card and nothing else. When the main light is directly behind you this is difficult, and it is on such occasions that an incident-light reading is more reliable. When taking an incident-light reading, however, be sure that you are standing in the same lighting as the subject.

An average subject – one that averages out to a mid-tone – should give a reading to within half a stop of that taken from a grey card. You may well

36 Two widely-separated tone ranges. A general reading, avoiding undue influence from subject or background is essential to record everything without loss. With a carefully controlled printer, subject and background can be reproduced realistically.

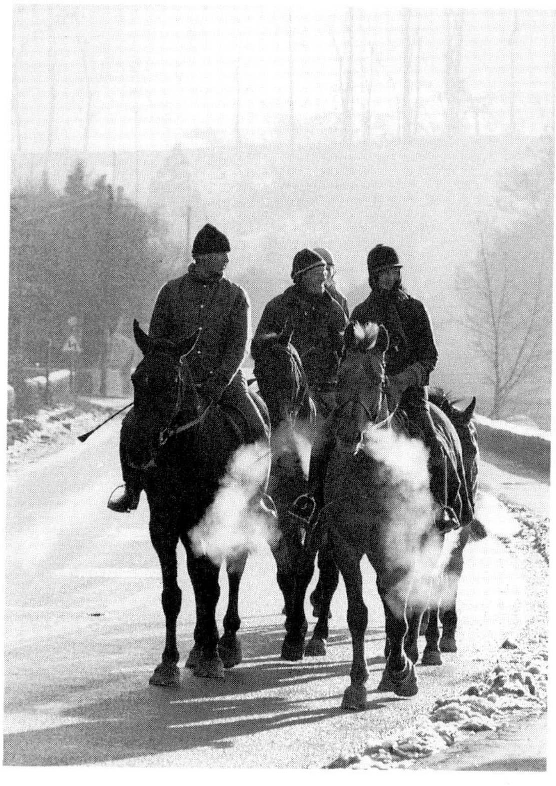

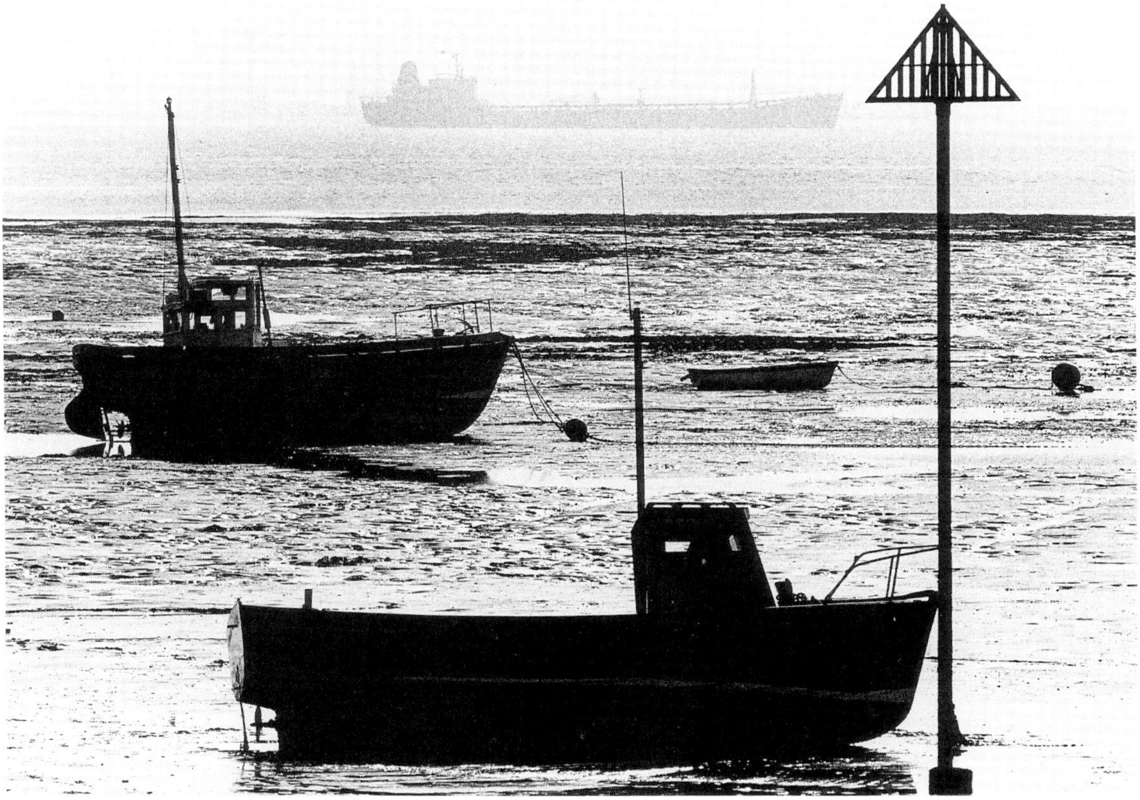

37 A lot of deep shadow and plenty of mid-tones. A normal reading could well lead to overexposure.

38 A high-contrast subject, but one that the modern SLR with centre-weighted metering might handle reasonably well.

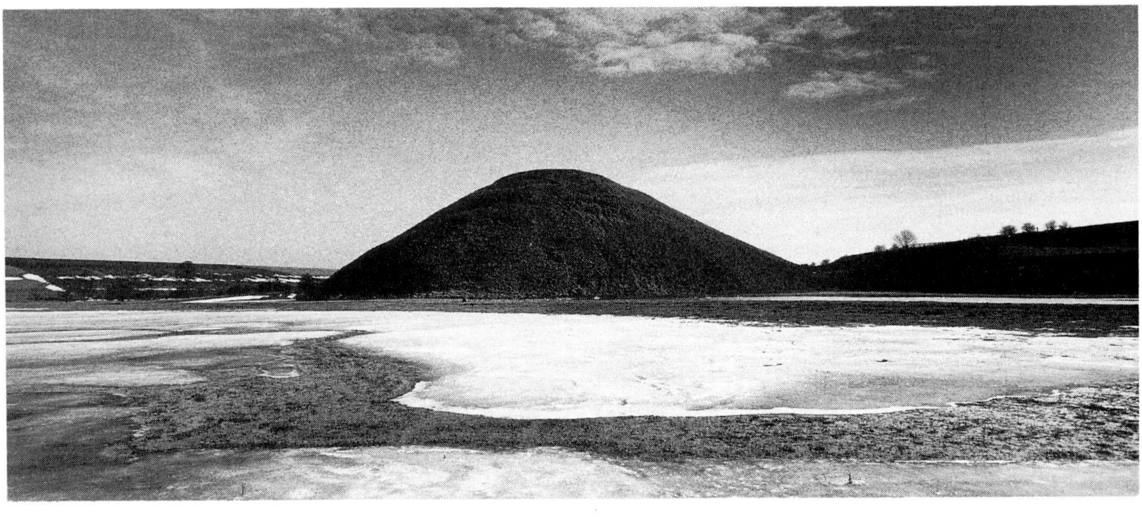

be surprised to find how many do, and how many more are within one stop and are therefore well within the latitude of negative films. You may occasionally be surprised, too, to find that a scene you would confidently classify as average turns out not to be so.

Interior plus exterior

Now turn to some subjects that are obviously not average and learn to assess how far from average they are. You want, say, to picture somebody looking out of a window. It is more or less a portrait, so you want a reasonably accurate flesh tone. You would also like at least an impression of the scene outside.

Take a general reading of the outdoor scene from the window. Take a grey card reading in the area of the subject's face or other flesh tone. On a bright day with clouds, there could be six stops difference between the two readings. Is the picture possible?

You do not want the interior and exterior scenes to look as if they were in the same lighting, so underexposure of one or overexposure of the other is acceptable. It is evident, however, that neither can stand a difference of six stops. With modern films, the outdoor scene may be able to withstand an error of two or three stops, especially if you allow for the exercise of some control in printing. This still leaves the interior at least three stops underexposed, lowering the flesh tone to Tone 4. As the part facing the camera must be somewhat shaded, you might accept Tone 5, but 4 is too low. The alternative is to let the outdoor scene go to four stops overexposure. Depending on the nature of the scene, that might just be acceptable, with some localised control over the print.

Exposure and development. The problem is basically one of contrast. Can you adjust exposure and development? You can in theory, but not very easily in practice. You really need a soft-working developer or a two-bath treatment – fine if you are using sheet film or expending a whole roll of film on this or similar subjects.

Soft-working developers are useful for high-contrast subjects in which you wish to reduce the contrast. They usually contain metol as the only developing agent, omitting its usual hydroquinone companion, and are only moderately alkaline, relying on sodium sulphite alone or sometimes adding just a little sodium carbonate. Their aim is to bring up the shadow densities more strongly than the highlight densities. Water bath and alkali bath methods are also effective, indeed often better. The water-bath method would be particularly suitable for this type of subject, if feasible.

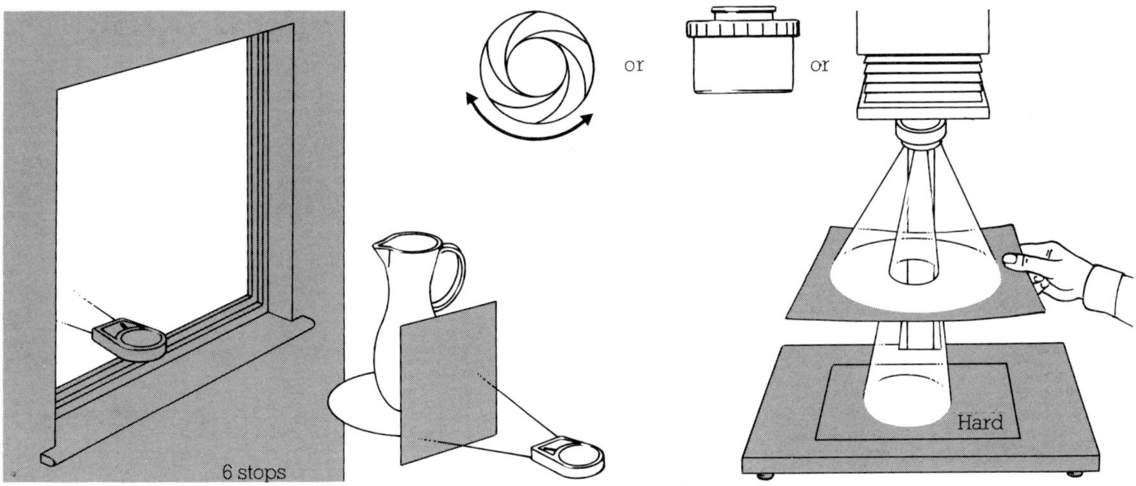

8.1 There could be six stops difference between a meter reading of the outdoor scene and the subject, but you want both rendered more or less normally. You could try various exposure and development adjustments but it is generally better with modern materials to use control in printing. With colour, the only answer is to increase the interior lighting.

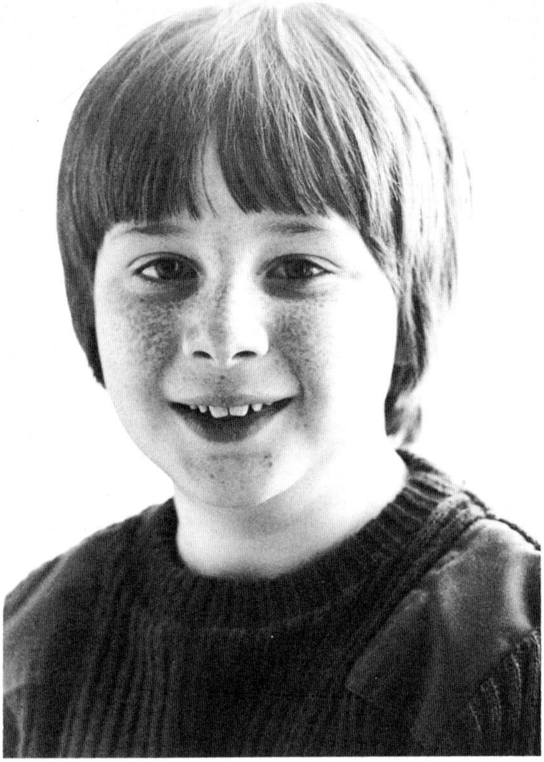

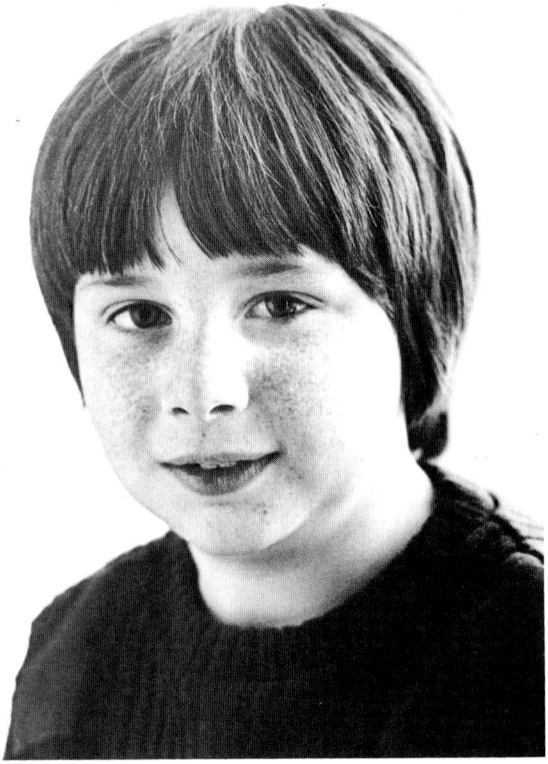

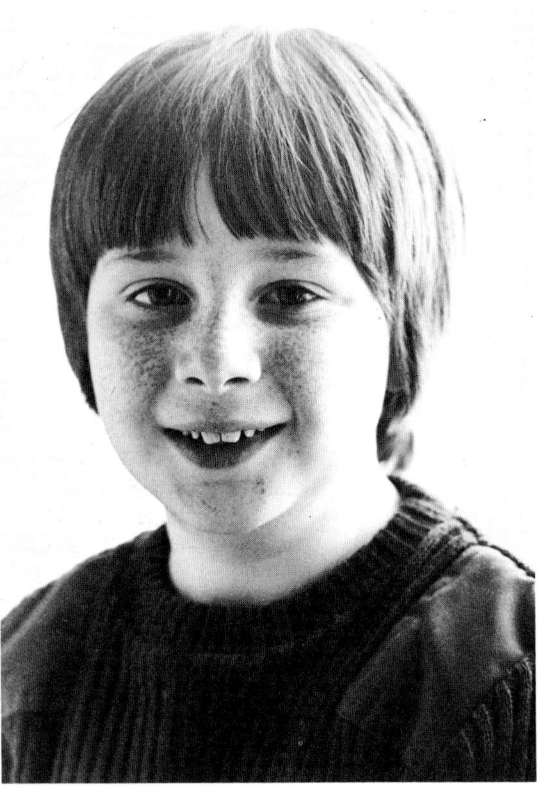

39-41 Portrait by window light. From left to right, window light alone gives uneven lighting. A white reflector improves matters by throwing light back on to the front of the face. Fill-in by flash bounced off the ceiling gives a more even overall light that is more suitable for colour.

A further technique is to increase exposure and curtail development, though in this case it is not well suited to the subject. With this method, you effectively place all tones one step higher than normal and bring them down again by shortening the development time. The idea is that the increased exposure has little effect in the highlight area (the shoulder of the characteristic curve), but helps to build density in the shadows. The underdevelopment has a greater effect on the denser areas of the negative (ie, there is proportionately less development there). Highlight and middle tones are therefore slightly compressed, while shadow detail is retained. Overall contrast is reduced. This treatment is not particularly effective with modern films, which tend to have longer straight line portions and to be without pronounced toe and shoulder regions. Nevertheless, some combinations of film and processing technique work well, so it is worth carrying out your own tests.

If you decide that adjusted film development is not the answer, you are left with printing control. That is probably the best solution for this particular subject. In printing, you have two possible techniques: using a softer grade of paper to reduce contrast, or printing-in the outdoor scene while shading the interior part. Which you use depends on the nature of the subject. If the two scenes blend one into the other, with the figure and, perhaps, curtains and furnishings overlapping the outdoor scene, printing-in could call for considerable skill. Without that level of skill, a softer grade of paper is the only answer. The ideal answer is probably a combination of both treatments.

Thus, the subject which, at first sight, seems nearly impossible, is not necessarily so. You must decide in advance, however, what method you are going to use to produce the final result. The camera exposure must be based on that method. If you decide, for example, that you must use only printing controls, the exposure must be such that printing-in is possible. You cannot expose for the indoor scene alone. Six stops overexposure of the outdoor scene is likely to produce densities in the negative that cannot be satisfactorily printed. On the other hand, the densities for the interior scene must not be so low that they require a high-contrast grade of paper to print properly. You have to assess the exact compromise necessary. In this case, two stops underexposure of the indoor scene is about the limit.

Finally, this subject is virtually impossible in colour, and particularly for a colour slide, without sacrificing detail at one or other end of the tonal scale. Drastic adjustments of exposure lead to noticeable colour distortion, and there is very little opportunity to control contrast by adjusting the film processing. The only real remedy in that case – and you might well decide that it is the only sensible course in monochrome, too – is to adjust the lighting. It may be enough to move the subject nearer to the window or to introduce a large white reflecting surface just out of the picture area to throw light back at the figure. That would probably not be enough for colour and the answer would then be to use extra lighting on the subject. Any such light used, however, must be of the same quality as daylight. You can't mix two different light sources in the same colour picture. In practice, you would almost certainly use electronic flash (see Chapter 12).

42 (Overleaf) a total distortion of subject tones with processing and printing for full contrast.

Sunshine and shadow

Now for a different type of problem. The scene is a wooded area with autumn foliage and strong sunlight throwing shafts of light through the branches. The leaves are transilluminated, showing delicate detail and colour, and the beams of sunlight are reasonably well defined. The overall lighting is good, and grassy patches are strongly

8.2 Sunshine in woods. If readings from sunlight through foliage and from darker parts of trees are within a six-stop range, adequate exposure should be obtained by adding three or four stops to the reading from the trees.

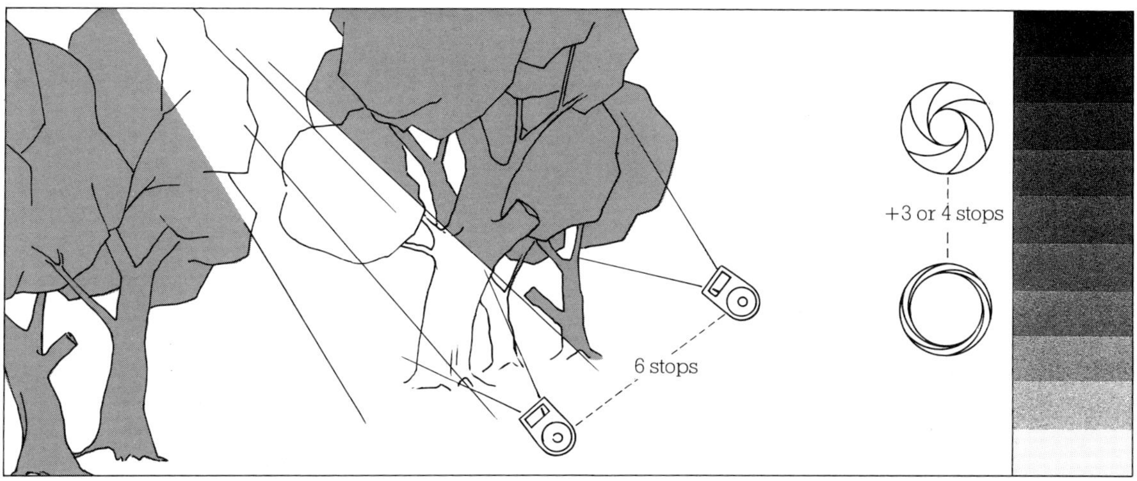

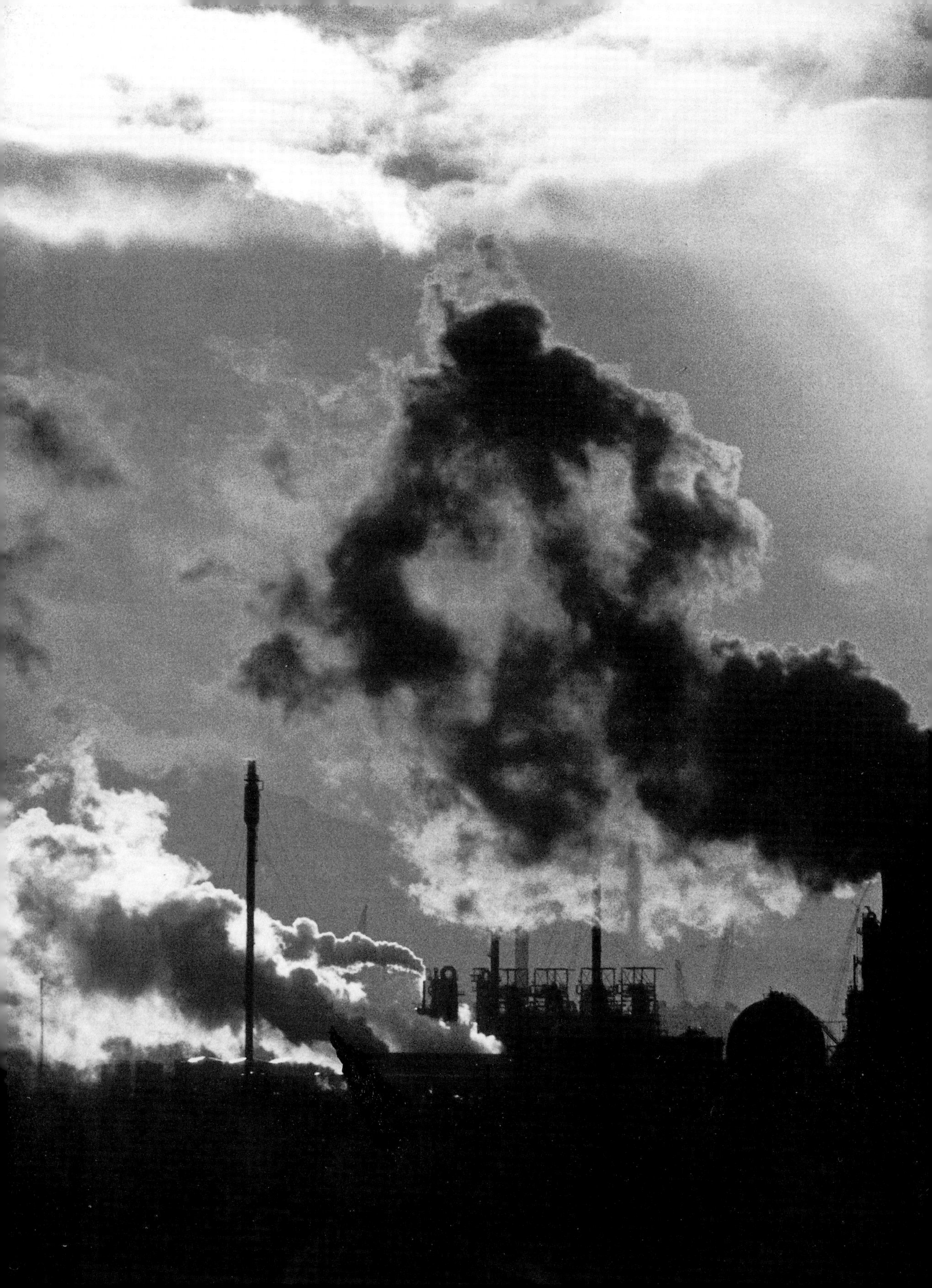

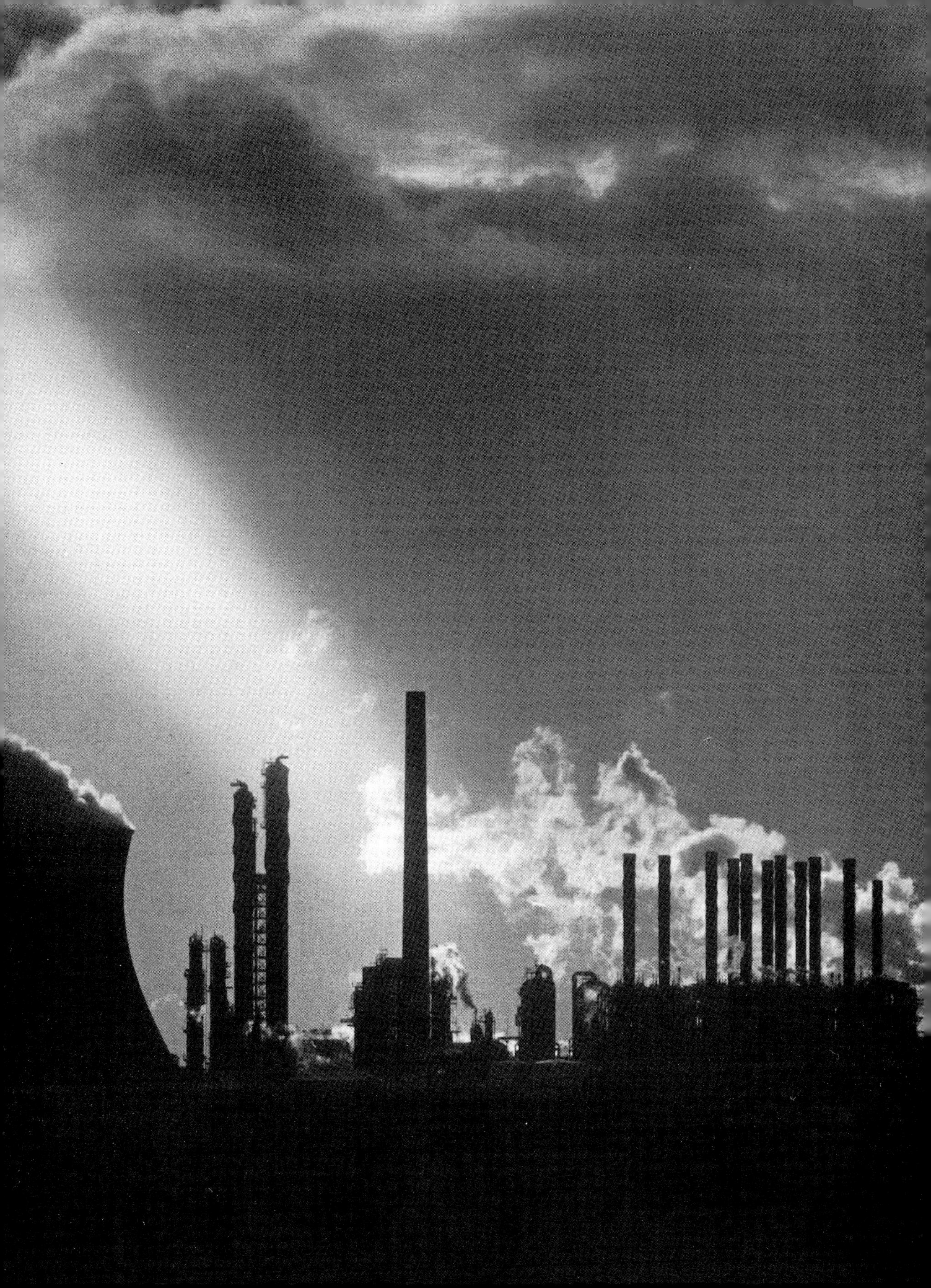

lit. What kind of picture are you going to produce and what exposure does it need?

You might well decide that the sunbeams and the finely-detailed foliage are the main attraction. The tree trunks and the ground area are simply a backdrop. The whole scene would quite possibly integrate to grey, so a direct meter reading would give you a possible exposure. The result would be well-defined tree trunks, ground area and general surroundings, with the leaves bright and the sunbeams broad shafts of light merging into the background and into one another. The overall effect would be of a light airy scene – but without any particular appeal. In colour, the highlight areas might well be almost devoid of colour and lacking any fine detail.

That is not the impression you get if you view the scene through half-closed eyes. You become more conscious of the contrast between the sun's rays, the foliage and the general woodland scene. The tree trunks and most of the ground area look darker, the sun's rays are more narrowly defined as shafts of light rather than broad bands, and the foliage appears as a delicate tracery. The scene sparkles. You may decide that this is the impression you want to convey.

It is then evident that you need to maintain the contrast, perhaps even to increase it. You do not need the ground and tree bark detail that your eyes so readily adjust to. You want to see the scene as with unaccommodating eyes – through a fixed iris, like the camera lens. The tree trunks might look like Tone 4 or 5 as you adjust your vision to them but they would be quite satisfactory as Tone 3 or even 2. You cannot readily assess the tonal value of the sun's rays or the leaves, but you can decide how you would like them to appear in the print. You would probably want the leaves at about Tone 7. You would not want the sun's rays to go beyond 9.

You now have a range of about six or seven stops, just within the capability of the film. Take a close-up reading of a tree trunk. Then point the meter at the brightest area of sky plus foliage. The chances are that the reading will be near enough the value of the sun's rays in the picture area. If the two readings are within the six or seven stop range, you have every chance of getting the picture you want by pegging the exposure at that estimated for the trees.

Your close-up reading for the tree trunk recommends an exposure to reproduce it as Tone 6, although it is probably actually about Tone 4. You want it as Tone 2 or 3. So, if you set your exposure at 3 or 4 stops less than the reading from the tree recommends, you should get the picture you want.

You have effectively placed the Tone 4 of the tree in the Tone 2 or 3 position. Consequently, all other tones are also brought down. The bright rays of the sun and the transilluminated leaves have been saved from overexposure and should retain detail. Any sky area visible may be a little over-bright, but that is not important. Parts falling into deep shadow will probably show no detail at all. That, too, is acceptable for the type of picture we are seeking. Now, the overall impression will be of strong sunlight in a shady woodland scene and there will be much more warmth and depth to the picture.

Transforming the subject

Progressing further, how do you transform a scene to make it reproduce in a particular manner? You are sitting on the beach on a brilliantly sunlit day. Sky, sea and sand are reflecting enormous amounts of light. Figures with unbelievable energy are racing along the beach at the water's edge. It hurts your eyes to watch them and the glare is such that you can barely make out their shapes at all. Can you show that?

You can, in fact, by careful handling of exposure. You could not make much of it as an ordinary exposure. Normal detail in sand and sky would call for an exposure so short that the figures would go into at least partial silhouette – a possible picture in some circumstances, but not very striking. Shorten the exposure still further and you will get darker-than-normal tones in the sky, sea and sand, the figures in full silhouette and maybe dancing highlights on the sea: possible again.

What would a wider aperture do? It could produce an interesting result, lightening the general surroundings perhaps to the point of obliterating detail. You would get detail in the figures but little contrast. You could get them nearer your painful view of them, however, by using the shutter speed setting to provide the extended exposure. Suppose you set an exposure time that allows the moving figures to blur quite noticeably – say to about a quarter of the figure width? In other words, the images of the figures move appreciably during the exposure. What happens, in fact, is that part of the figure moves into an area of the film that has already been exposed to the very strong backlighting – and part moves out of an

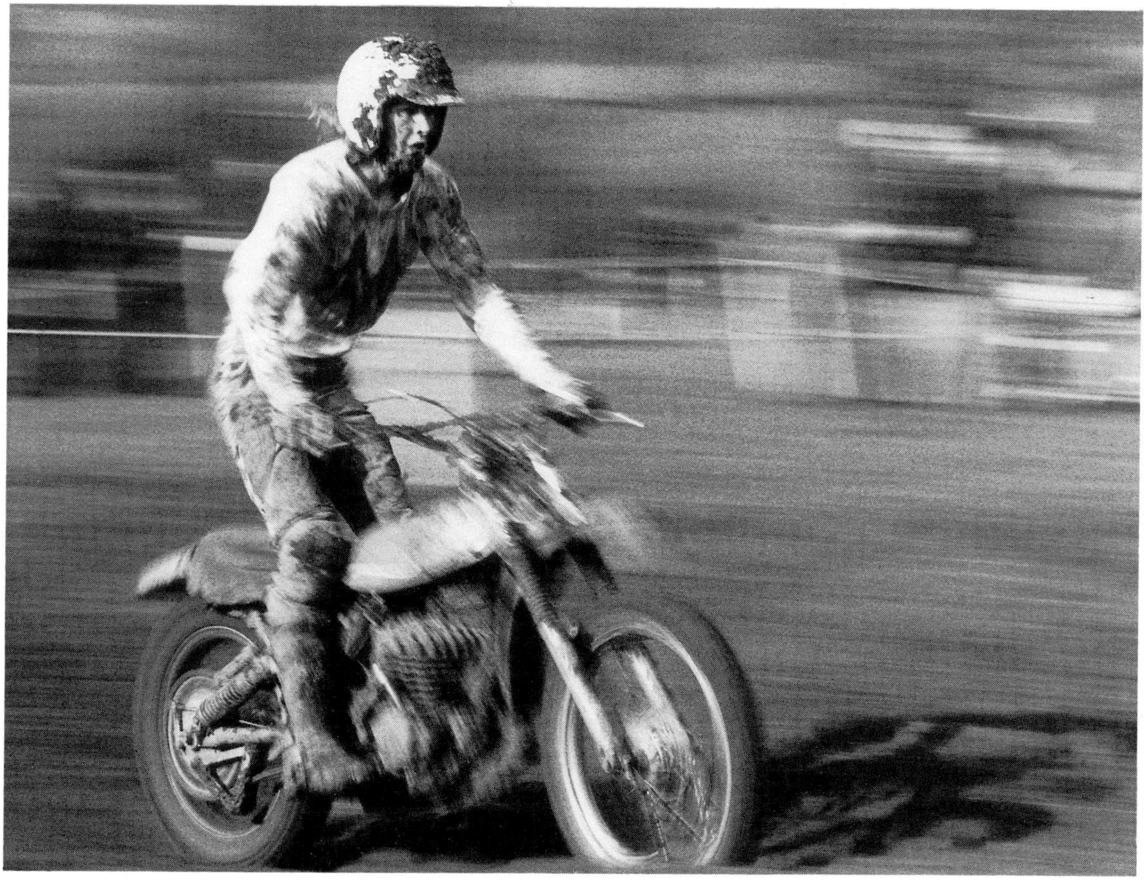

43 Use of a slow shutter speed to 'smudge' subject and background and emphasise movement.

8.3 Underexposure and overdevelopment. A reading from Tone 8 gives an exposure that would reproduce it as Tone 6 with normal development. Extended development may compensate to bring it up to Tone 7.

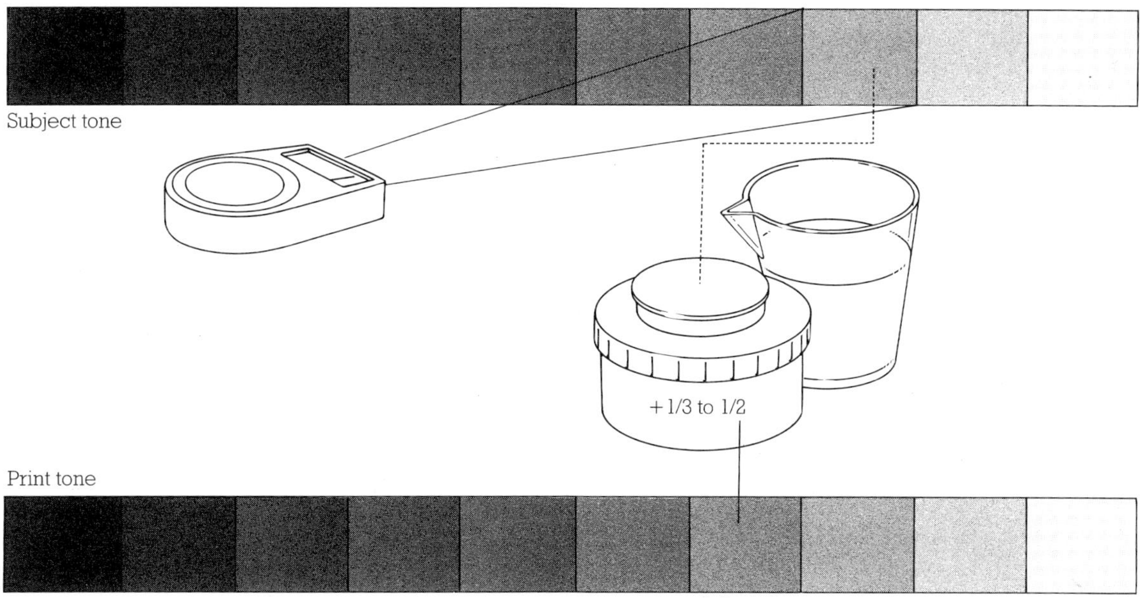

area that is subsequently exposed in a similar manner. The result is that the edges of the figures disappear and each is trimmed down to a 'slim line' version rather similar to what you see with unprotected eyes.

The trick is to get the exposure time right. If it is too long or the figures move too fast, they will virtually disappear. You generally need a shutter speed of about 1/15 to 1/30 sec, perhaps 1/60 if the figures are exceptionally energetic.

The limits of processing variations

Finally, what are the conditions in which adjusted development can be of some value? We have already indicated that generous exposure and curtailed development may have uses with some films in reducing contrast. The main drawback is that you do not often shoot a complete roll of film, particularly 35mm, under such conditions. You may well be out on a rather dull day when the light from a grey sky is very flat. Modelling is almost non-existent. Very weak shadows make buildings look like cardboard cutouts and faces uninteresting. Then you can think about the reverse technique – curtailed exposure and extended development.

These are relative terms. We talk loosely about overexposure, underexposure, etc. in terms of the norms laid down for average subjects in sun-plus-cloud conditions. These norms do not apply when the conditions change. The main difference between 'normal' and dull lighting is in the shadow areas. With sun-plus-cloud, the average shadow value is about Tone 6, or a standard mid-tone, perhaps a little darker.

Exposure in dull light. For the sake of comparison, take average shadow values as Tone 6. In dull conditions, such shadows could be about two stops lighter, corresponding to a Tone 8. So a normal exposure places them there, too light to give any real modelling. You want them to reproduce darker without too much effect on lighter tones. You cannot expect to simulate sun and cloud conditions, but you can improve matters a little.

In this respect, bear in mind that the dull lighting conditions do not affect the relative tones of areas in the same lighting, ie, the unshaded areas. The difference between white and black is still the same proportionately whatever the intensity of the lighting – or near enough so in the conditions that concern us. It is only the difference in shadow values that causes the changes in contrast.

To return to our subject in dull light. Take a reading from a mid-shadow area (not the deepest of the shadows). This gives an exposure for reproduction as Tone 6, which would be a two-stop underexposure compared with its true value of 8, but only one stop for its intended value of 7. Set your camera controls to give the exposure indicated by the shadow reading, so pegging the shadows at a value of Tone 6. Treat all exposures on the roll of film in the same manner. If the sun comes out, do not shoot, or change the film.

Try not to use the method on changeable days. It is chiefly suitable for the dull day with very little chance of sunshine.

Processing. When you process the film, the aim is to bring the shadows exposed as Tone 6 up to Tone 7. That will call for something like one-third to one-half increased development time, or treatment in a higher-contrast developer. Both treatments give the characteristic curve of the film a steeper slope. The light shadows and other mid-tones are better separated, while the few really dark and light tones are little affected. It should be easy to make a brighter print that shows improved modelling.

Do not be too ambitious with this treatment and don't try it with colour negative film. Modern films have rather less pronounced toe and shoulder portions of the characteristic curve than older versions had. You cannot make a flatly lit subject look as if it were shot in brilliant sunlight. The best you can do is to heighten the contrast in the mid-tones and deepen the shadows slightly to make a brighter print. To do so satisfactorily, however, you need to know your materials. Chapter 17 details tests for both film and developer, so that you know exactly what you can and cannot do.

9 EXPOSURE AT CLOSE RANGE

You will be aware that (apart from the choice of shutter speed) the amount of light reaching the film is controlled by the size of the lens aperture. Glass reflects some light, and also absorbs some. This means that some of the light that reaches the lens does not reach the film.

Effect of lens extension

In certain circumstances, there are further losses, due to what is known as the lens extension. For distant subjects, the lens is at a more or less fixed distance (the focal length) from the film. You move it in and out a little when focusing, but the movement is very small in proportion to the focal length. When changing focus from 1m to 10m with a 50mm lens, for example, you move the lens no more than about 1.5mm. When focused as far away as possible (infinity), a 50mm lens is 50mm from the film. When that same lens is focused on a distance of 0.5m, it moves about 6.4mm forward from the 'infinity' position, ie, further away from the film.

When you get really close, the lens needs to be moved an appreciable amount away from its infinity position, and the light emerging from the back of the lens has to travel further to reach the film. The further it travels, the weaker it becomes. Thus, exposure is affected by lens extension. In general photography, as we have seen, the extension is a small fraction of the focal length at normal distances. It is only about 13 per cent at 0.5m for a 50mm lens. As you move closer, however, the lens movement increases rapidly. At 0.1m (10cm), the extra extension required is about 50mm, or 100 per cent of the focal length.

The extra exposure required for additional lens extension is calculated by dividing the total extension of the lens by its focal length (the standard extension), and squaring the result. That gives an exposure factor. Extending a 50mm lens to 56mm, for example, gives (56/50), or 1.25. The effect, therefore, is negligible, and a normal exposure meter reading is perfectly adequate over the normal focusing range of a lens. Many modern lenses, however, particularly zooms, have a so-called macro-focusing capability, allowing them to produce images at about one-third life size. The added extension in such a case is one-third of the focal length of the lens, and the exposure factor is 1.78. That is significant, particularly with colour slides, and a normal exposure meter reading would not be adequate for such a subject. Naturally, a TTL meter reading *would* be accurate, because the internal meter receives only the same amount of light as the film.

When you get to real close-up work with extension tubes or bellows, the effect of the extra extension becomes much more important. With a life-size image, for example, the extra extension required is equal to the focal length. This means that the length of the light path is doubled and the exposure factor becomes 4, which amounts to two stops extra exposure. Again, a TTL meter reading is capable of noting the effect of the extra extension. In these circumstances, however, it might not give an accurate exposure recommendation. Close-up subjects are often non-average and can give misleading readings with any type of meter. It is generally best to take a reading from a grey card in the subject position, applying the appropriate exposure factor if a separate meter is used.

Exposure factors and magnification

No matter what lens is used, exposure factors are related to the size of the image. A life-size image always requires the lens extension to be double its focal length. In other words, the extra extension needed is equal to the focal length. The same applies to all image sizes. If you want a twice-life-size image on the film, you have to add extension equal to twice the focal length. For an image one-third life size, you need to add extension equal to one third of the focal length of the lens used. In all cases, the magnification is 1 per cent of the percentage additional extension.

As the relationship between added extension and focal length is always the same for the same image size, so is the exposure factor. A life-size image always needs four times the exposure indicated by a normal meter reading (given an average subject). An image one-third life size always needs about two-thirds of a stop extra exposure.

Thus, it is easy to compile a table of exposure factors allied to image size. The last column in the table indicates the practical adjustments that can be made because most exposure meters are marked with the standard range of film speeds that double up at each setting, with two additional marks between each setting. These intermediate marks are equivalent to one-third of a stop setting so, while working at a given magnification, the meter can be set to an appropriate film speed to take care of the close-up factor. For an image at 0.7 magnification (70 per cent life size), for example, set the meter to a film speed figure that is four one-third stop divisions lower than the actual film speed. You then get one and one-third stops extra exposure by simply following the meter reading.

Extension percent of length	Magnification or reduction	Exposure factor	Stop value
15	0.15	1.32	1/3
20	0.2	1.44	1/2
30	0.3	1.70	2/3
40	0.4	1.96	1
50	0.5	2.25	1
60	0.6	2.56	1 1/3
70	0.7	2.89	1 1/3
80	0.8	3.24	1 1/2
90	0.9	3.61	1 1/2
100	1.0	4.00	2
110	1.1	4.41	2
120	1.2	4.84	2 1/3
130	1.3	5.29	2 1/3
140	1.4	5.76	2 1/2
150	1.5	6.25	2 1/2
160	1.6	6.76	2 2/3
170	1.7	7.29	2 2/3
180	1.8	7.84	3
190	1.9	8.41	3
200	2.0	9.00	3

Close-ups with telephoto lenses

Extreme close-ups are usually taken with relatively short focal length lenses, because the longer the focal length, the longer the added extension needed for a given image size. The occasional advantage of using lenses of longer focal length, however, is that they allow a greater shooting distance for the same image size. For a life-size image, the subject-to-lens distance is the same as the lens to film distance – 10cm with a 50mm lens, 40cm with a 200mm lens. The problem is that the 200mm lens will almost certainly be of telephoto construction, with a foreshortened light path. That can affect the exposure factor for close-ups. The third column in the table should, therefore, be viewed with some caution when using telephoto lenses. The factors could be considerably greater.

Similar considerations can apply to the so-called macro-focusing lenses, including zooms. The extra focusing ability may sometimes be achieved by altering the focal length of the lens without relating the change to the aperture control settings. Some internal focusing lenses may pose similar problems. These are all modern lenses specifically designed for use with TTL meters. If they are to be used at close range with external meter readings, it is advisable to conduct a few tests first.

Copying by reflected light

Even when you are not close enough to make a significant difference in exposure (or when you use supplementary lenses, which do not affect exposure), you have to be careful with metering. Copying is a popular form of close-up work and the subject is often far from average.

When copying printed matter, for example, a straightforward meter reading does not give a correct exposure unless the printed matter is in heavy type and very closely set. Average newsprint integrates to a tone 1-1 1/2 stops lighter than a grey card, magazine pages 1 1/2-2 stops. An exposure at the level indicated by a meter (even a TTL type) would give a negative that is very difficult to print. You need to increase the exposure to the level of a grey-card reading. If you use a separate light meter, you then need the further increase for the lens extension, if any.

Even magazine illustrations generally read lighter than a grey card, because they rarely have deep black tones. Good photographic prints, on the other hand, should read in relation to a grey card much as you would expect the original subject to read. Of course, in all these cases, it is assumed that you are taking pains to avoid specular reflections.

In copying material of this nature, it is rarely wise to stint the development. Generally, an exposure just short of full (no more than half a stop under) plus slightly increased development (up to 10 or15 per cent) gives the best results. You want at least to maintain the contrast of the original and sometimes to increase it. Do not overlook the influence of lens flare and the basic density of the film.

44 A typical close-up subject, needing extension tubes. Meter readings, except TTL, must be adjusted to allow for the extra extension.

45 Still life using a 105mm lens. Sometimes in such situations extension tubes are used to allow the lens to focus closer than its normal minimum but are not long enough in most cases to affect the exposure.

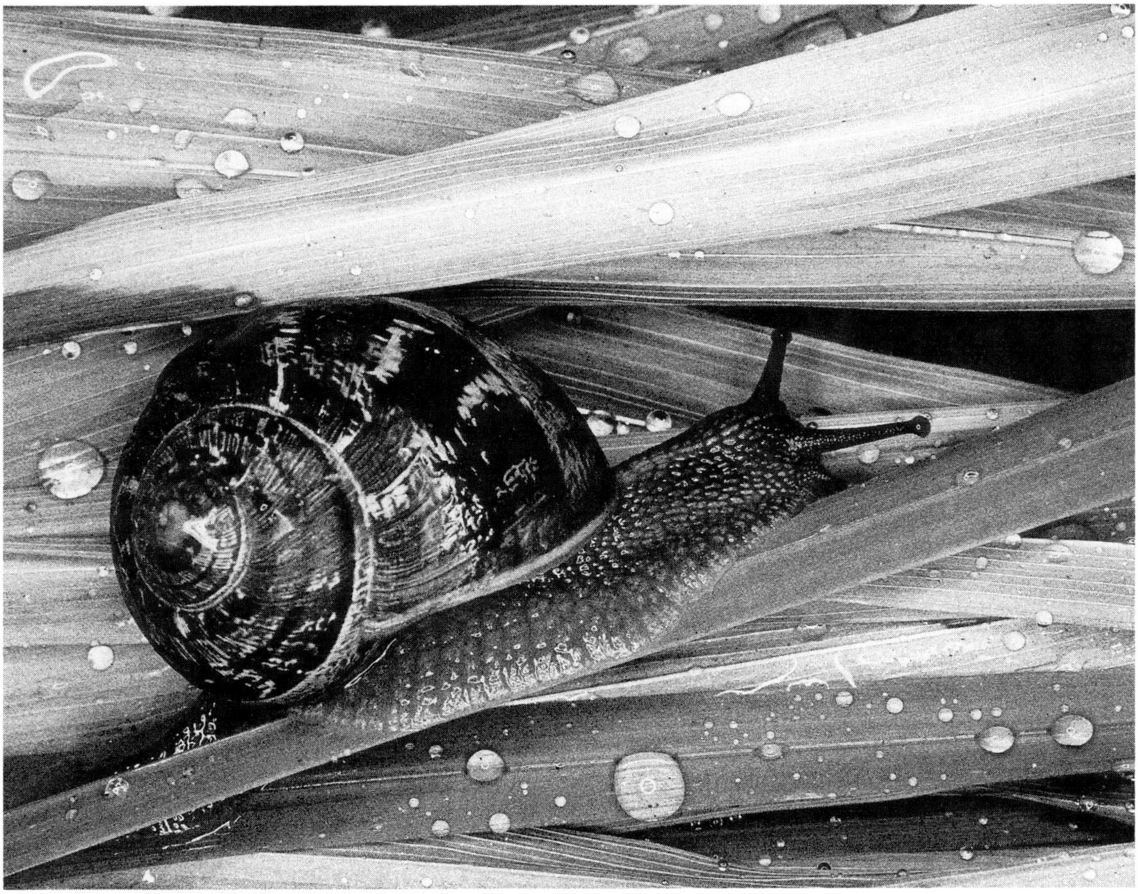

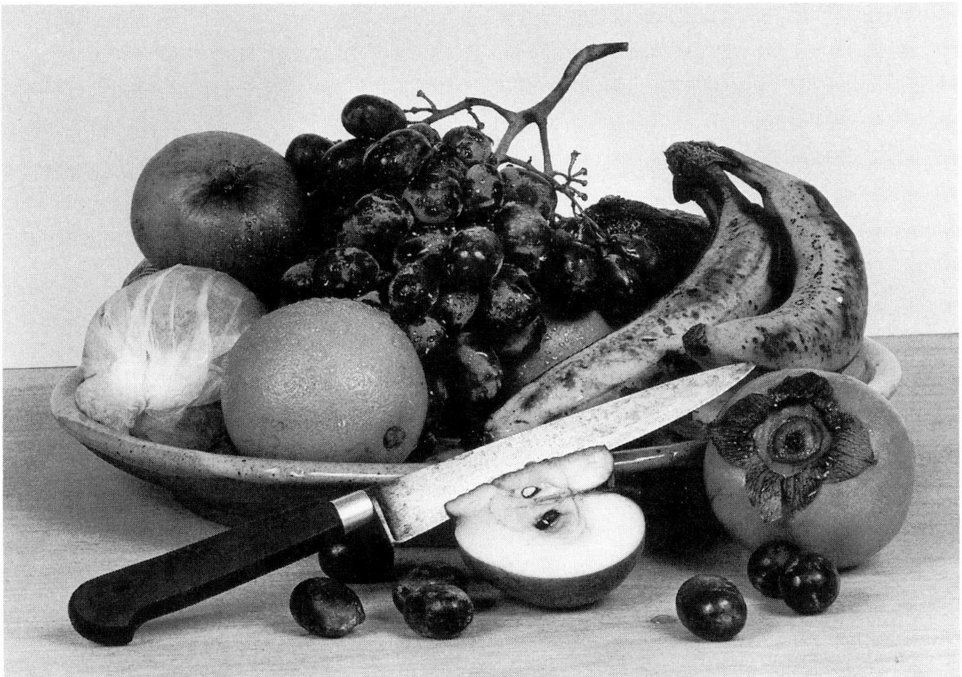

No matter how good the lens, the image never retains the full contrast of the original with standard exposure and processing. Similarly, some unexposed silver halide particles always develop, so contrast is, at least minimally, reduced. In copying most subjects, you must do nothing that will further lower the contrast.

If you are copying pure black-and-white material, you should use a suitable high-contrast film if possible. Failing that, a high-contrast developer used with a normal slow film should provide negatives that will print on the harder grades of paper.

When copying a mixture of printed matter and half-tone (continuous-tone) illustrations, a grey-card reading should form the basis for exposure. Adjust for the exposure factor, if required, and then close the lens down by half a stop. Full development or possibly 10 or 15 per cent extended development should give an adequate result with only a trace of background tone.

Printed matter on a coloured base is more difficult to handle. If, as might be expected, the colour of the print contrasts with that of the base, you may be able to improve its rendering by using a filter of the same colour as, or deeper than, the base colour. With red on yellow, for example, the yellow can be totally eliminated by a suitable yellow/green filter which leaves the red largely unaffected. If the lettering is white on a coloured ground, you need a filter of the opposite colour to the ground, ie, yellow, orange or red for a blue base, for a clearer rendering.

Exposure then becomes tricky. In addition to the close-up factor, you have to make a further allowance for the filter. Chapter 11 deals with the use of filters. It is only necessary to note here the fact that filters often have exposure factors printed on the rim, such as x2, x1 etc. You need to multiply this factor by the close-up factor. A factor of x2 for close-up and x4 for the filter becomes a factor of x8.

Further adjustment could be necessary. The effect of a filter on the eye, an exposure meter and the film can vary considerably. It can also vary for different *types* of exposure meter and under different lighting conditions. In this area, therefore, you cannot be precise about exposure until you have fully explored the characteristics of your filters with your lenses, exposure meter and film. Without this experience, base your exposure on the filter factor and then make two other exposures at half and one stop each side. This technique is known as 'bracketing', and is often frowned on by the purist, but a very necessary precaution when you have insufficient information or experience to be sure of the required exposure.

TTL metering can usually cope with filters and give reasonably accurate readings. Similarly, you can place the filter to be used over an external meter window. In neither case, however, can you rely totally on the readings so obtained. It is unwise to use such methods with the deeper coloured filters, with factors of x3 and greater, unless you have checked that, in normal conditions, the reading obtained ties up with the factor quoted for the filter.

Copying transparent originals

You cannot always copy by reflected light: trans-illumination is obviously necessary, for example, in slide copying. There is no great problem as far as exposure is concerned but, as transillumination is likely to lead to higher contrast than reflected light, you can run into trouble in that area. For slide copying and most other photography of translucent materials, you need to expose and process to give a reduction in contrast.

Copying transparencies in colour is catered for by special copying film with lower contrast characteristics than general-purpose colour slide film. For copying in monochrome, there is no such specialised material. There is a temptation to use the slowest available film, but that is not generally the best method. Such materials have high contrast and restricted exposure latitude. If you do use them, a low contrast developer is essential. Medium speed materials are easier to handle and give perfectly satisfactory resolution and grain size if properly exposed and processed. Exposure should be a little on the full side and development curtailed.

The difficulty with transparent originals is that *too* full an exposure can lead to *lack* of contrast, particularly with tungsten illumination. Highlights do not easily burn out in the yellowish light, while shadow areas are often far from opaque. It is, therefore, vital to meter the slide as accurately as possible.

Measuring exposure. A slide is small, so hold the meter as close to it as possible. You have no problem with throwing shadows on to it. The selenium type of meter with a large cell can actually be placed in contact with the slide. Provided that the area then measured integrates reasonably well to a mid-tone, the reading can be taken as the basic

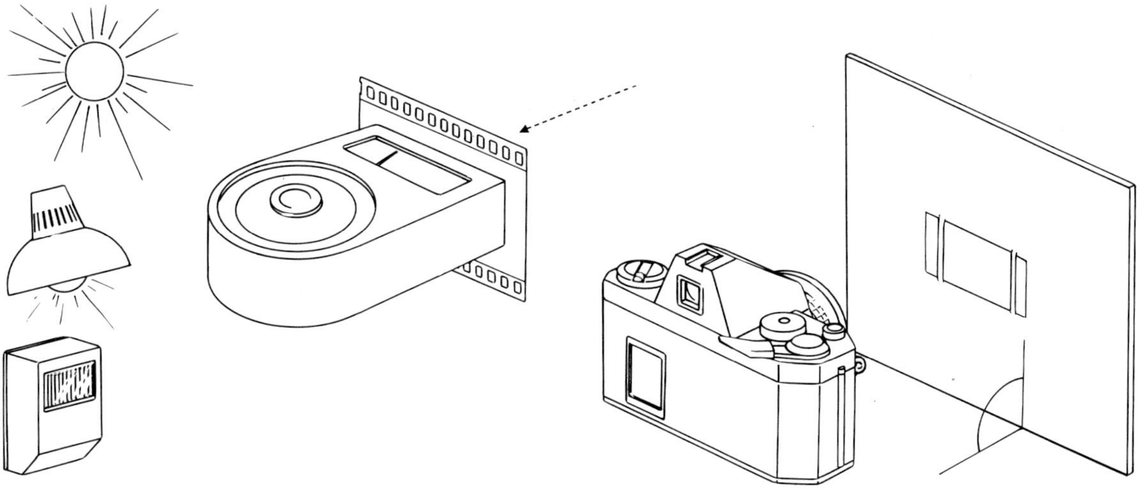

9.1 Copying slides is close range photography with transillumination. Any light source can be used for black and white, but daylight or electronic flash is generally preferable for colour. Direct meter readings are normally accurate. Slide and camera back must be kept parallel and focusing is critical.

exposure. If the subject is obviously non-average, it is advisable to take a reading through another slide of similar density but with a more balanced tone range, and use that reading as your basic exposure. The same advice applies, of course, to TTL meters, which are just as easily misled by non-average subjects.

Slides of varying densities pose no problems provided that they are average subjects. If they are not, you are again in the realms of guesswork, unless you have an average slide of similar density. Even then, when you are in some doubt about the correct exposure, bracketing is a sensible precaution. Take a few extra shots at half-stop intervals around the estimated exposure.

Once you have the basic exposure, you simply have to adjust for the magnification (except with TTL meters). Same-size copying means a x4 exposure increase over the external meter reading. At other magnifications, calculate the exposure factor carefully.

When processing your slide copies, cut the development time by 10 or 15 per cent, compared with the time recommended for average subjects. If you are prepared to work with more than one type of developer, use a low-contrast type.

Colour slides can also be copied on to colour negative film for the production of colour prints. Some prefer that method to direct colour printing from slides. Again, special copying materials are available, but they are not commonly stocked and are a little difficult to handle. Ordinary medium speed colour negative film can give quite successful copies and, in this case, a 10 per cent or so curtailment of the developing time seems to handle the contrast problem quite well.

Exposure levels in copying

There is no need to use powerful lights in monochrome copying. They may make the subject brighter to the eye, but they have no effect on contrast. You can make just as good copies with household lamps and relatively long exposures as with powerful floodlamps. Excessively small apertures should not be necessary either. Most lenses give their best performance at two or three stops below maximum and, as you are not concerned with depth of field, there is no need to stop down further.

It is better to use lenses constructed for, or known to be suitable for close range work (preferably not those with an added 'macro' facility). Genuine macro lenses are used stopped down for metering purposes. There is much to be said for pursuing this practice with other lenses, even though your camera is primarily designed for full-aperture metering. It makes more sense where exposure is critical to meter at the shooting aperture rather than to allow an electronic intermediary to predict lens transmittance. Check your instruction book first, however, because there are some lenses designed for full-aperture metering that do not give accurate readings when used stopped down.

Reciprocity failure. The main argument against low-light, long-exposure copying is the possibility of failure of the reciprocity law. This is the law that says that mathematically equal exposures have the same effect on the film, ie, 10 sec at *f*/22 is the same as one-quarter of a sec at *f*/4. In practice, most films react differently to low-light exposures of more than a second or two. That means low light on the film, not necessarily on the subject. Excessive stopping down can bring about failure of the reciprocity law. The effect is progressive underexposure as the exposure time increases. So try to keep exposures to a maximum of one second if possible, particularly with colour, where inaccurate exposure also causes a colour shift.

Theory and practice

A fact of life that must be borne in mind when dealing with the critical exposure problems likely to arise in copying is that theory is one thing and practice is another. We need the theory, because without it we have no basis on which to work. But that is all theory can do – provide a starting point. To expose the film, light has to pass through a lot of glass in modern lenses. F-numbers are marked to indicate light transmission but they in themselves are theoretical and it is not at all uncommon, for example, for an aperture marked *f*/2 on one lens to act like *f*/2.8 on another. Lenses vary in many ways and it is never wise to assume that light transmission is exactly what it should be according to the theory. If you expect to do a lot of critical copying work, standardisation of materials, processing and working methods is the best route to success.

Wherever possible use a standard lighting set-up, the same camera settings, the same type of film, and process it in the same chemistry using the same procedure. That way, you learn how lenses, film and chemistry interact and can undertake any task with confidence.

46 A,B With a macro lens, any changes in effective aperture when adjusting these lenses for use at different distances are compensated automatically by a TTL meter. For external meter readings, tests should first be made at various focused ranges.

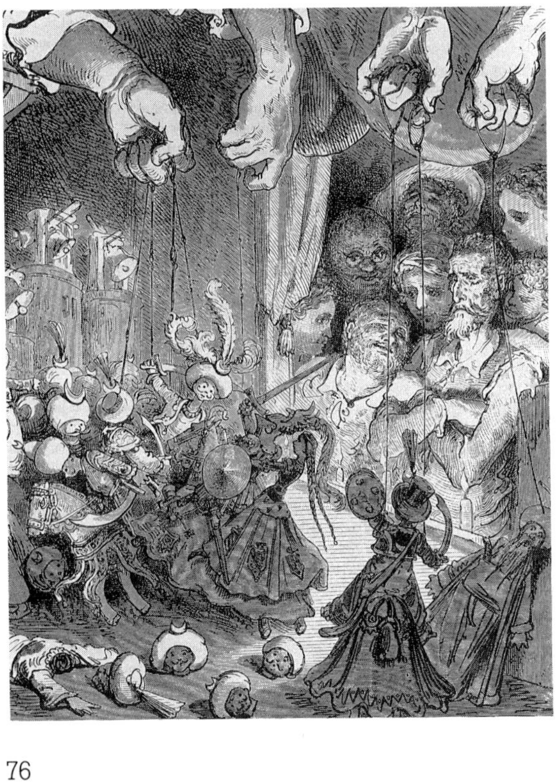

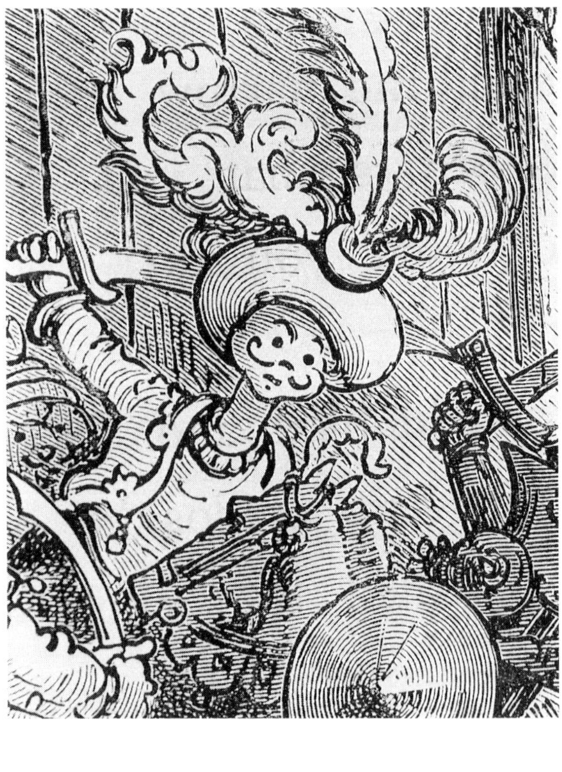

10 USING DAYLIGHT INDOORS

Indoors, exposure is as much a question of lighting as of camera settings. In natural light (window light), you can encounter extremes of contrast, which can be useful for some effects but are useless for representational photography, ie, the way we perceive the subject. Even in a room with large windows and light coloured furnishings, there can be as much as 10 stops or more between meter readings in important highlight and shadow areas – a range of 1:512. The eye can handle such extremes easily, because it adjusts almost instantly from the strong sunlight near the window to the deepest shadow, and sees ample detail in both. The film can manage most of the range, perhaps with the sacrifice of a little detail at one end or the other, but the resulting negative would be very difficult to print.

Replace the furnishings with darker colours and make the windows smaller or the room larger, and the range of luminances becomes too great for any film. Even the eye then has to adjust consciously from one extreme to the other. In such conditions, a truly representational picture of the room is impossible. No detail can be retained in any but the lightest mid-tones without burning out the sunlit areas completely.

Using window light

Nevertheless, very fine portraits can be taken by window light and nothing else. It can also be used for a variety of other subjects that demand soft illumination. In these cases, however, direct sunlight through the window is unacceptable unless large reflecting surfaces (or other windows, as in a bay) are available to throw light into the shadow areas.

Sunlight can be used if representational effects are not required. A shaft of sunlight through a window spotlighting a face, ornament, picture, etc., with only hazy detail in the very dark surroundings, can make an effective picture. A harsh room interior with high contrast lighting, with totally burnt-out highlights in windows and other brightly lit areas can create an atmosphere to enhance the aim of the picture. It would not be very effective with a daintily-furnished bedroom, but it could help to emphasise the story line in a dilapidated, paint-peeling slum kitchen. As ever, the problem is to set the camera exposure at a level that provides the result you want. The auto-exposure camera generally has no place in such a scenario, and an exposure meter is essential. It takes experience to assess subjects like these and obtain entirely predictable results.

Representational photography by window light

To begin with the relatively easy treatments that aim more or less at representational results, let us consider a portrait by window light. We need not go into great detail about the arrangement of the model or the use of reflectors, supplementary lighting, etc., as this subject is dealt with extensively in other books in the series. Whatever your set-up, however, you are likely to be faced initially with higher contrast than normal in portrait work. The general problem is that the window-lit side of the face or figure is much brighter than the other side. Your model should not be in direct sunlight, which is unsuitable for this type of picture. You are not aiming at any particular effect – just the rather pleasant appearance of smooth, diffused lighting.

Identifying the tones. The only real problem, therefore, is to identify the tones you wish to reproduce. Naturally, you want the window-lit flesh tone, and you want detail in at least some of the shaded areas. So meter both of these, and note the difference between the lightest and darkest areas in which you expect to see detail. It might be three stops. The window-lit flesh tone you will want to reproduce as about Tone 7. If you do, the shadow areas will reproduce as Tone 4, which is darkish but with some detail. If that is acceptable, an exposure of one stop more than a close-up reading of the window-lit part of the face should be adequate.

If there is a difference of more than three stops between the two readings, you are on the border line of showing no detail at all in the shaded area. If that is unacceptable you will need to employ a reflector or supplementary lighting, unless your tests have shown that you are still within the range where exposure and processing adjustments can be made.

47 Shadow 'self-portrait' using an 8mm fish eye lens. The camera was placed on the floor, directed upwards and triggered by self-timer. Overhead illumination was weak enough to lend slight animation to the subject.

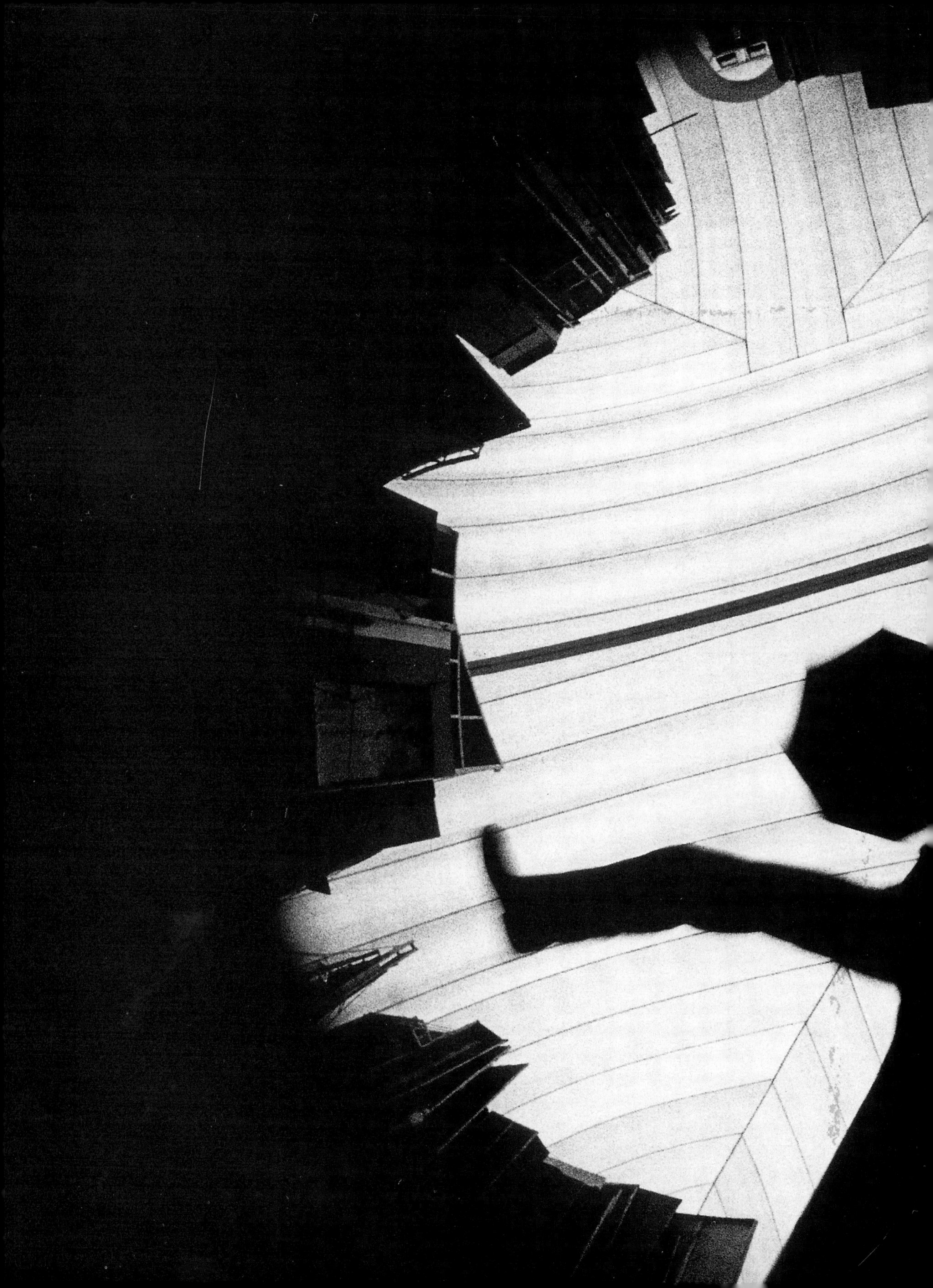

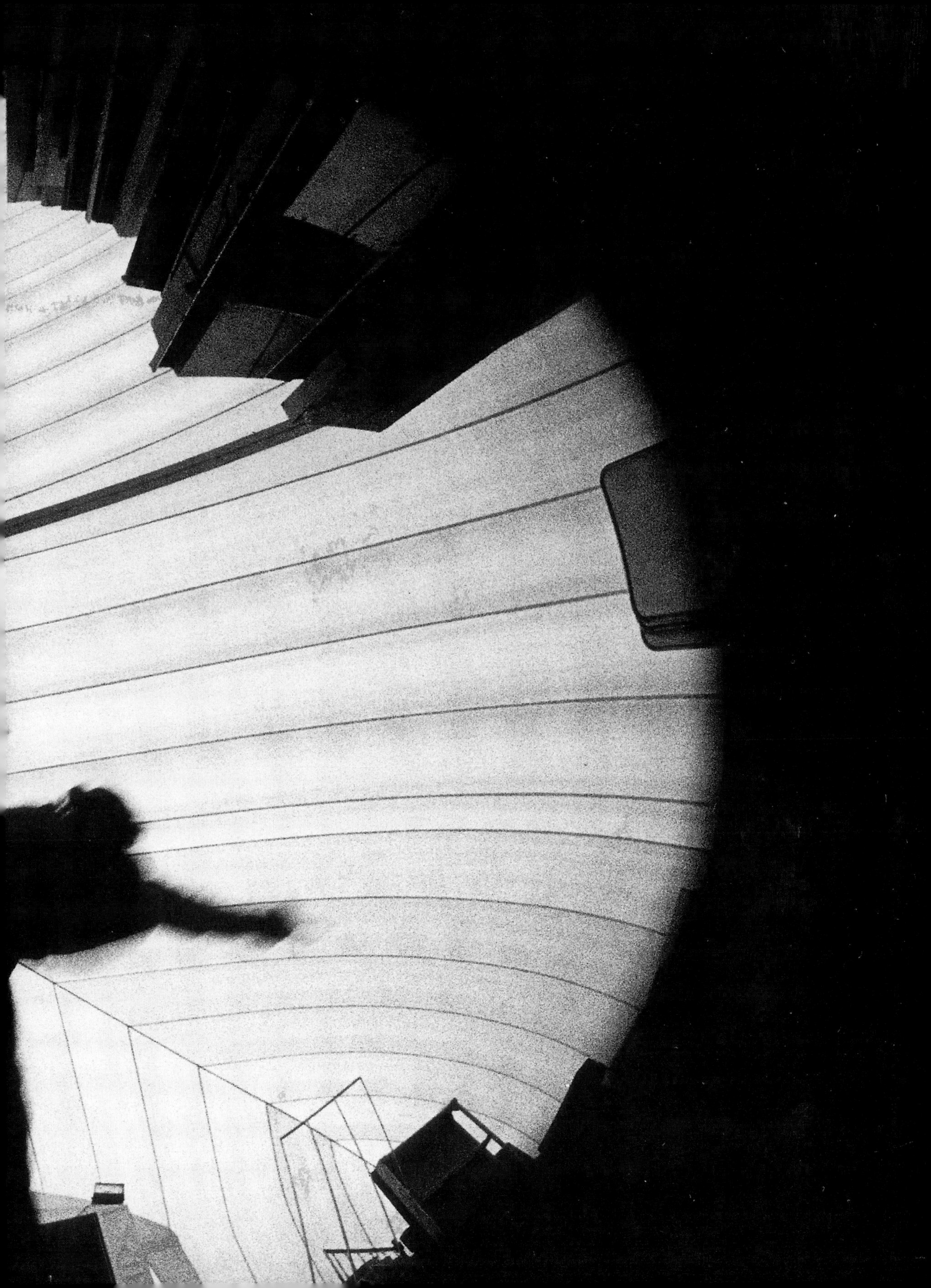

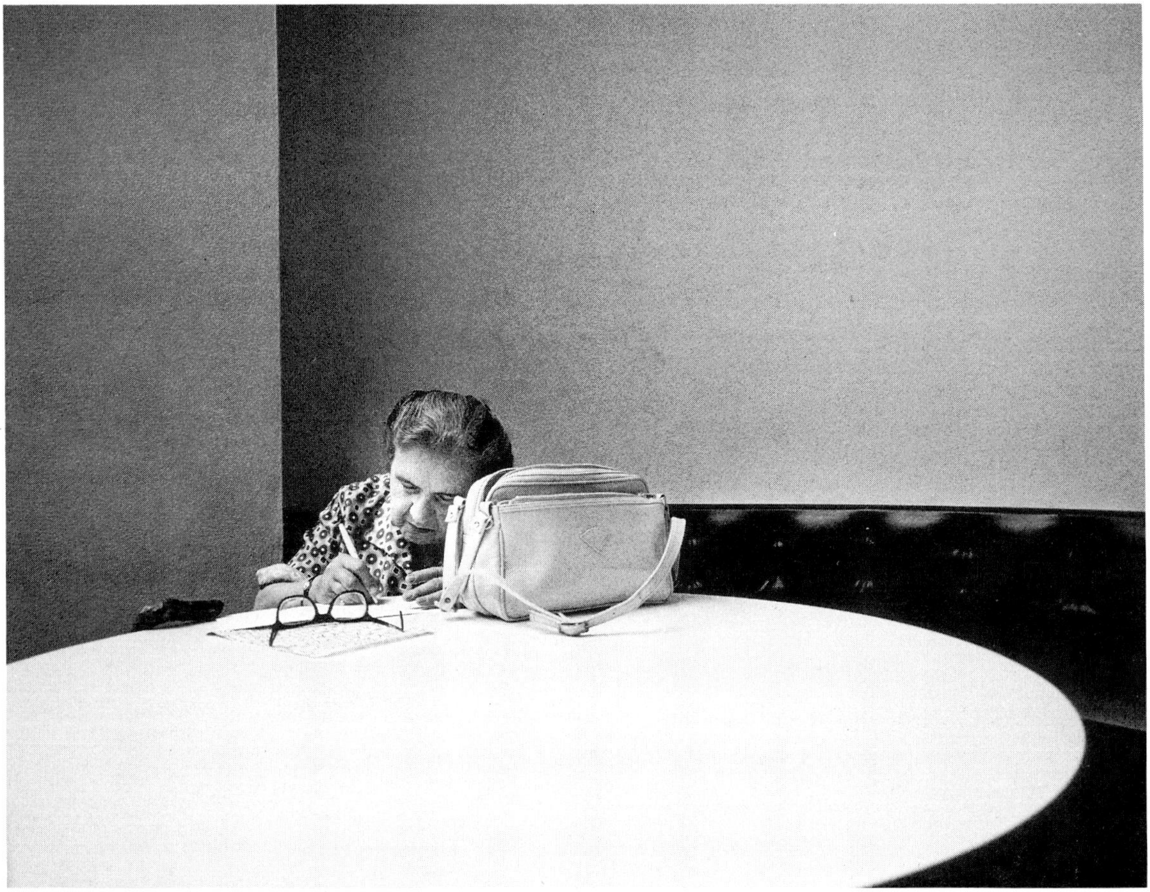

48 Window-lit portrait. A direct exposure reading averaging all tones in the picture. Lack of detail in the table adds to the geometrical feeling of this composition.

You may have found, for example, that you can place the window-lit flesh tone as Tone 8 by a longer exposure and then bring it down again by reduced development. It then reproduces correctly as Tone 7, with some compression of other tones, retaining a little of the extra exposure given to the lower tones. This does not work if the shadow tone is a long way out of range, say five stops from the mid-tone.

If you think the procedure will work, give two stops more exposure than a close up reading recommends for the window-lit flesh tone and cut development by up to one-third. The same treatment applies to virtually any attempt at representational results by window lighting. Large windows on overcast days provide very useful light sources for the photography of small objects. Placed close to the window, they escape the drastic fall-off in lighting that affects a large figure, even in the dullest of daylight, but they retain some modelling.

Non-average subjects. As with all small objects, exposure has to be calculated in relation to the subject, which is often non-average. When using a separate meter, be very careful to point it along the camera lens axis and, even if the subject does seem to be average, preferably use a grey card or an incident light reading. This should give you the correct exposure for virtually any subject (after allowing for the lens extension, if any). It is best to use one of these indirect metering methods in preference to your TTL meter. You could also need to adjust the reading for the subject in special circumstances. If it is glass, for example, with fine, faintly-modelled detail, overexposure must be avoided at all costs. A slightly reduced exposure is preferable and, if you can also extend the processing time by 10 to 15 per cent, so much the better.

On the other hand, a dark object with some very light texture calls for a full exposure. An extra half stop might be advisable.

The window as a spotlight. Breaking away from representational photography, how do you deal with subjects positioned well back in the room and illuminated by shafts of sunlight as from a theatrical spot? In many cases quite simply by a direct reading from the illuminated subject alone or from a grey card in the subject position. This is suitable where the surroundings are dark and you need the minimum of detail in them.

With lighter coloured surroundings, there is more light but the camera may not be as conscious of it as the eye. Meter various parts of the surroundings and compare the readings with that from a grey card in the subject area. The readings tell you how they should reproduce. If the wallpaper, for instance, reads two stops lower than the grey card (which is in sunlight), it will reproduce as Tone 4, which is darkish, but nowhere near black. If you want it darker, you have to be prepared to let your main subject go darker. In the case of a figure, this might be acceptable.

Should you decide that the wall is to reproduce no lighter than Tone 2, you have to let the figure go to Tone 4 (or 5 if you can bring in processing control). This may sound a bit too dark, indicating that the lighting is not really suitable for the idea you have in mind. Perhaps the wall is reflecting too much light. You might try to adjust the lighting by partly drawing a curtain or erecting a barrier out of the picture area.

49 Window light can be a perfect source for small objects, where fall-off with increasing distance from the window is of little importance.

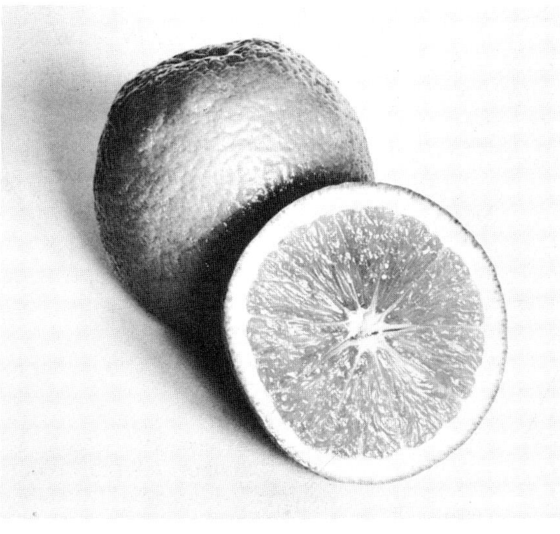

Metering with backlit subjects

In another situation, you might use sunlight through the window for backlighting, shooting directly at it with the subject between the camera and the source of light. Now what effect are you after? Do you see the subject again as a figure? Perhaps not, in which case you have to adapt the following procedures to your requirements.

First, what is the most important tone in the picture? At what level should it be reproduced? The probability is that you would choose the highlight tone on the figure – the touch of rim lighting provided by the window light. In that case, what tone should it have in the final image? Much lighter than the average flesh tone seems reasonable – say Tone 8. It is not easy to meter the actual rim light but it should be nearly the same as that on the back of the subject, so meter this instead. If you use the exposure now showing on the meter, the rim-lit area will reproduce as Tone 6 – the standard mid-tone. You want it as Tone 8. The indication is that you need two stops more exposure than the meter recommends.

That might be all you are concerned with. Perhaps you are prepared to accept the tone on the front of the figure as shadow. But you can also get an idea of what the other tones should be. By placing the rim-lit area at Tone 8, you are giving a relatively short exposure, but it should be enough to burn out the actual window area completely. The illumination on the front of the figure depends almost entirely on the size of the room and the tone of the furnishings. Meter it directly, and compare the reading with that from the rim-lit area, which is to reproduce as Tone 8. At four stops less, it will be noticeably lighter than black, with fair detail, especially if any parts are significantly lighter or darker, such as eyes or clothing. At five stops less, the darkest parts are approaching black and any greater difference gives you a silhouette.

Similar measurements taken from areas of the floor or other parts that fall within the picture area can give you a clear impression of how each will reproduce. Except with the strongest sunlight and the lightest tone, none should be completely burnt out.

This is the type of subject with which the full use of Ansel Adams' Zone System would demand adjustments in exposure and processing to control contrast, or where you would use different developers. But in this situation, you could be taking pictures that need opposing treatments all on the same roll of film. It is possible to cope in

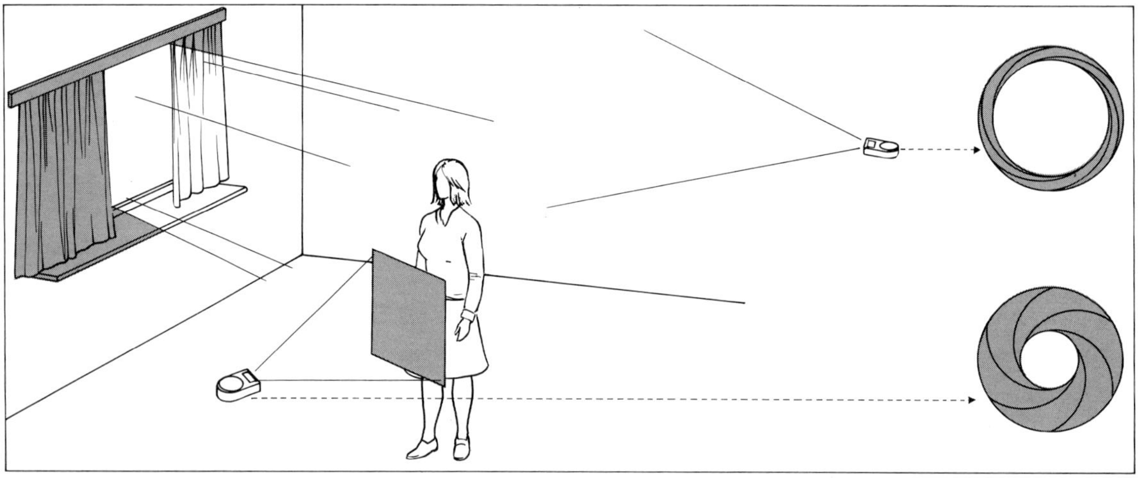

10.1 Curtains are a useful control over the contrast of window lighting. A large difference between readings from subject and background can often be corrected by adjusting the curtains.

35mm by organising your shots so that you shoot all of one type of picture first, and leave an empty frame before those of another type, and so on. Note the number of the blank frame, wind the film back, wind it on again to the blank frame and cut it in the darkroom. With rollfilm, use separate films for each type of shot.

Identifying the key tone

The way to solve the exposure problem when shooting by window light is to identify the tone that must be reproduced at a certain level and the tones that you can – or wish to – sacrifice. The most important tone is not usually difficult to identify. Having done so, decide which in our list of tones is nearest to the level you want your important tone to be in the final picture. To ensure that it will be at this level, take a close up meter reading from it. If you were to give the exposure recommended by your meter, you would reproduce your 'key tone' as Tone 6. So you simply set the exposure the same number of steps higher or lower as the difference between Tone 6 and the tone you want. If, for example, you want your key tone to reproduce as the lightest possible tone with some detail (but probably little or no colour), you give three stops more exposure to bring it to Tone 9.

You can then check how other tones will reproduce by comparing direct readings of them with the reading from your key tone. In this case, as your key tone is to reproduce as Tone 9, anything with a higher reading will be dead white. Anything required to be dead black must be eight or more stops darker – which is a little unlikely.

Again, remember that these predictions of tonal values depend on the characteristics of the film and the processing technique. They are close to what might be expected from a general-purpose film developed according to the manufacturer's instructions. To be able to forecast the results you will get with your own materials and technique, you must make tests before you start and as you go along. That is particularly important with colour film, which is constantly changing as the emulsion chemists strive for ever 'better' colour. The trend is to increase colour saturation as much as possible, even at the cost of separating it from its 'grey' tonal value in nature.

50 The window spotlight effect. A large window provides adequate, though rather contrasty illumination. The flesh tones provide the obvious metering area.

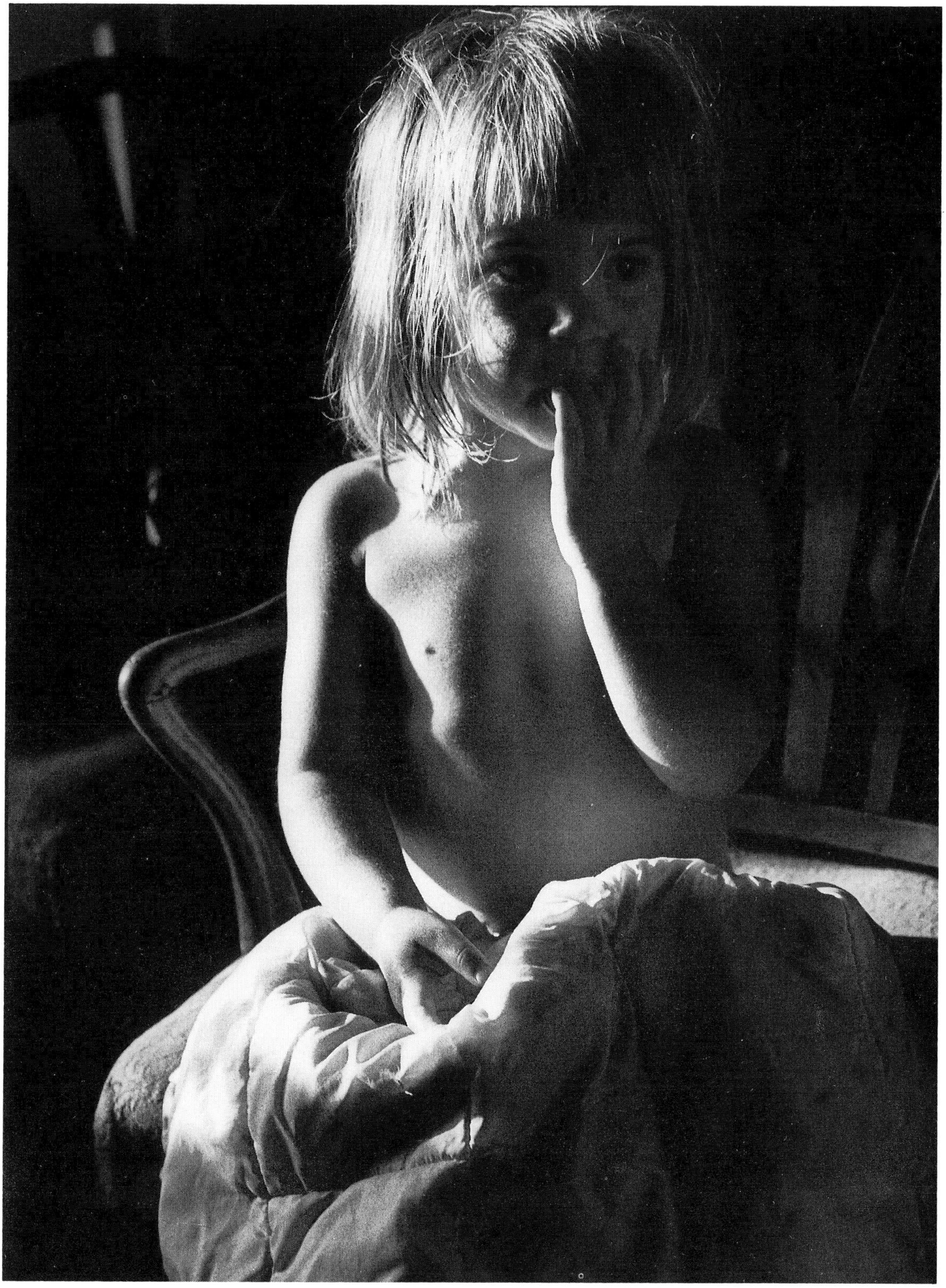

11 HOW FILTERS AFFECT EXPOSURE

Sometimes you cannot get quite the exposure you want in terms of lens aperture and shutter speed. In bright sunny conditions, for example, with an ISO 125/22° (ASA 125/22 DIN) film in your camera, you perhaps want to use a large aperture to restrict depth of field, but at *f*/5.6 you have no exposure time short enough. It would be worse still if you were using ISO 400/27° (ASA 400/27 DIN) film. But can you do anything to allow you to use *f*/4 or *f*/2.8? Yes, if you use filters.

The prime function of a filter is to change, in a selective manner, the colour of the light reaching the film. It does this by transmitting light of its own colour and absorbing light of all other colours to a greater or lesser degree. It can thus change tonal values in monochrome photography, or correct an overall colour cast in colour film.

Filter factors

The amount of light absorbed by a filter is specified by the manufacturer in the form of a filter factor, such as 1.5, 2, 4, etc. The factor indicates that, when you use the filter, you should multiply the normally indicated exposure time by that figure. With a filter factor of 2, you should give twice as much exposure, ie, one stop extra, to compensate for the light absorbed by the filter.

This may seem a little odd, because you are transmitting all the light of the filter hue and then giving it extra exposure. The remaining light, which is partly absorbed, gets extra exposure to bring it back to near normal again. In practice, it does not work quite like that because filters are not generally of pure colour and very few colours in nature are pure.

The average coloured filter transmits light of all hues but absorbs some of them much more strongly than others. A red filter, for example, has relatively little absorption effect on yellow or orange, rather more on green and a strong absorption of blue and violet. As virtually all colours in nature are mixtures, any given filter is likely to have some effect on most colours.

In the use of a yellow filter for darkening a blue sky to allow a white cloud formation to show up more clearly, some of the blue light from the sky is absorbed. But the white cloud has a blue content, as do, to a lesser extent, the green grass and foliage and even many reds, browns and other colours. So you have to increase exposure to avoid underexposure of parts of the scene, but the increase is not sufficient to restore the full tone of the colour most affected by the filter.

All filter factors are approximate. They need testing under the given conditions. The light reflected from white paper in tungsten lighting is yellowish, because tungsten lighting has a much lower blue content than daylight. A x4 orange filter might absorb rather less than a quarter of it.

11.1 Filters absorb colours selectively. A red filter, for example, transmits virtually all red light but absorbs other colours more strongly the further they are removed from it in the spectrum. Blue and violet are absorbed most strongly.

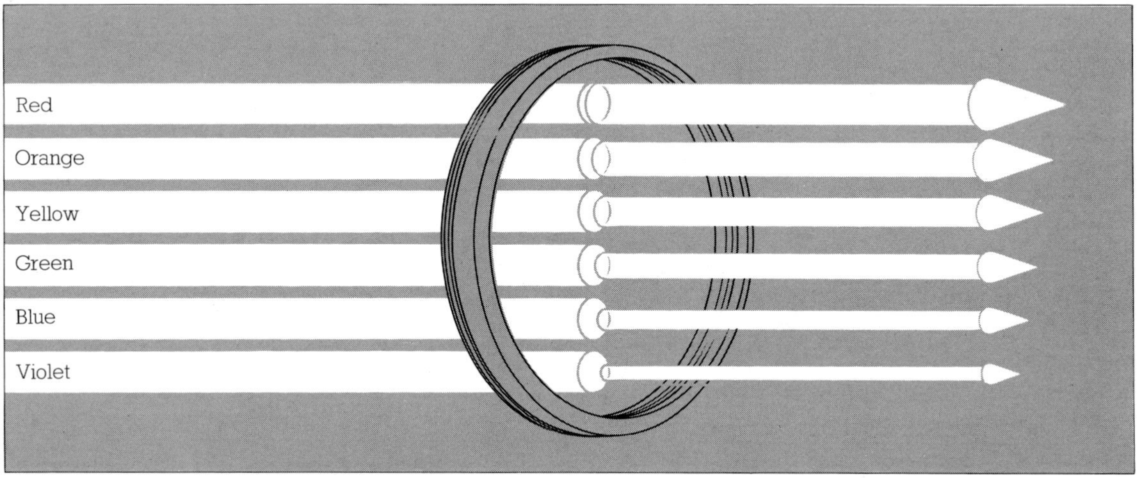

Under blue or green filtering of the illumination, more than three-quarters of the reflected light could be absorbed by the same filter. Under different conditions, you may have a factor that is anything from about 1.5 to 4 for the same filter. Even in daylight, a yellow filter may have a factor of 1.5 in brilliant sunshine, but of 2-4 in a shady place under a deep blue sky.

Controlling exposure with filters

Whatever the conditions, any coloured filter absorbs some light and lowers the overall intensity of the light reaching the film. It can therefore be used to control exposure and, in the example we started with, a x4 filter would allow you to shoot at *f*/2.8 instead of *f*/5.6. A filter factor of 4, however, generally means a deep orange or red filter. This cannot be used with colour film, unless you want a special effect of a pronounced red cast overlaying all the colours. Even in monochrome, such a filter has a strong effect on tonal values. A blue sky becomes virtually black; other blues, greens and mixtures containing those colours are considerably darkened. Red, orange and yellow are reproduced much lighter. If your picture can stand such alterations in tonal values, you can shoot through a coloured filter to allow you to use either larger apertures or longer exposure times than would otherwise be possible.

Neutral density filters. If you cannot accept such tonal changes or are shooting in colour, there is a way out. Filters are also produced with neutral density, ie, with density but no colour. These are specifically designed for exposure control purposes and are available in various densities. You can use more than one, multiplying their factors, or you can use them in conjunction with coloured filters. A x2 orange filter plus a x2 neutral density (sometimes referred to as 0.3ND) would allow you to increase exposure by two stops, assuming that the orange filter lives up to its factor in the given lighting conditions. The factor of an ND filter is accurate in any conditions because it absorbs light of all colours equally.

51-52 The effect of using a red filter on red and green peppers in daylight, left, and tungsten lighting, right. The red pepper is on the left.

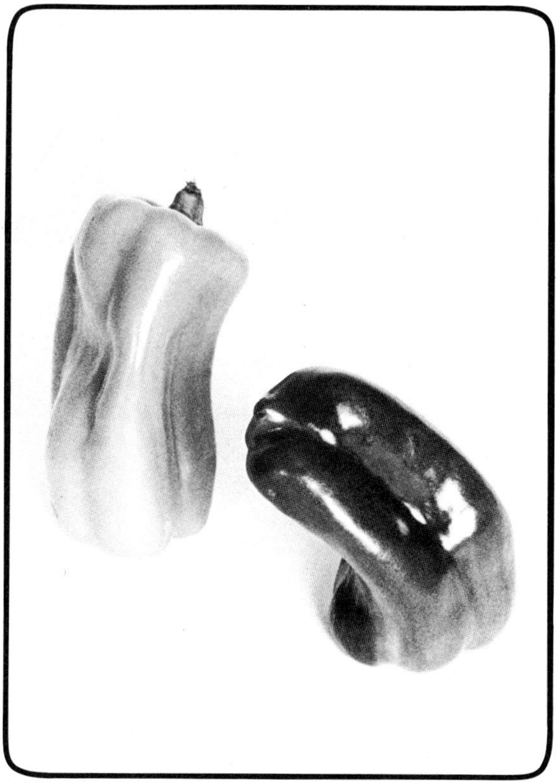

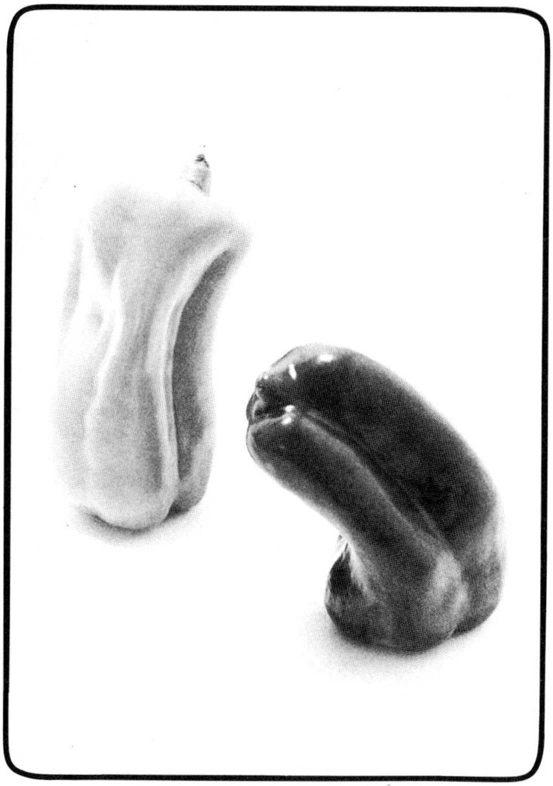

Testing filters. You can check filter factors with reasonable accuracy by measuring the light passing through them with a selenium meter, which has a colour sensitivity closely matching that of modern films. For practical purposes, however, you need to make a series of test exposures with and without the filter in various lighting conditions.

Graduated and other filters. One specialised type of filter would appear to meet the requirements of changing the tone of the sky without affecting a landscape area, and therefore allowing unchanged exposures. This is the graduated filter, with colour or neutral density shading across the filter to clear glass (or plastic). The general idea is that, with the coloured part toward the top of the lens, the sky area is filtered and the land area is not. Unfortunately, most filters designed for this purpose are usually situated too close to the lens to prevent the effect spilling over into the whole picture area. That does not matter much with monochrome, but these filters are intended primarily for colour work. It is generally advisable to use only the lightest pastel shades if brilliance of colour in the foreground is required. As such filters do affect the whole picture area, they generally have a factor greater than unity.

What the true factor is depends entirely on the result required. With a yellow graduated filter for monochrome, you darken the sky area but only slightly affect the land area if you make little or no exposure adjustment. If the sky tone becomes too dark, applying a filter factor of 1.5 or 2 may give the result you want.

With the types designed for colour film, the effect varies widely with exposure. It is best to find by experiment the level of exposure that provides the most satisfactory result. TTL meters are not sufficiently reliable for this purpose.

Polarising screens

Polarised light 'vibrates' in one plane only, as opposed to the vibration in all directions along the line of travel of ordinary 'random' light. Polarising screens can be used to polarise light or to control the amount of polarised light allowed to pass through them.

Light reflected from a polished, non-metallic surface is partially polarised. Skylight may also be partly polarised (by reflection from solid particles in the atmosphere) and can be darkened by a polarising screen. Polarised skylight generally appears deep blue to the eye, but it is less so to the film, which tends to be a little disproportionately sensitive to blue. The use of a polarising screen can restore the visual effect or, if required, exaggerate it. The screen has no colour but has some density, so it absorbs some random light while impeding some polarised light. Thus, a polariser always has an exposure factor. As with a coloured filter, the factor varies with the conditions, but the polariser's own natural density ensures that it is rarely less than 3. Depending on the

11.2 Bracketing exposures. When exposure cannot be determined with confidence, make one shot as the meter indicates and then give other exposures on either side of the 'correct' level, at one-stop intervals for black and white and half-stop intervals for colour.

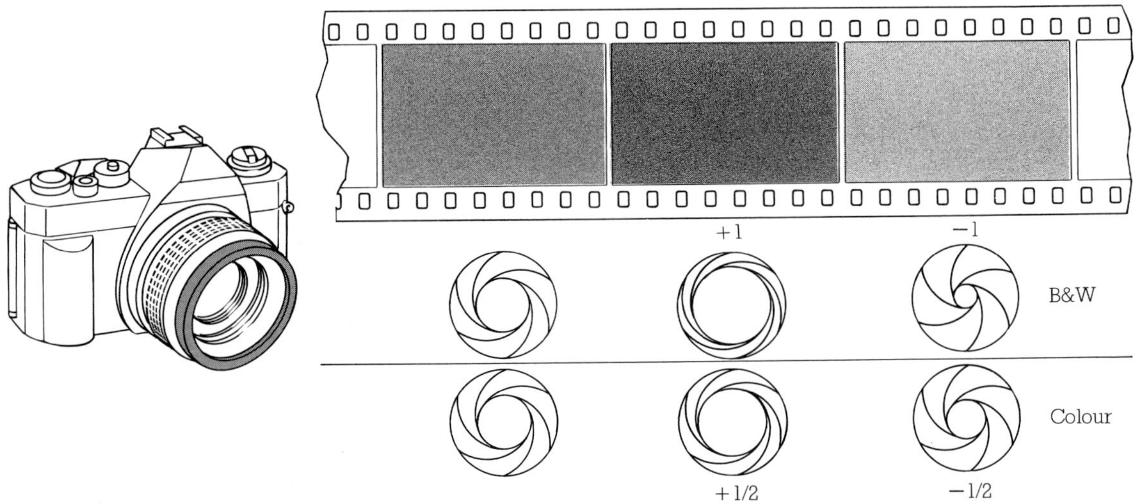

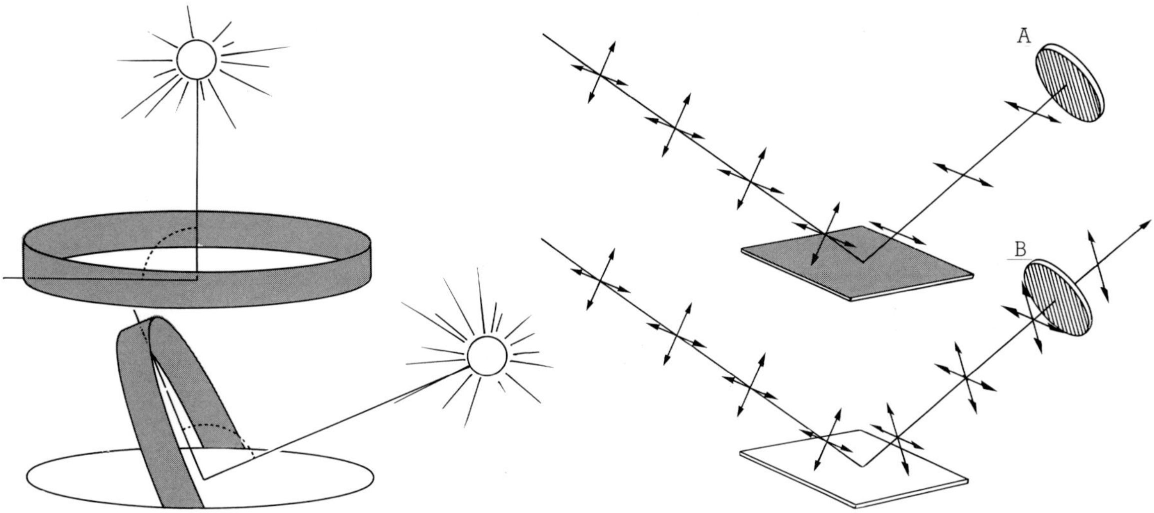

11.3 Skylight can be polarised only at 90 degrees from a line between the viewing position and the sun. Thus, the polarised area varies with the elevation of the sun.
Random light (vibrating in all directions) can be plane polarised when reflected from some surfaces. A polariser can eliminate such reflections (A). Not all random light gets through the polariser (B), which therefore has an exposure factor.

amount of polarised light it absorbs, it may reach 4 or slightly higher.

Filters and meter readings

Filter factors are applied to the exposure indicated by a separate exposure meter or by the camera meter before the filter is placed over the lens. A TTL reading through the filter gives a reasonable indication of correct exposure in most cases, but it can lead you astray when you use deeply coloured filters. That is because the meter cannot match the colour sensitivity of the film exactly. Most are a little over sensitive to red. That can be corrected to some extent by filtering the light reaching the light-sensitive element, but it is seldom fully corrected – probably for reasons of overall sensitivity. A reading through a deep orange or red filter is therefore likely to be over optimistic, leading to slight underexposure and possibly producing a negative that is difficult to print with the required sparkle.

It is thus advisable, at least with the deeper colours, to make your meter reading without the filter and then to apply the filter factor recommended by the manufacturer or that determined by your own experiments. With modern films, errors brought about by applying an inaccurate filter factor may have minimal effect on exposure, but they could prevent the filter having the effect you were aiming at.

If you use deeply coloured filters with an automatic exposure control camera, it is wise to switch to manual control or use the backlight or exposure compensation switch, as appropriate, to give the extra exposure above the filter factor. If the camera is totally automatic with TTL metering but with no manual setting or exposure compensation facility, you can still control exposure by adjusting the film speed setting (assuming the manufacturers have not completely hamstrung you by providing only DX coding). If the meter appears to read the factor as x2 but it is marked x4, set the film speed one marked setting lower, ie. ISO 64/19° (ASA 64/19 DIN) instead of ISO 125/22° (ASA 125/22 DIN). You have then calibrated the meter to recommend one stop extra exposure. Finer control can be exercised if necessary because the film speed scale usually has dots between the marked settings representing

53 (Overleaf) A perfect example of choosing the tone to suit the interpretation plus heavy printing up at the printing stage.

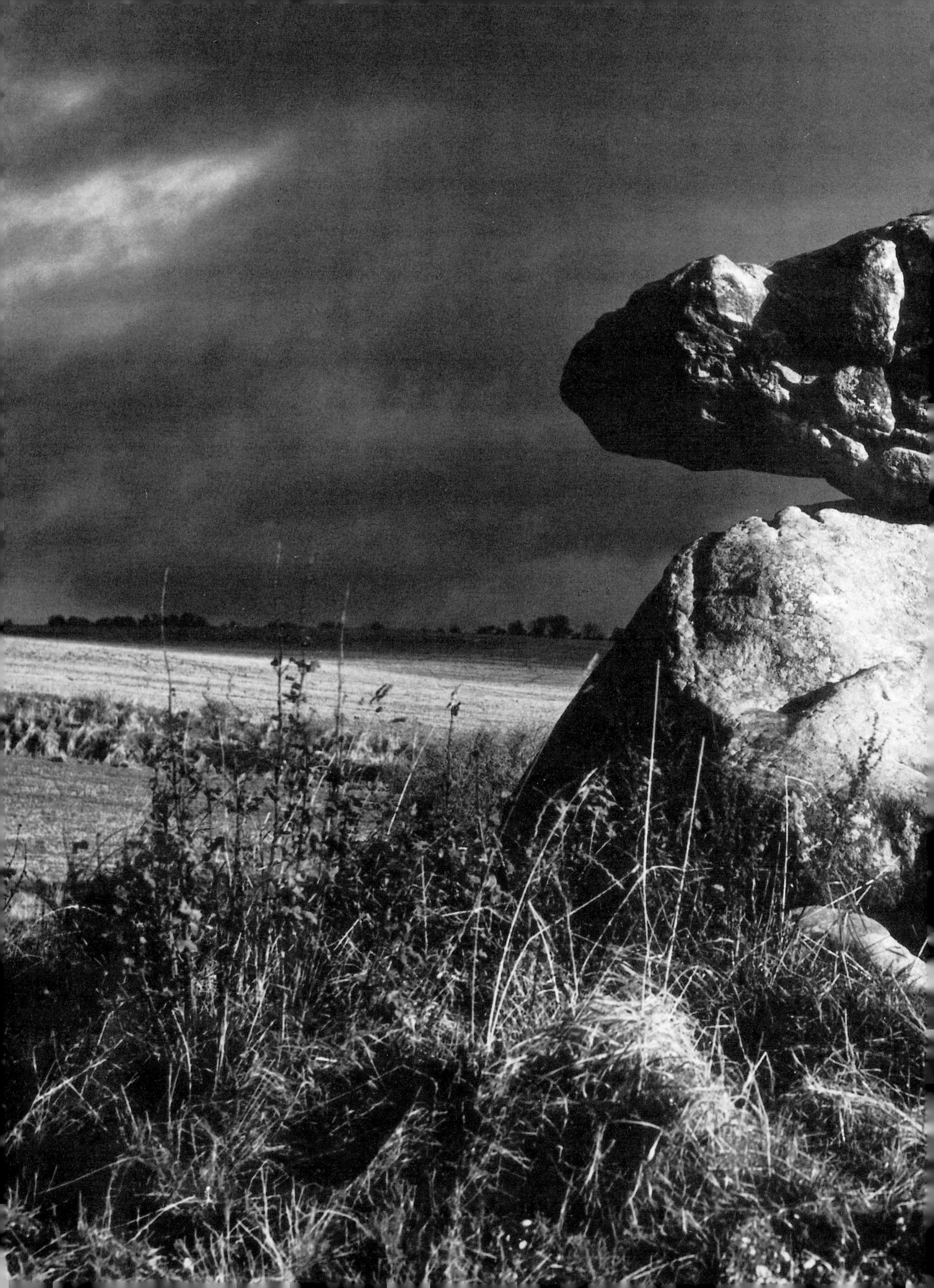

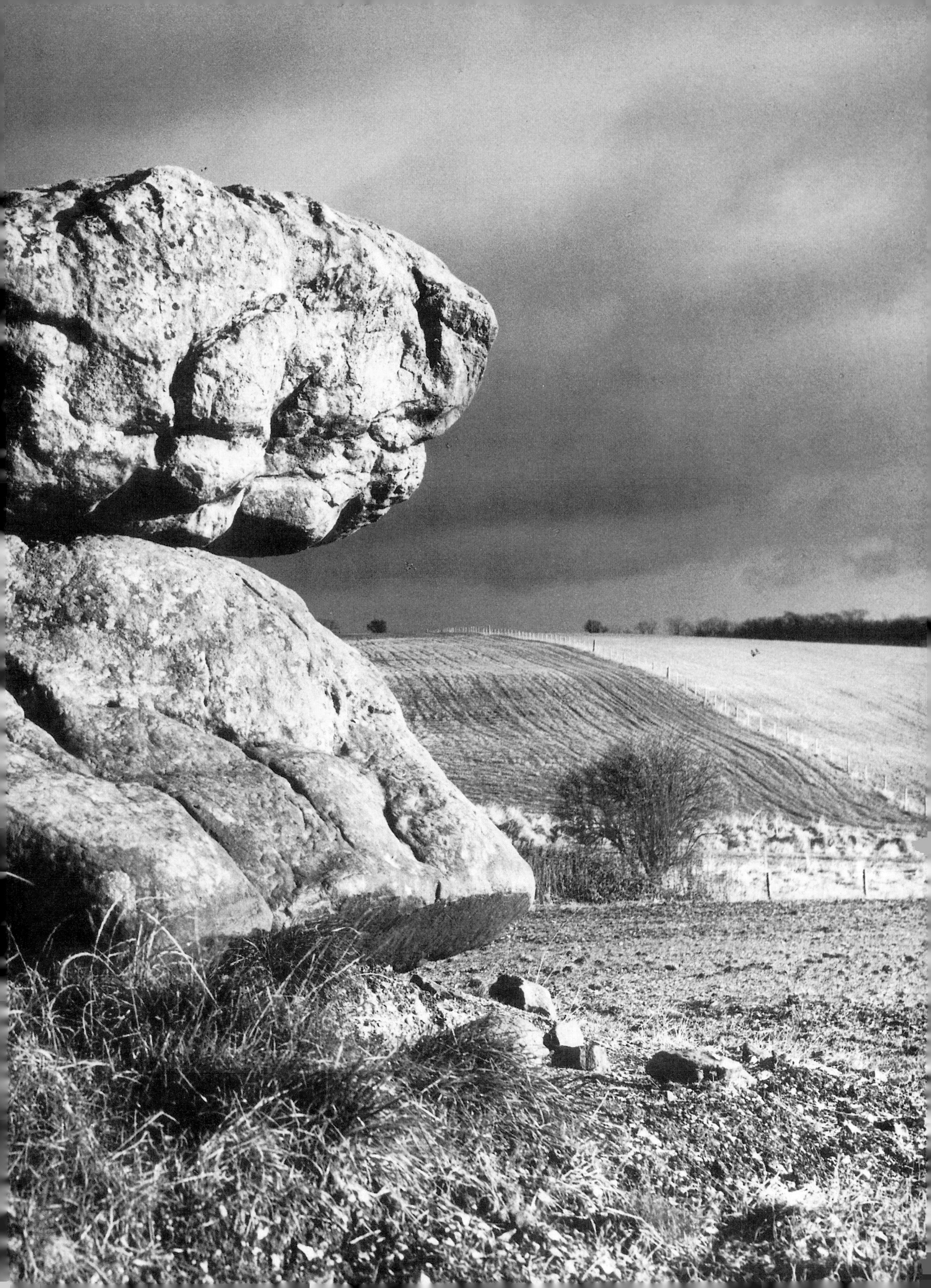

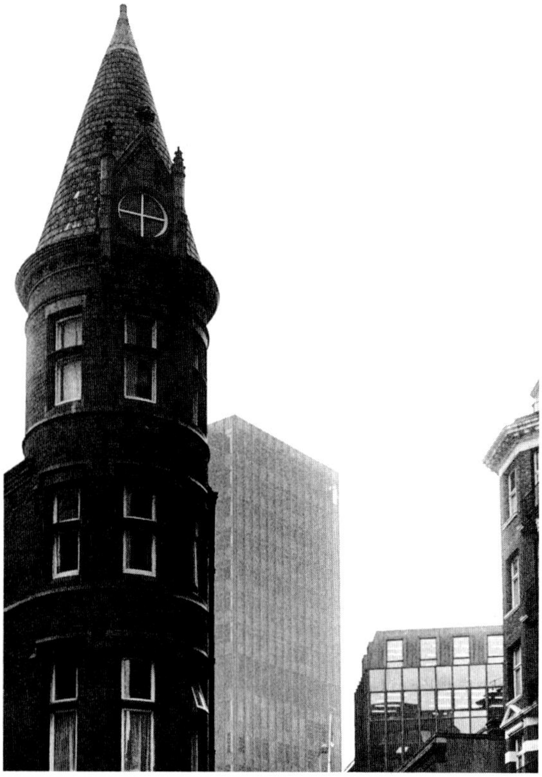

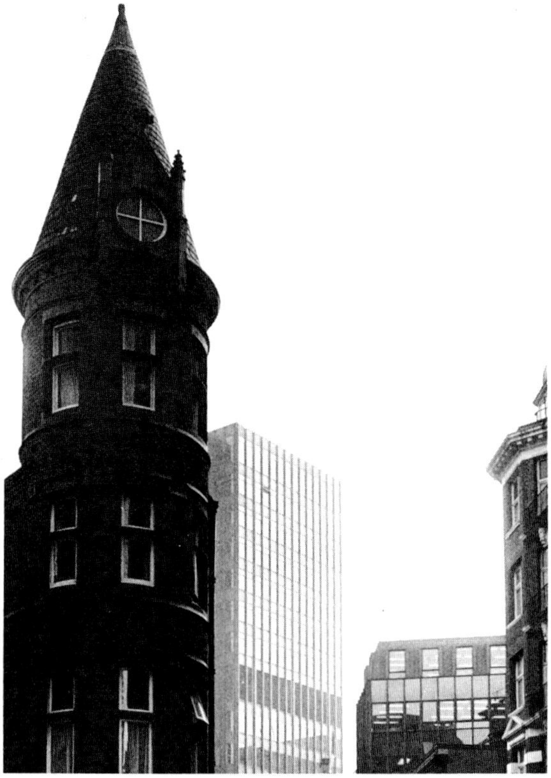

54-55 Use of a polarising screen to eliminate reflections. It works most effectively at an angle of about 30 degrees from the reflecting surface. It has no effect at 90 degrees.

increments in exposure of one-third of a stop.

For automatic exposure cameras that do not read through the lens, you can divide the film speed setting figure by the filter factor. With a x4 factor and an ISO 400/27° (ASA 400/27 DIN) film, set the film speed to ISO 100/21° (ASA 100/21 DIN). The meter is then informed that it is dealing with an ISO 100/21° film and gives four times the exposure normally appropriate to an ISO 400/27° film.

Exposure latitude with filters

Exposure is more critical when you use filters, and the latitude even of monochrome films is considerably reduced. The fact that you are using a filter generally implies that there is a lack of tone differentiation or contrast in the subject. No matter how you expose, certain tones are so alike that you cannot separate them adequately. Filtering can alter one of them so effectively that printing is easy. But if you attach the filter and then get the exposure wrong, you could nullify the effect of the filter or overemphasise its effect on the darkened tone.

Overexposure tends to weaken the effect of a filter, whereas underexposure may exaggerate it. However, underexposure can also lead to lack of detail in the darkened tone and an overall lack of contrast. Unless you are absolutely sure of the effects your filters have, there is a good case for bracketing exposures whenever you use a filter. Two extra exposures at one stop over and one stop under your calculated exposure should be adequate for monochrome work. In colour, filters are rarely strongly coloured and bracketing at half-stop intervals is more appropriate.

Filters and reciprocity law failure

There is one special kind of filter that deals with a special kind of problem with colour film, namely the failure of the reciprocity law. In effect, this law says that a given amount of light has the same effect on the film whether it be made up of a short exposure at a large aperture or a longer exposure at a smaller aperture. In other words, 1/30 sec at *f*/1.4 has the same effect as 4 sec at *f*/16. The law holds good on most occasions, but fails with most films when exposures are longer than 1 or 2 sec.

The problem is greater with colour film because it has three separate emulsions. If the law does fail, it will fail to a different extent for each emulsion. The result is a shift in colour rendering, because the relative amounts of red, green and blue light that make up the various colours of the subject are distorted. The remedy is to increase exposure to compensate for the underexposure and to add a special filter to correct the colour distortion.

Unfortunately, you do not obtain that kind of information on the little leaflet packed with the film. You need to get it from the film manufacturer or distributor. Even then, the filters used are rarely available from the average photographic supplier. On the whole, therefore, it is best to avoid long exposures with colour film when colour fidelity is important. Do not close down the lens aperture excessively in the hope of getting sharper results, or for greater depth of field than you really need, unless the exposure can be kept to no longer than one second.

Colour photography at night or in dimly-lit interiors may well call for long exposures, but some apparent colour distortion may then be accept-

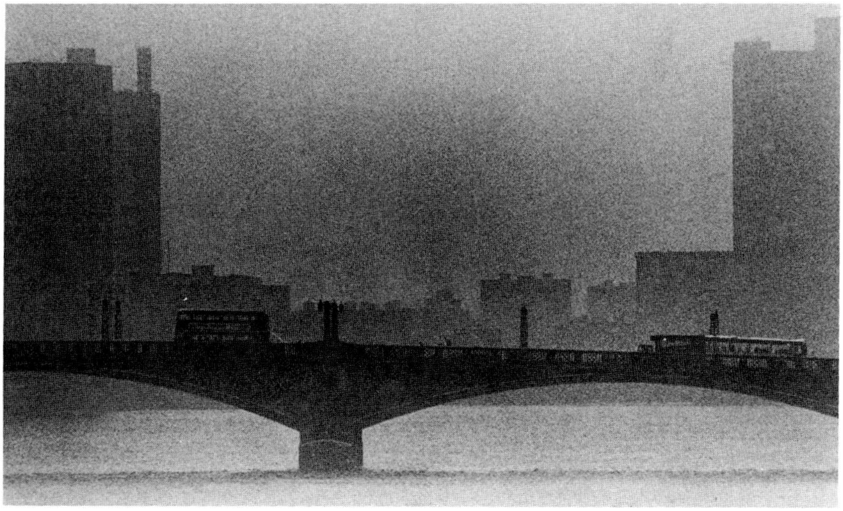

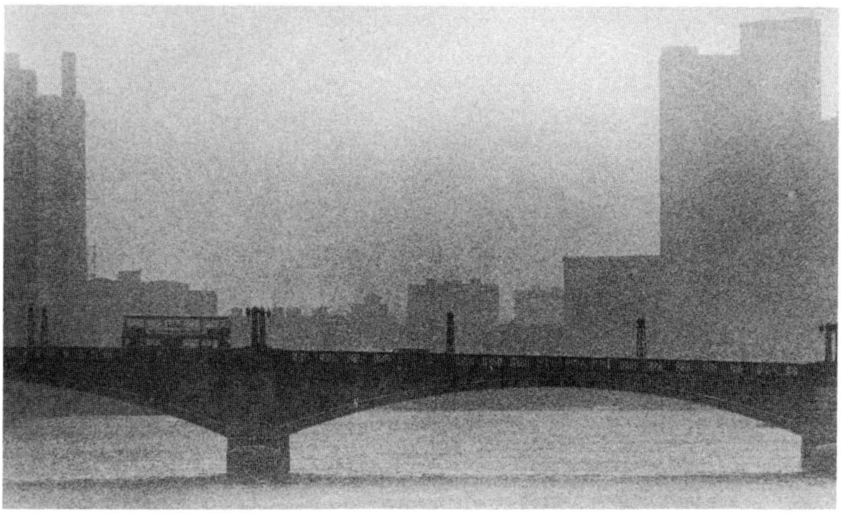

56-57 UV filters are not designed to cope with heavy mist or fog. At best, they give a marginal increase in contrast that is generally achieved just as efficiently with increased development and/or a higher-contrast print material. The filtered shot is at the top.

able. We do not see colours clearly in dim light and we are generally prepared to accept that the camera is similarly handicapped. We are also well acquainted with the fact that few lights are white in such conditions and can happily accept the effect of coloured light on familiar objects.

Dealing with UV radiation

Finally, we should perhaps mention the one filter that has a factor of unity, and therefore no effect on exposure. This is the colourless so-called UV filter. Actually, it is a UV-*absorbing* filter, reversing the principle that we call all other filters by the name of the colour they *transmit* most freely. The common type is designed to absorb the invisible ultra-violet radiation to which all films are sensitive.

UV radiation (it is not light, either) is of very short wavelength and is scattered by solid particles in the atmosphere to form a bluish haze (to the film) in distant shots. Nevertheless, not all such haze arises from UV radiation. In by far the majority of cases, and certainly if it is visible, distant haze is caused by the scattering of blue light. Both types of haze can be eliminated on monochrome film by the use of a pale yellow filter. With colour film, the pale pink filter generally supplied under the name 'skylight' is equally effective. In practice, such filtering is often neither practical nor desirable. We are quite accustomed to seeing a bluish haze in the distance and, unless we really need the detail, there is very little point in eliminating it.

In some circumstances, however, UV radiation is less scattered and reaches nearby objects in sufficient strength to put a blue cast over the whole picture, although we cannot see it in the subject. Then, we need to do something about it, and the usual remedy is the colourless UV-absorbing filter. It can improve the quality of pictures near large areas of water or at high altitudes, where there is likely to be less solid matter in the atmosphere and, therefore, less absorption of the UV radiation.

There is no need for exposure adjustment because the UV content has a negligible effect on overall illumination and does not materially affect meter readings. Some slight adjustment is necessary, however, if the filter has any coloured tint. Pinkish or straw-coloured filters are often sold as 'haze' filters. They, too, absorb UV radiation, but also some visible blue light and affect the exposure to some extent.

12 FLASH, THE PREDICTABLE LIGHT SOURCE

The one great advantage of flash as a light source is that its intensity and duration are predictable, resulting in the removal of at least one variable from the exposure problem. Flash now almost invariably means electronic flash and, with most units, an automatic exposure facility. This is achieved by putting a light sensor in the body of the unit and connecting it to an incredibly rapid switching circuit. The sensor picks up light reflected from the subject and, when it calculates that the film has had sufficient exposure, the switching circuit cuts off the flash discharge.

Automatic exposure flash

At very close range, depending on the power available, the cut-off circuit of an automatic flash unit can switch in very early and reduce the actual exposure time to as little as 1/40,000 sec. Normally, at full power, most flash units have a flash duration of about 1/1000 sec. As the fastest speed of most inter-lens shutters is considerably less than this, the full duration of the flash is invariably used. With focal plane shutters, the flash must be fired when the film is totally uncovered, and this restricts exposure times according to the design of the shutter. Although extremely rapid synchronisation speeds are being attained with modern, fast-moving shutters, shutter speeds of 1/60 sec or slower must be used with some cameras.

Automatic exposure flash units are available in a variety of designs. In the simplest case, automatic operation is available only at one lens aperture. More expensive units may allow two, three or anything up to the full range of lens apertures to be used. Some have tilting and swivelling heads, leaving the sensor facing forward to allow the flash to be directed at a reflector for 'bounced' flash and 'brolly' techniques.

Dedicated units

Many flash units have additional contacts sending signals to special circuitry in the camera to provide other automatic facilities, the simplest being automatic setting of the camera shutter speed to the mandatory synchronisation speed. Another facility might be a 'ready' signal in the camera viewfinder when the unit has drawn sufficient power from its batteries to fire. There may also be a confirmation signal when automatic exposure is deemed to have been successful. These are known as 'dedicated' units and some of them are extremely sophisticated. Unfortunately lack of standardisation in the camera industry means that each camera manufacturer has his own system of dedication, with contacts in different positions in the camera accessory shoe. As a result, warnings are commonly issued that only the camera manufacturer's own-brand flash units must be used.

12.1 The guide number of a flash unit is the product of *f*-number and distance. As shooting distance increases so the lens is opened to keep the product the same.

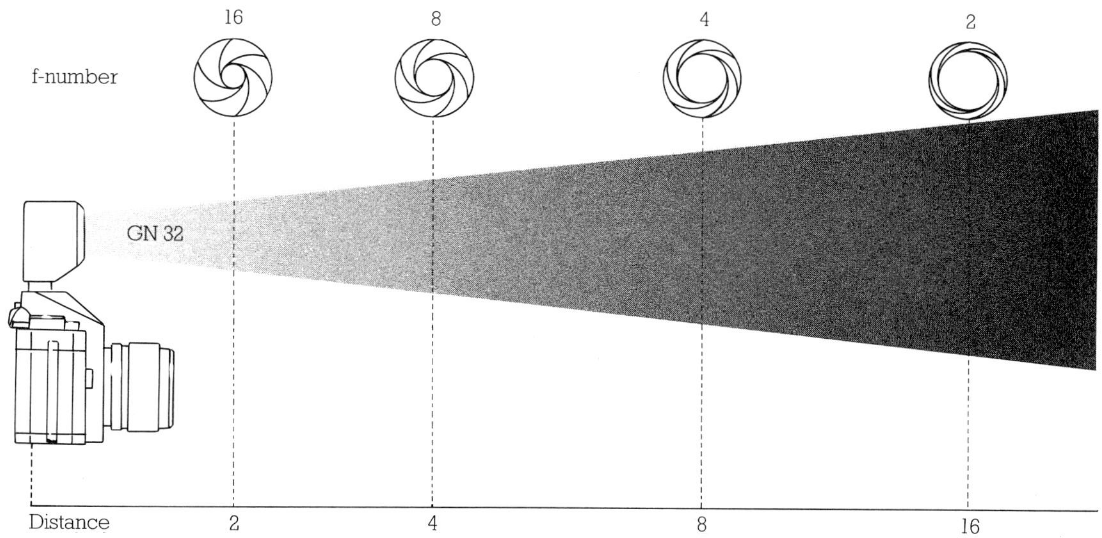

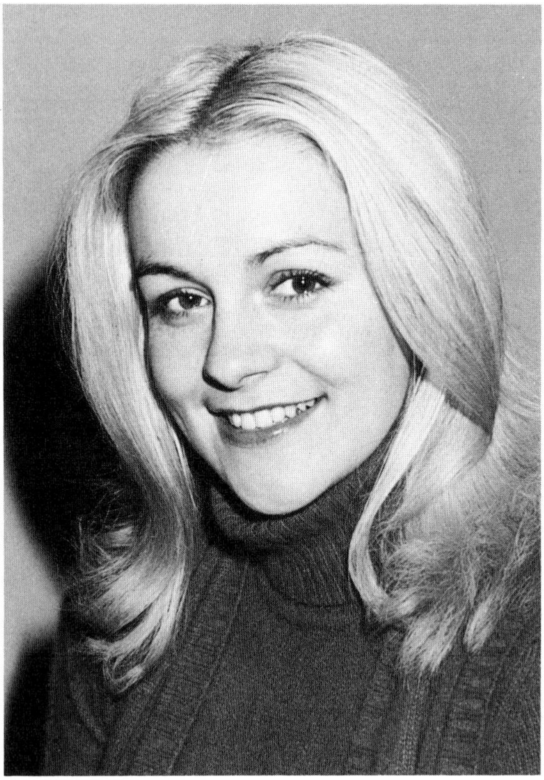

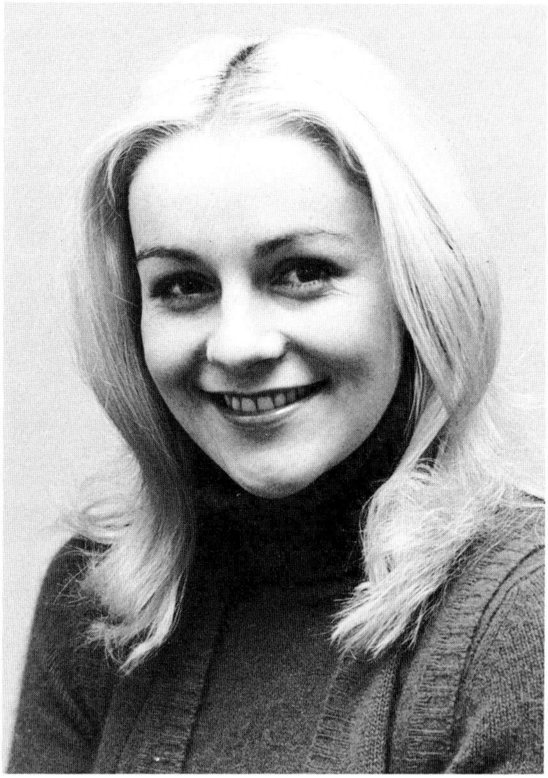

58-60 Direct, on-camera flash causes harsh shadows. Totally indirect lighting with flash bounced from the ceiling gives soft lighting overall (above right). Bounced lighting plus a weak direct flash on the camera restores a little modelling.

12.2 Multi-sockets can be used to connect more than one flash to the camera for simultaneous firing, but problems could arise with units of different makes. A more reliable method is to connect a slave unit to each off-camera flash. The flash connected to the camera will then activate all units simultaneously.

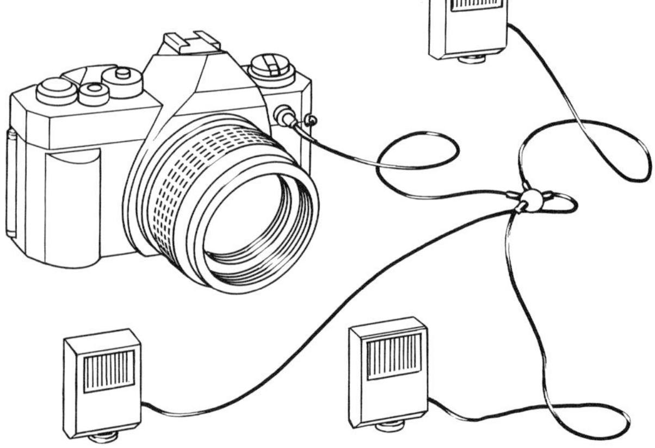

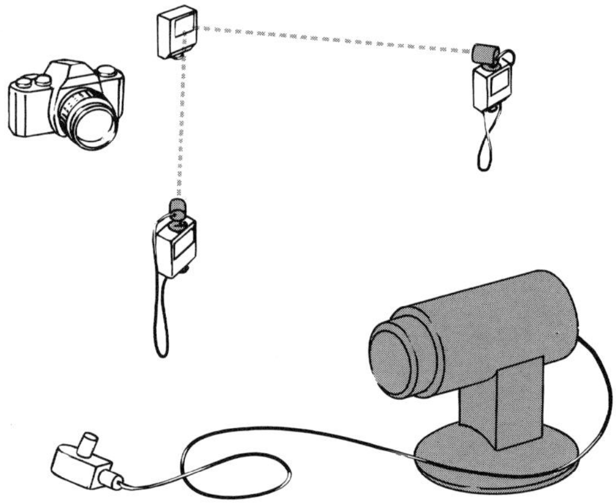

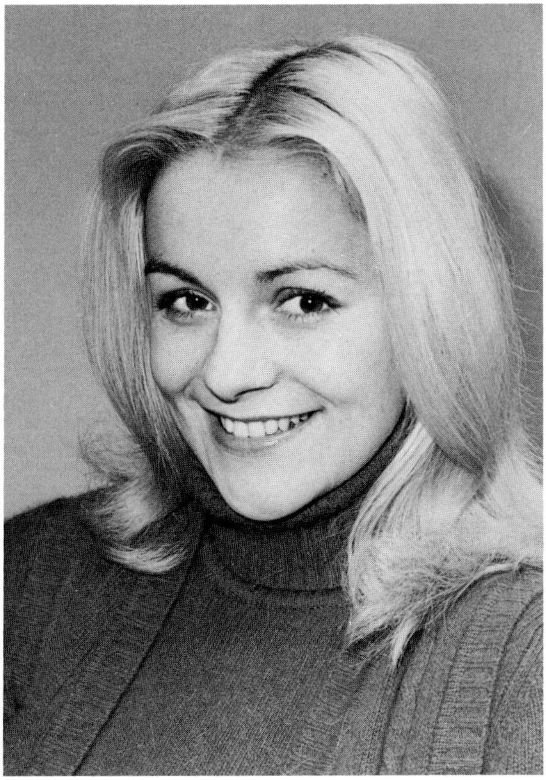

Using an independent unit, of which there are many, could invalidate the guarantee. That is a natural precaution for the manufacturer to take, but the danger of damage with the correct design of unit, properly used, is virtually non-existent.

Among the dedicated units are those taking their exposure reading through the camera lens instead of via a sensor in the flash unit. That has obvious advantages for multiple lighting sets, but the necessary linking cords and connections can be quite expensive. It avoids the necessity for a separate remote sensor, as supplied for some other units, but any kind of off-camera operation for dedicated units generally needs a special accessory cord to transmit the required signals from flash unit to camera.

Exposure guide numbers

With or without automatic facilities, the predictable output of a flash unit makes it a relatively easy light source to operate manually. With the camera shutter set to its obligatory flash synchronisation speed or slower, the only variable on the camera is the lens aperture. As with other forms of artificial light, however, there is also the variable of the distance of the light source from the subject, which affects its intensity at the subject plane.

Both lamp distances and lens *f*/numbers work on a law of squares with respect to illumination. So, with a given flash unit used with a flash of given speed, the amount of light reaching the film is the same when the product of distance and *f*/number are the same. In other words, exposure is the same with a flash at 10ft and the lens at *f*/4 as when the flash is at 5ft and the lens at *f*/8. Each pair multiplies up to 40, which can be taken as the 'guide number' for that unit used with a film of the given speed. Naturally, the guide number varies with the speed of the film in use and the aperture range for automatic operation may change with it. Many dedicated units, however, automatically set the flash unit to the film speed set on the camera.

Flash meters

Multiple lighting set-ups or the repeated use of a single flash can sometimes make exposure assessment a little difficult. There are complicated formulae to work out the effective guide number of a flash unit used at an extreme angle, or for two or more units used close together, but a more effective method in this case is to use a special kind of exposure meter. The ordinary meter cannot react fast enough to give a reading of flash illumination. With special circuitry built in, however, the intensity of even the shortest burst of flash illumination can be measured. Such is a flash meter.

A flash meter works on incident light, ie, the light falling on the subject, so it is placed in the subject position, facing the camera. Generally, it is set to the appropriate film speed and gives a recommendation of the lens aperture appropriate to the illumination received. Being an incident light reading, it is not affected by the nature of the subject or the background.

Factors affecting flash guide numbers

The predictability of flash can be overstated. As soon as you start to use it as a serious light source, you can run into difficulties. To use flash seriously, you have to position it away from the camera, or restrict the one on the camera to fill-in use, with another unit or head as the modelling or 'key' light. In these conditions, the camera distance is unimportant. It is the distance of the key flash from the subject that matters.

Flash units give a harsh light compared with skylight or large floods. To soften the effect, you can use diffusers or reflectors. If you do, you need to know their effect on the subject illumination. In most circumstances, you make use of reflectors whether you are aware of it or not. The flash bounces off nearby reflecting surfaces, such as walls or ceilings, adding to the direct illumination from the flash head itself. The maker's quoted guide number allows for a relatively high level of such reflected light. It assumes that the flash is used in a medium sized room with reasonably light-coloured walls and ceilings. In large rooms or halls, or in any room with predominantly dark tones, the guide number is therefore optimistic. Outdoors, where there are no nearby reflecting surfaces, it may be wildly so. In such conditions, the operating range of an automatic exposure unit may also be reduced.

Quoted guide numbers assume more or less frontal lighting, where few shadows are cast on the subject, and such that are, are of little importance. Move the flash 30° off the lens axis and strong shadows are introduced – shadows that you may not be prepared to accept without at least some detail or tone. The guide number could then be half a stop or more too high for your purposes. Unless you can afford a flash meter, the problem begins to look much more complicated than the guide number system would lead you to believe. It is not quite as bad as that.

If you require nothing more than casual snapshots indoors, you can use a single unit on the camera, firing directly at the subject or, better, aimed at the ceiling to provide 'bounced' illumination. In the first case, use of the guide number will give acceptable results. In the second, an estimate of the average distance from flash to subject via the reflecting surface is the figure that has to be divided into the guide number to give the lens aperture required for correct exposure. We are more concerned, however, with the problems that arise when using flash in studio fashion, ie, instead of tungsten floods and spots.

Using more than one flash

A popular method for colour work is to use a single flash fired into a large white umbrella, which throws a uniform flood of light back on to the subject. It works very well and exposure is simply a matter of applying the guide number allocated to the 'brolly-flash' combination or conducting tests to determine such a guide number. Monochrome work generally needs more modelling than such methods can provide and may be carried out with two, three or more flash units firing simultaneously.

There are two basic methods of synchronising more than one flash unit with the shutter operation. One uses a separate cable to each flash connected to the camera socket via a multi-adaptor. It can be an unreliable method and trailing cables are a potential hazard. Except with true studio equipment, moreover, the cables are flimsy and the connections insecure.

A more reliable method is to connect only one flash unit to the camera shutter contacts and to attach light-operated switches to each of the others. These switches are quite inexpensive and are commonly called slave units. This is yet another photographic misnomer, because it is actually the dependent flash units that are the slaves. However, the so-called slave unit contains an electronic switch that reacts with remarkable rapidity to any sudden significant rise in light level. It closes a circuit that fires the flash to which the unit is attached. Any number of slaves can be fired from one 'master' flash, provided each has its attached switch or is connected to such a switch. That is possible with slave units that carry extra connections.

The method has many advantages because it allows you to use any combination of units from various manufacturers and of varying powers. Modern slave units are extremely sensitive and can work with quite weak triggering flashes. In the average room, it is possible to put the least powerful unit on the camera as a fill light and to trigger more powerful units placed well away from, and even behind, the camera. Line of sight between master and slave flash is not necessary.

Exposure for this kind of multiple flash work is not nearly as complicated as it might seem. A possible set-up is a lamp at 30-45° off-axis as the key light, another of lesser power or at a greater distance from the camera and more or less on-axis as fill light and, perhaps, another on the background or as a back light. *The back or background light has no effect on exposure.* A background light aims to bring the background up to a level of illumination that the main light cannot provide. It does not affect the subject. A back light illuminates parts the main illumination does not reach and the camera cannot see. Its aim is generally to provide outline or rim lighting to separate the subject from a similarly toned background.

But how much should you add to the guide

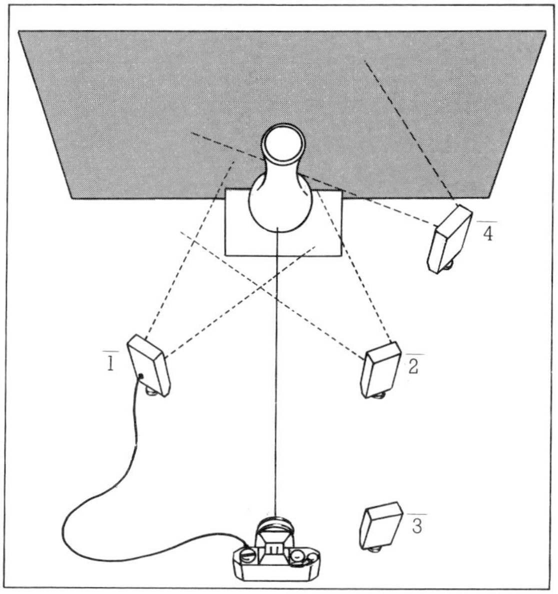

12.3 In a multiple flash set up, the key light (1) is generally within a 30-45° angle from the lens axis. The fill light (2, 3) can be at a similar angle or nearer to the axis. Its power can be varied by in-built switching, diffusion or distance. The background light should normally be positioned to avoid overspill on the subject.

number of the main light for the effect of the frontal fill light? If the lamps are correctly arranged, with the intensity on the subject much greater from the key light than from the fill, you can generally ignore the effect of the fill. It is simply lifting the shadows cast by the off-axis key light. Its effect on overall illumination is minimal. There can be occasions, however, usually in colour, when you use a rather strong fill light, almost to the extent of cross lighting. This time, the fill does affect overall exposure, because it is now almost a secondary key light. That may seem to raise a serious exposure problem, because it takes some rather complicated mathematics to work out the result of combining two different guide numbers of lamps used at different distances. Yet the margin of error is obviously small. You cannot be doubling the illumination on the subject, so your required exposure adjustment must be less than one stop. If you give half a stop less, you must be within a smaller fraction of a stop of correct exposure.

The need for experiment

Exposure for multiple flash work is always a matter of experience or experiment. Now that rollfilm and 35mm are universally used in hobby photography, tests usually take the form of bracketed exposures while actually shooting. In our case, very little bracketing is actually required. One exposure based on the key light guide number and another at half a stop less should cover you adequately and provide useful information for future similar set-ups. If you are really fussy, you can make it two extra exposures at one-third and two-thirds of a stop less, instead of just one at half a stop, but the difference is not likely to be significant.

Tests and experiments are necessary with flash work, because so much depends not only on the intensity of the light, but also on its nature. The size of the tube and its reflector, the distance the unit is used at, the nature and tone of nearby reflective surfaces and so on, all play their part. Wherever possible, standardise your lighting set-up or at least work around a standardised practice, so that you can get to know the effect of the individual lights. Occasionally, modified processing is also called for. With some lamps, particularly the larger types, flash lighting tends to be rather flat. An extra 30 per cent on the developing time may help.

Exposure is always a matter of compromise, and flash exposure is no exception. You need experience with your own equipment to teach you the compromise that provides the type of result you want. If you do a great deal of flash work, you need ancillary equipment to provide spot and flood effects, and guide numbers then become a bit hit-and-miss. They form a useful basis for experiment, but that is all. A flash meter is essential for serious work, just as the ordinary exposure meter is with continuous light sources. You can work without a meter if you keep to a few well-tried lighting set-ups, but a meter is still helpful in the assessment of the effect of small adjustments in lamp position. It also allows you to measure the intensity of each lamp separately and avoids the necessity for complicated calculations when you use reflected flash illumination.

Close-up with flash

Flash is useful illumination for close-range work, if only because the light sources are so much more easily handled and they do not get hot. Tiny units are available that are particularly suited to close-range work, where the power of the average electronic flash unit might well be too great. It is not too difficult to fabricate an attachment to place one such unit on each side of the lens or the camera body, connected individually to a multi-socket or with a slave unit on one.

Even the smallest of these units can be too powerful for some applications. With a guide number as low as 12 (metres) for your chosen film, two units add up to a guide number of about 17 (guide number x the square root of 2). The extra lens extension for a life-size image reduces that to about 8.5. The flash would need to be one metre from the subject for an aperture of *f*/8, or half a metre for *f*/16.

Manual control of exposure is always advisable with close-ups. Flash guide numbers can be highly inaccurate for this type of work. The ratio of reflected light from nearby surfaces is usually much lower, while subject and background can often influence meter readings by their tone. Close-up subjects are frequently 'non-average' in exposure meter terms. Additionally, of course, the ordinary auto exposure flash unit cannot be aware of any extra lens extension you might be using. Shooting a life-size image entails cutting the effective power of the flash to one-quarter, owing to light lost as it travels twice the distance inside the camera.

The nature of the subject

You do not normally need to take account of the nature of the subject with manually-controlled flash exposures. Guide numbers and flash meter readings are akin to incident light readings, or to reflected light readings from a grey card. They are not influenced by the subject and should give adequate exposure whatever its tonal distribution. That does not apply, of course, to auto-exposure units. They work in much the same way as for a normal exposure meter, taking a reflected light reading from the subject. A very light subject will read too high and cause underexposure. A

61 A suitable subject for auto-flash exposure. With non-auto units, it is difficult to restrict the light intensity at such close range. The auto unit restricts its duration.

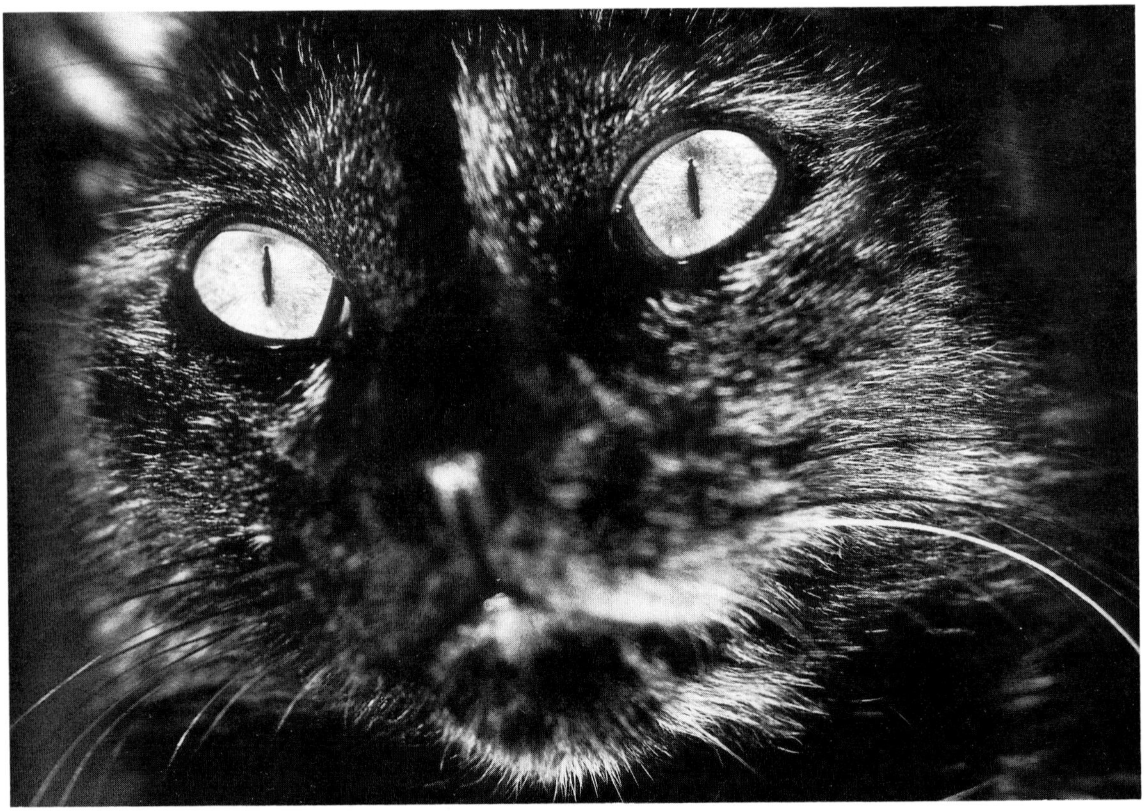

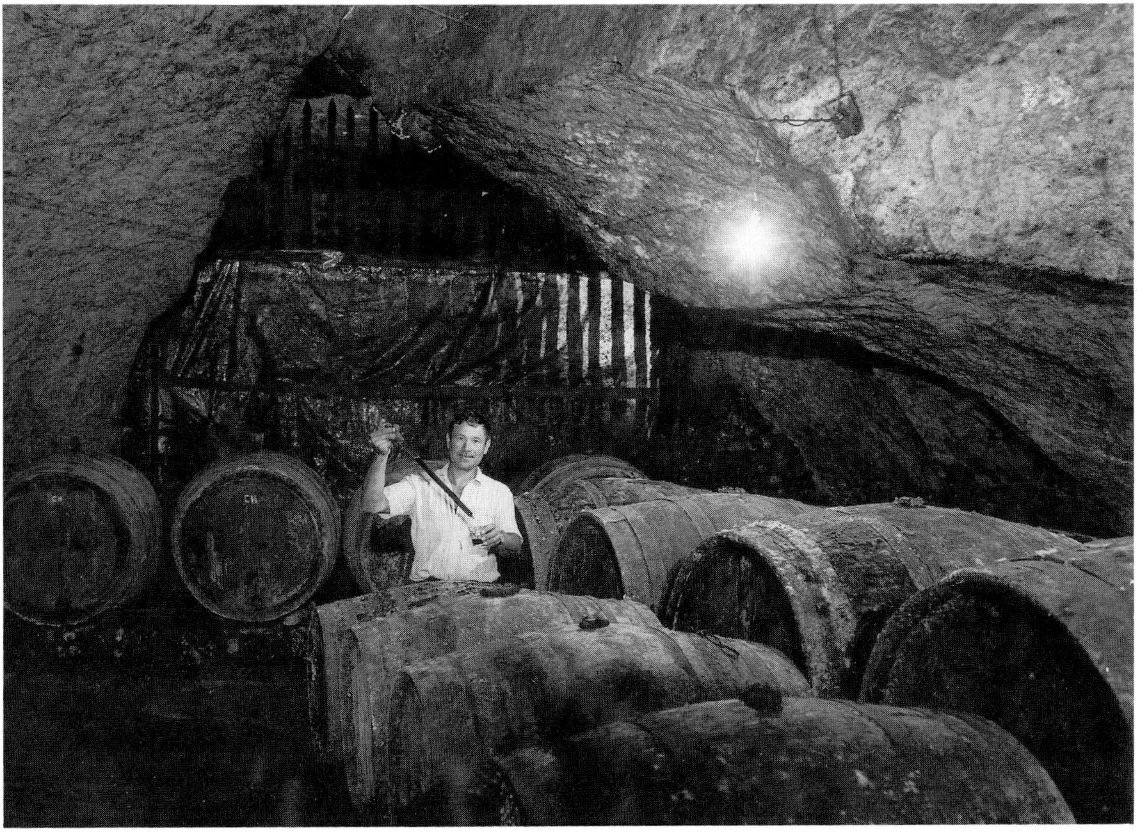

62 Wine grower in a cave. A one-second exposure was given with four flash heads on slaves. A typical example of applied multi-head flash lighting.

very dark subject may cause overexposure. You have to make the appropriate adjustment, which is most easily done by setting a larger or smaller aperture on the lens than on the flash unit.

Other factors *can* upset the guide number system, which relates primarily to frontally lit subjects. If the lighting comes primarily from well round to one side (to accentuate texture, perhaps) and little or no frontal fill is used, exposure needs some care. The prime consideration, as ever, is the effect you want. Oblique flash throws heavy shadows. Are they to be totally empty or do you want some detail? The effect of lighting positioned at 45° to the camera angle could be to demand up to one stop extra exposure for fully detailed shadows – but that could burn out the highlights. The effect of 'skim' lighting at almost 90° to the camera axis could be to demand two stops (or more) extra exposure, again, with the sacrifice of extreme highlights.

The decision you have to make is how much detail you need in the shadows and whether it is best handled 1, by a weak fill light because you want to retain detail in the highlights, or 2, by extra exposure because the highlights are small and can be allowed to burn out. In the former case, you can probably expose in accordance with the flash guide number and add fill-in lighting by reflector or heavily diffused flash at about one-sixth to one-tenth the power of the main unit. In the latter case, halving the guide number is likely to lead to satisfactory results.

High-speed reciprocity failure

We mentioned the reciprocity law earlier in respect of slow shutter speeds. In fact, a similar effect may occur with very short exposures, too. That rarely posed any problem before the advent of automatic exposure flash units, which control exposure by restricting the duration of the flash. When the flash unit is very close to the subject, the effective exposure can be as brief as 1/40,000 sec. That can lead to similar effects of failure of the reciprocity law as with low-light exposures – underexposure and colour shifts. Fortunately, the

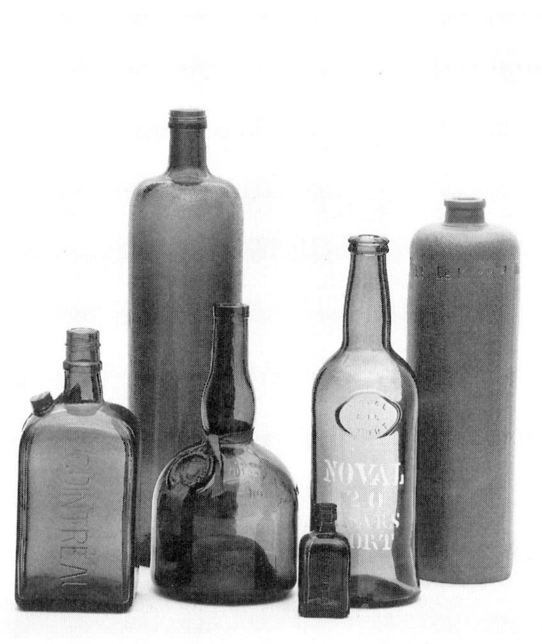

63 Example of shadowless illumination using flash from a wide-area source. An umbrella or tent have a very similar effect with small scale subjects.

effect rarely seems to be as pronounced as with long exposures and the colour shift is generally minimal. Experience with your own equipment and technique will indicate the corrections required, which may be no more than a half-stop wider aperture on the camera lens than on the flash unit.

Fill-in flash

A popular use for flash is as a fill light when the subject is strongly sun lit, typically in backlighting situations or with high contrast subjects, such as wedding groups. The heavy shadows cast by direct sunlight can be lightened by a relatively weak flash from the camera position.

The practice has had its ups and downs with 35mm SLR cameras, which are invariably fitted with focal plane shutters. The requirement that the film must be totally uncovered when the flash fires restricts the use of flash in daylight with such a shutter, because the only shutter speeds at which the film is totally uncovered are frequently 1/60 sec. or less, although 1/125 sec is now becoming the norm. Anything faster than that is, however, as yet exceptional and rather expensive. The result is that, in the type of lighting that calls for fill-in flash, the obligatory shutter speed can be too slow for the required or available apertures, and certainly too slow to stop any significant action.

Problems used to arise, too, from the immutable power of the flash itself. The aim is normally to add only about a quarter of a full flash exposure to the daylit subject. That entails doubling the guide number or heavily diffusing the flash output. The

12.4 In bright sunlight, with a shutter speed of 1/60 sec. (obligatory for flash on some cameras) you have to use a very small lens aperture, but you can still have problems with flash fill-in. Even a lower power unit might have an effective guide number for fill-in purposes of 140 or so, which means it would have to be used at least 9ft away at *f*/16.

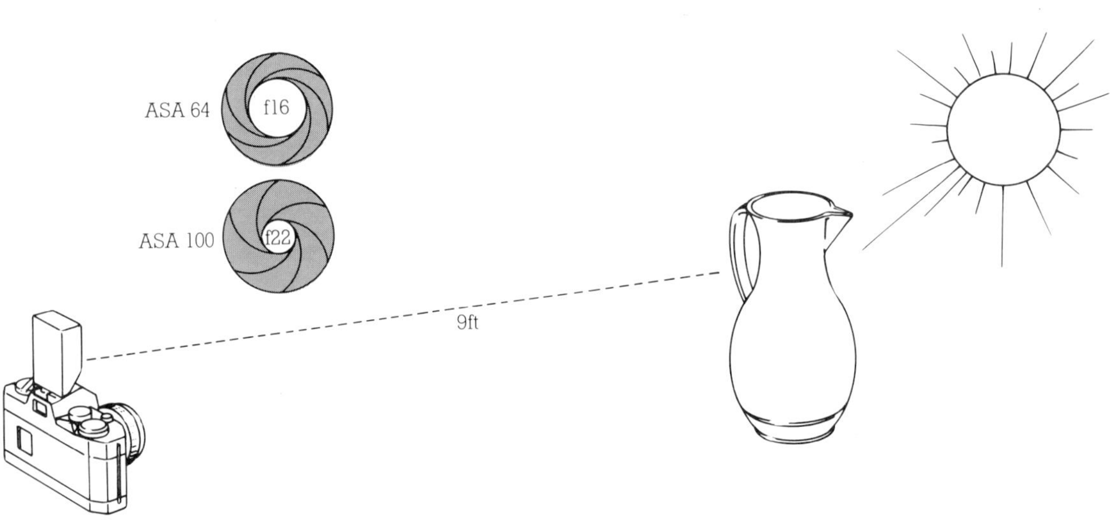

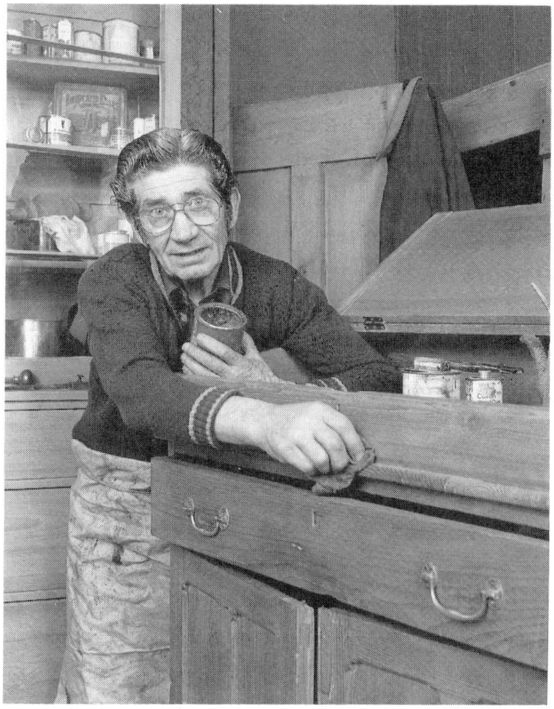

64A Furniture polisher. Umbrella flash provided even illumination with equal brightnesses on subject and surroundings.

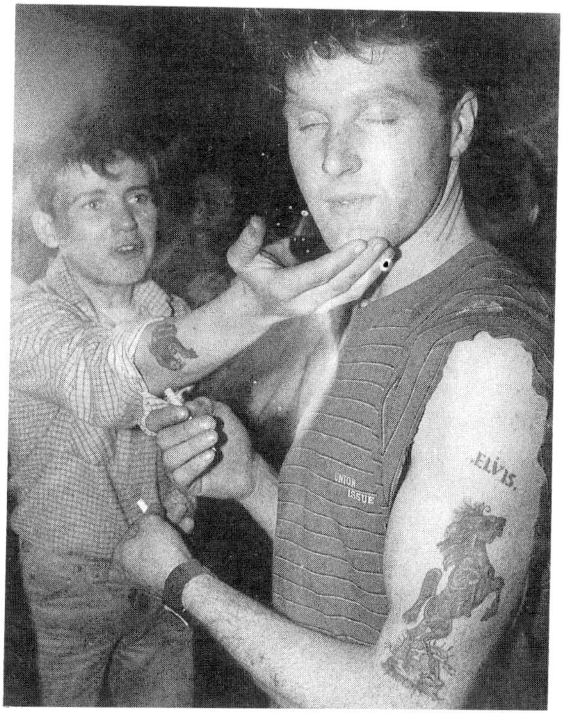

64B Pub scene. The flash gives side/front lighting which is more even in depth than when used on-camera.

auto-exposure unit can help in such a case because it is possible to 'fool' the flash exposure system by setting its auto working aperture to a larger figure than you have set on the lens. If your shooting aperture, for example, is *f*/11 and you can set the flash to *f*/5.6, you should be able to cut its output to one-quarter of a normal full exposure.

This is obviously an area for experiment. The actual settings required depend on the result you are looking for and how your particular unit reacts to being 'misinformed'. The aim should be to keep the fill lighting to the minimum. You don't normally want to light the shaded part (such as the face in an against-the-light portrait) to a level at which it looks frontally lit. That would look unnatural with scenes where the main source of illumination is very evidently located behind the subject.

13 SHOOTING IN LOW LIGHT

Modern films and lenses have almost put flash and other artificial light aids to photography out of business – or is that wishful thinking? Looking at the booming sales of electronic flash equipment, and the increasing incorporation of flash units into cameras, it probably is. In a way, that is a pity because, once we start boosting the natural light to take a photograph, we are creating something artificial. With the lost reality, we are also in danger of losing atmosphere, impact and interest.

Theatre, night-club, discotheque, even some everyday interiors, have characteristic lighting that creates a mood. In the past, books such as this often explained how existing lighting could be augmented by hidden floods or spots to provide enough light by which to take a photograph. Such methods were not really necessary even then. Now, with ISO 1000/31° (ASA 1000/31 DIN) and faster films available for colour slides or prints, with the possibility of uprating in reserve, with silverless image monochrome films capable of astronomic speed ratings, and no doubt even faster films to come, the proverbial black cat in a coal cellar becomes almost photogenic.

Add lenses with maximum apertures approaching *f*/1, and flash begins to look dated. Certainly, it is widely over-used. It has its place in simple cameras and many specialised fields; glamour and fashion studios apparently could not survive without it. Nevertheless, in much general photography in the hobby field, it is a mood-destroying escape from a few readily-soluble problems.

The problems of low light

Certainly, low light levels do create exposure problems. Night scenes and interiors rarely have the same distribution of tones as the average daylight shot. They are often of much higher contrast. You rarely encounter a dimly lit subject that does not have almost impenetrable shadows coupled with comparatively brilliant highlights. Almost any interior in daylight has windows that you would prefer not to render as blank white and deeply shaded parts farthest away from the window. With dark furnishings, the contrast is severe. Stage shows may spotlight an individual and throw the rest of the cast into comparative gloom. In a musical performance, instruments or costumes may produce brilliant reflections.

Apart from contrast, there is the relatively long exposure time that may be necessary if you need considerable depth of field. This raises the problem of movement and of reciprocity law failure. Yet how often in such circumstances are you looking for pin-sharp detail in movement or 'correct' colour – whatever that may be – in low light? Even the contrast problem is not as bad as it may seem because it is the faster films that handle high contrast situations best.

Your own problem

The real problem in low light photography is a personal one. What kind of result are you trying to produce? No matter what you do, you cannot reproduce the scene as the eye sees it. You cannot even do that in broad daylight, although you can approach it closely. At low light levels, the film

66 Weak toplighting in a restaurant is not ideal for a portrait but the relatively low light level on the front figure is acceptable in the context. A full exposure is vital.

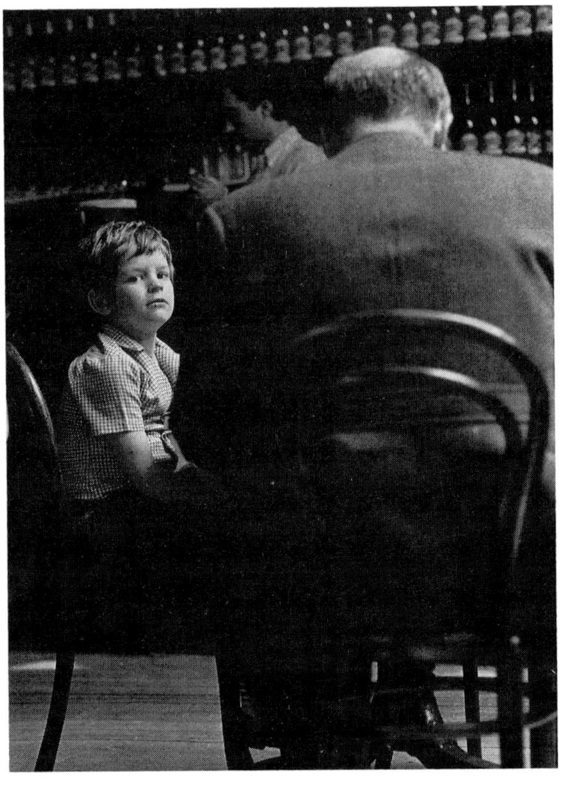

cannot alternately peer at light and shade and see colour and movement exactly as the eye does. In fact, the eye rarely sees what we imagine it does. It puts in its own features (in conjunction with the brain) to translate degraded colours, freeze movement, delineate features that are barely discernible, and so on. Quite often, the eye is working on 'memory pictures' stored in the brain.

You cannot reproduce photographically what the brain perceives, so you have to create an impression. Of course, you can go close, fire a flash at the exotic dancer and get a fully exposed picture of a figure in virtual isolation. But that would give nobody an impression of the scene as it actually appeared. A better impression might be created by a shot through smoke haze with a shoulder or head protruding into the picture area and the figure on the stage indicated rather than delineated.

You would not want to show a room interior with every corner, every fold in the curtains, every detail in the furniture and furnishings fully lit and pin sharp. Well, you might, for advertising or other commercial purposes. Generally, however, you want the room to look reasonably natural. So, as in most photography, you compromise. You trade one aspect against another to produce an image of the subject as you see it or as you want others to see it. Your exposure has to be assessed accordingly.

Facing the practical difficulties

Once you have decided how you want to present your low-light subject, you have to work out the exposure required in terms of shutter speed and aperture. Lacking experience in similar situations, you are lost without an exposure meter. Often, you are not much better off even with one, and still less so if it is only the TTL version in the camera. Taking a straight reflected-light reading, as the TTL meter does, is useless in most cases. Few meters are sensitive enough to give any reading at all for a night scene with relatively few lamps around, and many TTL meters still have viewfinder readouts that cannot easily be seen in low light.

When the overall light level is too low to provide a reading, you have to find something in the picture area that does persuade the needle to move or the light to glow. It might be a flesh tone, a reflection on a wet surface, the pavement below a street lamp, or even the lamp itself. You might have to introduce a suitable object into the scene purely for metering purposes. A white card (the reverse side of a standard grey card) is useful or, failing that, a newspaper or a handkerchief.

Make sure your reading is of the selected tone only, but take it into the lightest part of the picture area if necessary. This makes a separate meter virtually essential, except, perhaps, where you are photographing floodlit buildings on the opposite bank of a river. Then, a telephoto lens would give you a reasonable base reading on your TTL meter.

Back to the zone system

Once you have your reading, you have a base to work from. You have first to decide how the tone you metered is to reproduce in your picture. Going back to the tone or zone methods, what depth of tone would you expect, for example, in a flesh tone in the prevailing light conditions? You would not expect it to reproduce as in daylight, as an average skin tone, maybe not even as a standard mid-tone. It would be more like a Tone 5, perhaps. You need to consider this carefully. If the subject is standing right in the lamplight, then you want to be nearer the daylight rendering. Assuming that you want Tone 5, you give one stop less exposure than the meter indicates, remembering that the meter would aim to reproduce the metered area as Tone 6.

If you had to put in an artificial white tone, decide how you would expect such a tone to reproduce in the position you read it. You are not likely to expect brilliant white, unless, again, you were very close to a bright light source. It would probably be nearer Tone 8. So your exposure would be two stops more than the meter indicates, because it aims to reproduce anything it reads as Tone 6. If the only reading you can get is direct from a lamp or other light source, you go through the same procedure. If it is a street light, you must expect it to reproduce as empty white; a lightly curtained window perhaps Tone 9. So your exposure is three or four stops more than the meter indicates.

With a little ingenuity, and a lot of practice, you can get close to the exposure you want with such methods. You should always be able to get the tone you want in the area you meter, but you cannot be sure how the other tones will come out. It is always wise, therefore, to bracket your exposures. Four extra exposures for colour slides at half stop intervals and two extra for negative materials at one stop intervals should achieve the required result.

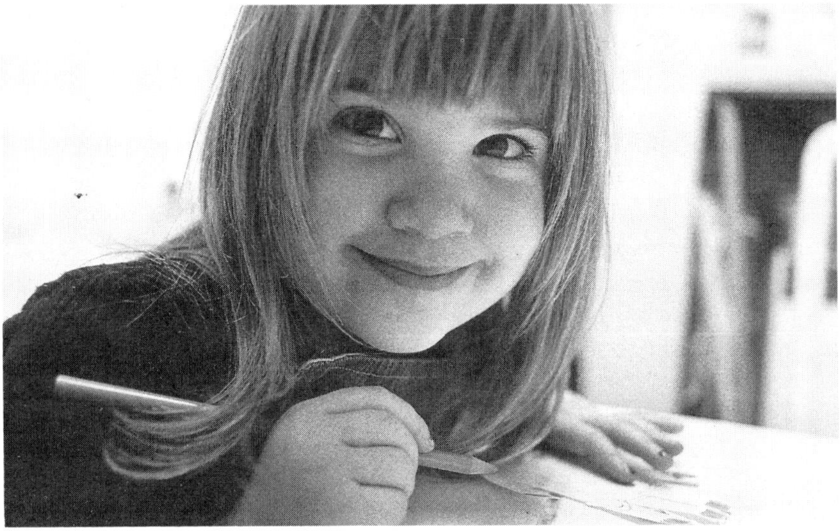

67 In poorly lit surroundings look out for useful reflecting surfaces.

Aperture or shutter speed?

In low-light photography, it is advisable to control your exposure as far as possible by aperture rather than by shutter speed. Particularly in colour, reciprocity law failure is likely to be a real problem if your shutter speed exceeds two or three seconds, demanding that you bracket your exposures extensively.

Wide apertures are often quite practicable in this type of photography. Your main subject is usually at a reasonable distance and, even at full aperture, depth of field increases significantly with increasing focused distance. Alternatively, shaded foregrounds may suffer little from lack of sharpness, while somewhat out-of-focus backgrounds for relatively close subjects are frequently acceptable.

The effect of lens extension

Do not forget that low-light photography does not necessarily mean that the subject is dimly lit. It could mean that you have to put in a lot of lens extension for close-range work and have to stop down excessively for depth of field. The level of illumination at the film plane can then be very low indeed.

The problems are not so great, however, because the subject can be well lit and you have no difficulty in taking a meter reading, unless you are confined to using a camera with stopped-down metering and a needle readout. Even then, you can take a reading at full aperture and convert it to the shooting aperture. With a hand-held meter, convert the reading as shown in Chapter 9.

You still have the problem of reciprocity law

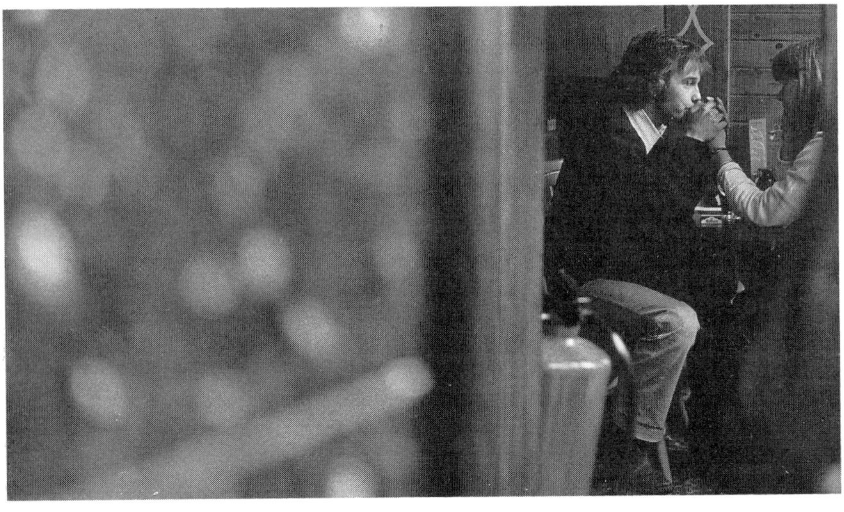

68 Scene in a café, as viewed through the street door – a situation calling, if possible, for pre-set prefocused shooting.

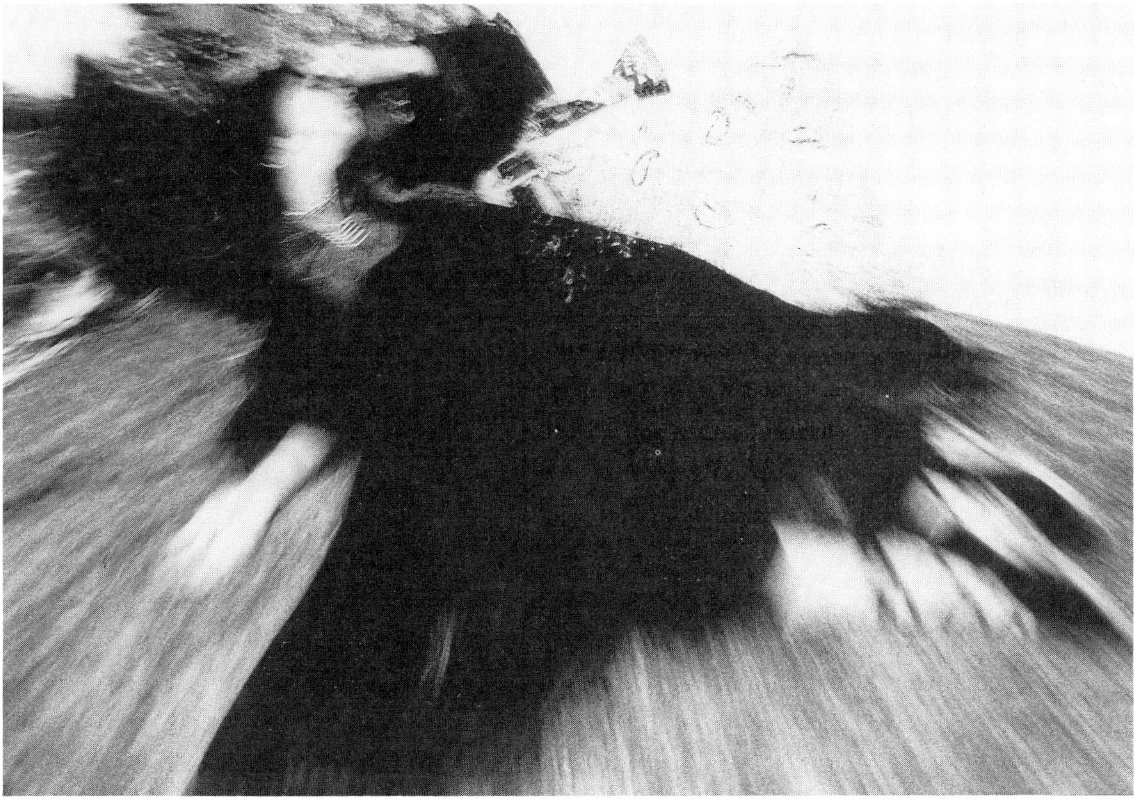

69 Low light and rapid movement. Without flash, there is no way to 'freeze' the movement. A suitable subject for impressionistic treatment. Development could be prolonged to retain reasonable contrast.

failure. It is more important in this type of work because you are not actually shooting in low light and colour distortion is less likely to be acceptable. If you find that your exposures run to more than a second or two, you would be well advised to seek some method of augmenting the lighting.

Experience is the best teacher
There is no real substitute for experience in low-light photography. In normal lighting, casual use of an exposure meter will always get you some sort of result and, more often than not, a satisfactory one. But in low light, few meters work very well. The specifications of some modern meters may lead you to believe that they can read candlelight in a field. In fact, the lower down the scale you go, the less accurate the meter becomes. You have to use it with considerable ingenuity and read it with more than a little scepticism. With no previous experience, you must bracket widely. With experience, you can take fewer shots and have a reasonable chance of success.

Experience has to be acquired, and it does not take very long if you go about it sensibly. The first rule is to stick to one brand of film, processed always in the same manner. Many films can be uprated and there is no reason why you should not do that if your first experiments show that you get satisfactory results. Once you have settled on a speed rating allied to a method of processing, stick to it. You will then soon learn how that film can be expected to behave in a variety of circumstances.

You cannot buy experience cheaply; you have to use a lot of film. Seek out your subjects at every opportunity. Do not wait for the occasional masterpiece to turn up. Shoot anything and everything in low light – streetlighting, floodlight, moonlight and so on. Try the impossible, using a dozen different exposures on it. Keep records of your exposures and any other relevant detail, such as light sources just out of the frame, meter readings, etc. Comparison of records and images at a later date will give you a bank of information for future use.

14 THE UNPREDICTABILITY OF DAYLIGHT

Daylight may be the most popular light for general photography, but it is the light over which we have least control. Dull winter light with a raincloud-filled sky is of little use to any photographer. Certainly, you can still take photographs by it and sometimes you have to. If you are a wedding photographer and your client insists on the traditional group outside the church, you have to make the most of it. If you are a press photographer assigned to a particular event on that kind of day, you cannot offer to go back when the sun is shining. If possible, you take along your own sun in the form of a powerful flash unit.

Bad weather shooting

Dull days, rainy days and general bad-weather days are part of life, and there are pictures to be made out of all of them. Wet slate roofs under a grey sky with smoke pouring out of factory chimneys form an evocative scene that has been depicted many times, with varying degrees of success. How do you go about calculating the exposure for such a scene? You can take a straight average reading and get a more or less perfect exposure, but the picture will be a rather dull-looking record. You want it to look like a dull, depressing scene, but you still want some quality in the print.

The whole scene is likely to be of very low contrast, and very low contrast prints made up almost entirely of mid-tones rarely appeal. What do you do? Make it darker, or lighter, or increase contrast? All are possible. If you reduce your exposure by two stops, all the tones are pushed two stops down the scale. Weak shadows go black, the sky gets darker, the sense of gloom is greater but, unless you have reasonably strong highlights on the wet roofs or pavements, you still have a flat, lifeless print. You really need a slight break in the cloud cover to provide that extra reflection. If you get this, then the darker treatment may work. If not, you can try increasing the contrast by extending development by 50 per cent or so. Then you might add print manipulation, using a higher contrast paper and printing up to a darker tone in sky and shadow areas.

You can go further. You can use a fast film, underexpose it by a stop or so and 'push' the development in a vigorous developer – perhaps even a print developer. This will give you even more contrast and a prominent grain structure. It should add a brightness to highlights that would otherwise be too little emphasised and, by virtue of the underexposure, leave deep black areas, especially if you print on a high contrast paper.

The way you treat it depends on the way you see it. Grainy, relatively high-contrast treatment is particularly suitable for many dull-weather scenes. A truthful rendering often has little impact, so you have to exaggerate the effect.

Picking out the telling detail

You can often create more impact by concentrating the interest for this type of shot. A bedraggled figure under a streaming umbrella at a bus stop certainly gives an impression of bad weather: but a close-up of just part of the umbrella and a few running droplets over an unsmiling face is better still.

Let us consider this scene in terms of exposure. There are a black umbrella, water droplets and flesh tones. Which is the most important? In this case, not the flesh tones, so a straight reading is out. You want some detail in the umbrella fabric and, if possible, in the water droplets. If you aim at giving the umbrella a little extra exposure, you should be successful. It would normally be one of the darkest tones in the picture, about Tone 2. We do not want it in the middle tone area, so Tone 3 would be about right. This means one stop more than a normal exposure for the conditions, and pushes the flesh tone up the scale to be reproduced a little lighter than usual, but still leaves detail in the water droplets. An exposure one stop more than a reading from a mid-tone should give you a negative that prints well on normal paper, with the opportunity to move up a grade if necessary.

Making the most of foggy conditions

Of all bad-weather conditions, perhaps fog is the most difficult to handle. A foggy scene can be pictorial, evocative, striking. It can also be dull and lifeless. The exposure level is often very important, despite the limited tonal range.

The advantage of fog is that it obscures detail. It reduces figures, buildings, etc. to mere outlines or eliminates them completely from the background, depending on their distance and the density of the fog. The disadvantage is that it flattens contrast almost to a monotone. You must have something to lighten the gloom in at least a small part of the picture.

London today is not as notorious for its fogs as in former days, when busmen used to walk in front of their vehicles with flaming torches; but fogs do still occur, and London is still the city of big red double-decker buses. A typical London fog picture could show a bus looming up out of the gloom at a temporary bus-stop sign so frequently used in those conditions. The temporary stop is on a column embedded in a block of concrete, and the actual sign is at about head height. If you shoot from close by in a fog, it will show up clearly with the bus only vaguely outlined as it approaches. The bus should have headlights and interior lights on. There is an exposure problem that could be repeated with similar scenes in many other cities.

In ordinary misty scenes, exposure is not too much of a problem, because the subject is generally very short-scaled. Most films have plenty of exposure latitude for such subjects. The difficulties arise chiefly with colour slides. The density of the mist or fog has a considerable influence, but a straight reflected-light reading should not be too far from correct. If it errs at all, it will be on the side of underexposure. You could compare the reading with an incident light or grey card reading. It does not matter much about the direction of the light or where you point the meter, as the fog will be all around you.

If the incident-light reading recommends that you give less exposure than a reflected-light reading, take its advice.

In the case of our bus-stop, the problem is a little easier. We have the bus-stop sign itself. It has a white tone that we can aim to reproduce as at least a moderate highlight – say about Tone 8. A close-up reading gives us an exposure that would reproduce it as a mid-tone (Tone 6), so we need two stops more exposure than this to give it its required tonal value. That should leave ample scope for the shape of the bus to be outlined against the fog, but what will happen to the lights is anybody's guess, as they will be heavily diffused.

We should not aim at reproducing the white too light. It would not look right and could raise the level of exposure so that the other tones – the red of the sign, the outline of the bus, and especially the lights – would also be raised significantly in tone and reduce what little contrast is present. The lights could also spread excessively.

14.1 A. In dull weather, normal exposure may give a flat, lifeless result.
B. Two stops underexposure with development increased by 50% or more increases contrast.
C. One stop underexposure plus extended treatment in a high contrast developer increases contrast and grain size to suit certain subjects.
Further contrast can be obtained at the printing stage if necessary.

Snow and frost

Wintry days can also bring snow, ice and frost. These can be difficult to handle, because reflected-light meter readings are meaningless. A blanket of snow over the landscape raises the general light level considerably as it puts natural reflectors on almost everything. A reflected-light

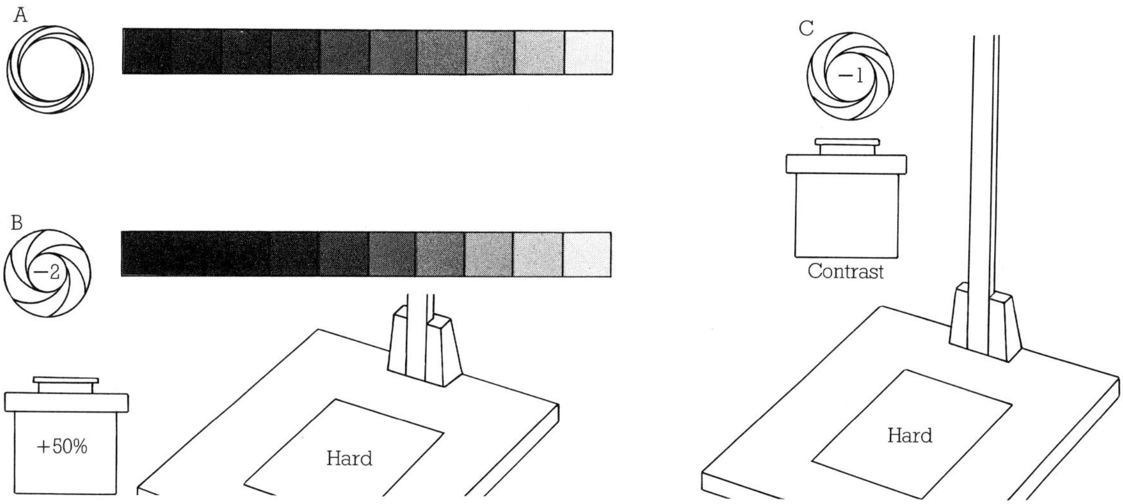

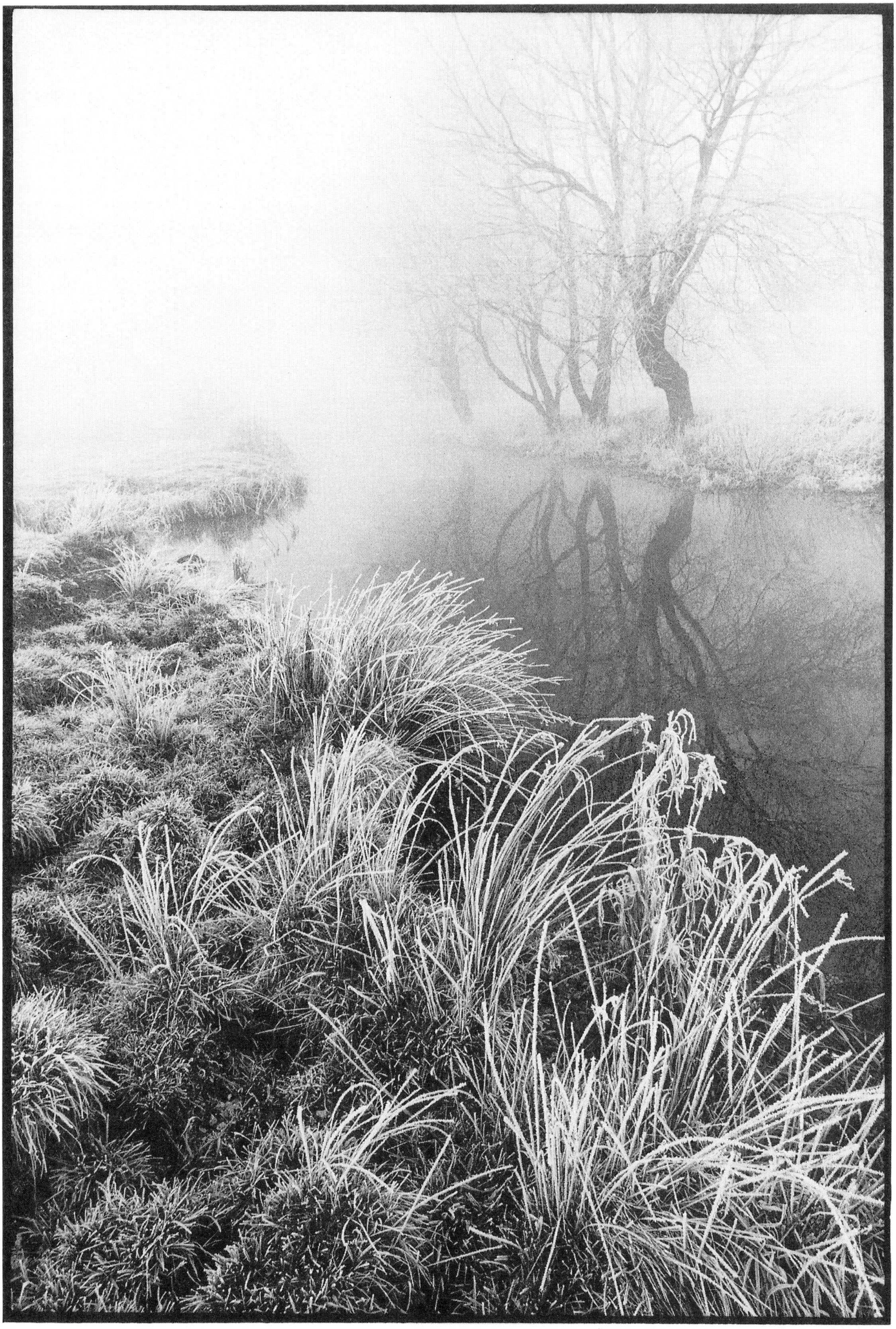

meter reading will indicate underexposure by up to two stops.

Snow pictures. The nature of the lighting is important. When you photograph snow scenes, you are not so much concerned with the snow itself as with the shadows in it. It is the shadows that provide the texture. There are always shadows in snow, even in the most diffuse light, because of its nature, but they are naturally much more pronounced in sunlight and even more so with a low sun. You have to judge the density you expect in the shadows in the final result. In low sunlight, it could be about that of the standard grey card, in more diffuse lighting one stop lighter and in fully diffused lighting another stop lighter.

If you can measure a fully shaded area of snow, base your exposure on that. Give the indicated exposure when the sun is low and direct, one stop more for sun and cloud, two stops for diffused skylight, when the shadows will be barely perceptible. These are the exposures for the snow only, of course, where the parts that are not snow-covered are relatively unimportant and you are not too concerned with retaining detail there.

Frequently, your pictures taken in snow conditions do not feature only the snow. Shots of winter sporting events are obvious examples. Then, ideally, you want detail in figures and faces as well as in the snow. That is not easy, especially with colour slides. Winter-sports shots generally show heavily suntanned sportsmen and women dressed in vivid colours. The sky is an unbelievable blue. In most cases, the effect is exaggerated by the nature of the light and the necessity, at all costs, to avoid overexposure. Snow reflects a considerable amount of light and, if you are to retain any detail in it at all, exposures must be kept as brief as possible. They generally need to be kept shorter than a meter reading from a grey card or a flesh tone would indicate. Such a reading might well give a satisfactory rendering of face, clothing, etc., but the snow would become a uniform mass of white powder. On the other hand, you cannot shorten the exposure unduly or you will lose all detail in the principal subject.

Exposure in such conditions is about as tricky as it can be, especially for a colour slide. Sometimes, such as when the sun is in front of the camera, the conditions are next to impossible. The film cannot handle the contrast, and texture in the snow has to be sacrificed. You can underexpose the figure by a stop or so and get darker complexions and more saturated colour in the clothing, but you can rarely picture the snow successfully.

With sun behind the camera, you have a better chance. You can meter a flesh tone or a grey card, or take an incident light reading and adjust the indicated exposure according to the particular effect you are after. In monochrome, you can probably underexpose by up to two stops, in colour up to one stop. You are then compromising at both ends, underexposing the figure and getting more saturated colour and slightly overexposing the snow, hoping to retain some detail. Naturally, your chances are better when some clouds are present and the harshness of the light is tempered by cloud reflection or slight cloud cover. You can then follow the same course but have a much better chance of picturing the snow more satisfactorily.

For more leisurely subjects, such as general snowscapes, when you want some detail in the foliage, buildings, etc. you can pursue more orthodox zone methods. You can decide how much detail you want in the foliage, tree trunk, stonework, etc. and place that tone accordingly. You might meter a tree trunk, for example, and decide that it could be satisfactorily rendered as slightly darker than usual, say Tone 3 or 4. That would indicate two or three stops less than the meter recommends. If this agrees with a reading from fully shaded snow, as already mentioned, you can go ahead. If not, you have to decide where to compromise, remembering that in monochrome moderate overexposure will not completely block up the highlights and you have the opportunity of printing up at a later stage. Underexposure is fatal, however. You cannot print detail that is not in the negative.

Posed portraits in the snow are not so difficult to manage as action shots, either. You can choose your spot to avoid the worst of the sun's glare and may, in fact, find it best to shoot in the shade. If that is not possible, try to increase the light on the figures to avoid overexposing the snow. Large reflectors, or fill-in flash are the obvious remedies, but careful choice of viewpoint could allow a snow-covered rise in the terrain itself to act as a natural reflector.

70 The sun struggling to get through adds a useful feature to a misty scene but it does mean that the sky area of the print needs heavy printing up to obtain the required result.

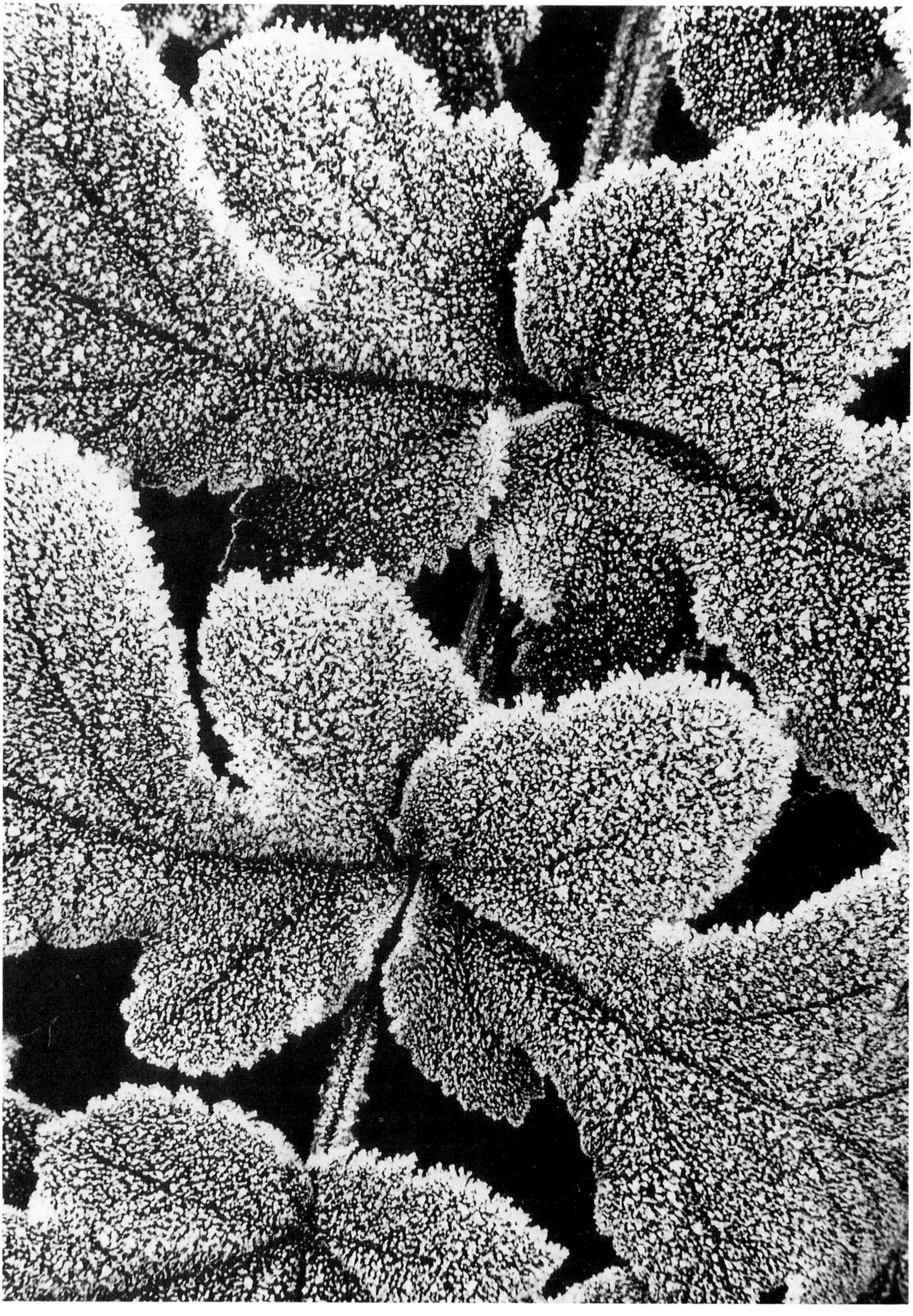

71 The frost is the most important part of the subject and your aim in metering must be to place that tone correctly.

Frost pictures. Frost is even more difficult. It generally provides a delicate tracery. Over-exposure is fatal in this case. All the tiny shadows are lost and the frost looks like flour or baby powder. Depending on the nature of the subject, a straight reading is likely to recommend under-exposure, which loses the contrast and the sparkling effect. As a general compromise, an incident-light reading is probably best; but it is better to search around for a more direct method.

Shots of subjects in frost generally have to be taken in sunlit conditions. The aim is to make the picture almost entirely out of the reflections from the tiny crystals. The surface on which the frost lies may be vegetation, iron railings, wooden fencing or a variety of other bases, but you rarely want much detail in these. If, therefore, there is a sufficiently large, frost-free area of the base, you can meter that and place it on the desired tone, perhaps Tone 2 or 3, ie, three or four stops less exposure than the meter indicates. Alternatively, if there is a large area of solid frost you can meter, you could aim at placing it at about Tone 9, ie, three stops more than the straight reading. As always, keep in mind the tone that you want to reproduce in the final result for the most important feature of the subject.

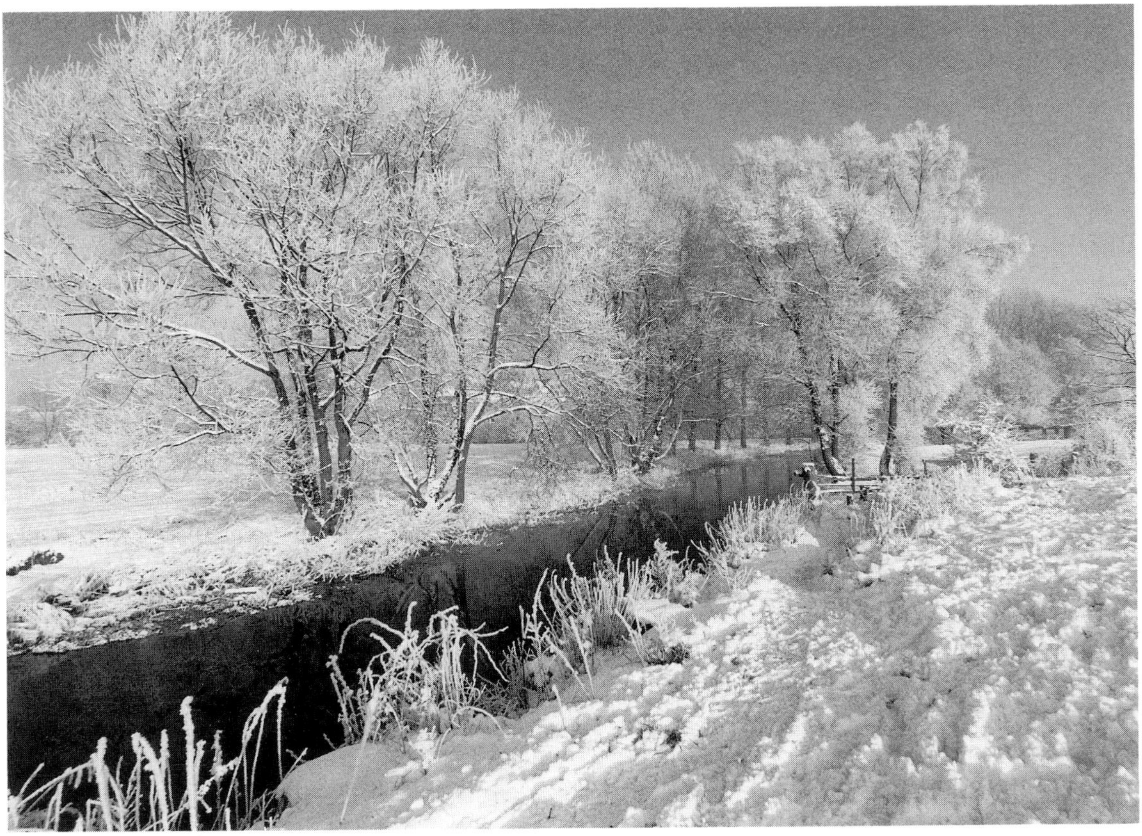

72 Snow is a classic example of a subject that fools the meter. Keep the reading shorter than that indicated but not so short as to lose all detail in the main subject.

Atmospheric conditions

If you do all your shooting in your home country, you get used to the effect of daylight in general on your photographs. Many people scorn the aid of exposure meters and claim to be able to get their exposures 'spot-on' in any conditions.

Depending on your interpretation of 'spot-on', that is not as impossible a claim as it might seem. Long experience can lead to the type of familiarity that breeds confidence. After all, many photographers in years past used such methods with complete success. Admittedly, they worked in monochrome only and they developed their plates or films by inspection, so that they could control matters to some extent at the post-exposure stage. They tended also to deal with one exposure at a time and were expert printers.

Even today, however, there are plenty of photographers who prefer to rely largely on their own experience, and come unstuck when they venture into foreign parts. The light in certain parts of the world has a strangely luminescent quality, as many an artist has remarked. There is an obvious difference between the light in a smoke-filled industrial valley and that on the surrounding mountain tops. There is a more subtle difference in other areas, as on many Mediterranean shores. Sometimes, it is due to the lighter colours generally favoured for the building materials or exterior decoration, sometimes to generally cleaner air. Whatever it is, the effect is often noticeable, but it does not fool an exposure meter.

There is a surprisingly widely-held opinion that exposure meters need re-calibrating to Mediterranean sunshine, and that all exposures need adjusting compared with exposure for similar scenes in Britain. That is not, of course, true. It is true, on the other hand, that light-coloured buildings, sea and sand reflect more light than the average landscape. That is the reason for the frequent underexposure problems encountered by visitors to Mediterranean holiday resorts. A switch to incident light reading would soon cure the problem, but TTL meters are not designed for that.

Using the zone or tone system is just as effective. If you carefully meter a principal tone, or another recognisable tone, and place that correctly, you should overcome all problems. You could meter a flesh tone, for example, and place it on Tone 5, 6 or 7, as you wish. Or you might prefer an open shade area as your key measurement (Tone 5 or 6).

Remember always that placing the tone correctly means giving more or less exposure than the direct reading indicates, according to the number of steps any desired tone is away from Tone 6. If you want your flesh tone on Tone 5 (dark skin), you give one stop less exposure than a direct reading indicates.

15 SHOOTING ON THE RUN

Many photographers may raise the quite legitimate objection to much of the discussion so far, that it assumes a leisurely approach to photography. It is true that the majority of photographers who concentrate on problems of exposure tend to produce more or less static types of picture, such as landscapes, architecture, posed portraits and figure studies – the type of subject one can study at leisure and plan in detail. Conversely, those who appear to treat exposure in a more cavalier fashion are apt to be photographers who shoot a lot of pictures in a relatively short time, in varying light conditions.

The two types are not as far apart as it may at first seem. The first relies on careful meter readings, allied to his system of working. The second relies largely on experience allied to the occasional use of a meter. But his experience is built on the results he achieves. He has learned how to deal with various lighting conditions to produce the type of result he wants. He may sometimes go wrong and, when he does, his is often the sort of spectacular failure that his more leisurely friend might never experience, but that is the nature of human fallibility.

There is now a third type, of course. That is the photographer who relies totally on the exposure meter built into his camera, either allowing it to take over completely on fully automatic working, or constantly changing his camera settings under the command of the meter readout. More often than not, that is also a perfectly satisfactory method but, again, when it goes wrong, failure is usually complete. It works only for average or close-to-average subjects.

The case for consistency

Nevertheless, calculated meter readings from specific areas, grey cards, zone systems and so on are not favoured by many photographers. The difference between the superb and the merely very good is, perhaps, not important to them. Nor is it practicable on many occasions to delve into a well-stocked gadget bag for incident-light attachments, grey cards, lists of zones, etc.

We have to differentiate between run-of-the-mill photography, including a great many snapshots not intended for posterity, and more serious attempts to produce something genuinely creative. In monochrome, purist opinions notwithstanding, exposure latitude is wide and it is possible to produce identical prints of many subjects from negatives that have had up to two stops difference in exposure. Even in colour, there is sufficient latitude to allow a certain casualness of approach to the average subject.

Colour slides. Colour slide work is more critical but a stop either side of the theoretically correct exposure does not ruin a picture that is well within the film's capability. In most cases, it simply leads to different levels of colour saturation and overall density. That can be a matter of individual preference, artistic licence or the power of the projector lamp.

There is a compelling argument in favour of a consistent approach to exposure in colour slide work. If you approach the matter casually and are prepared to accept varying densities of image, you must also be prepared to accept that you cannot present pleasing slide shows. It is extremely off-putting to see slides of similar subjects

15.1 Bright skies can affect a meter reading. If the sky area is more than about one quarter of the metered area, add one stop to the exposure indicated. Larger areas may need even more compensation.

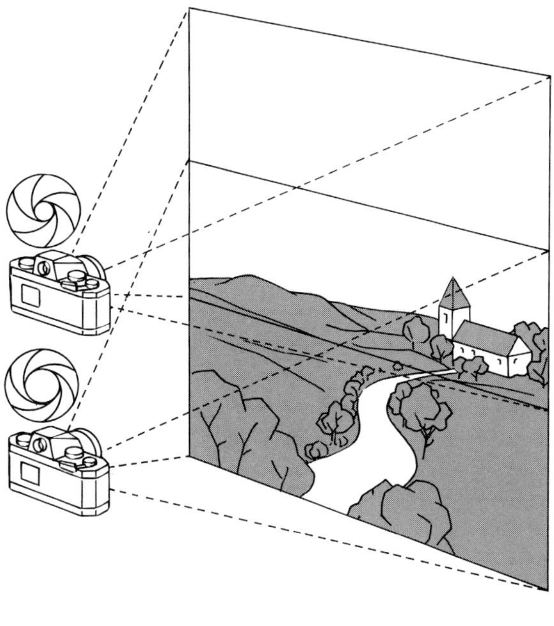

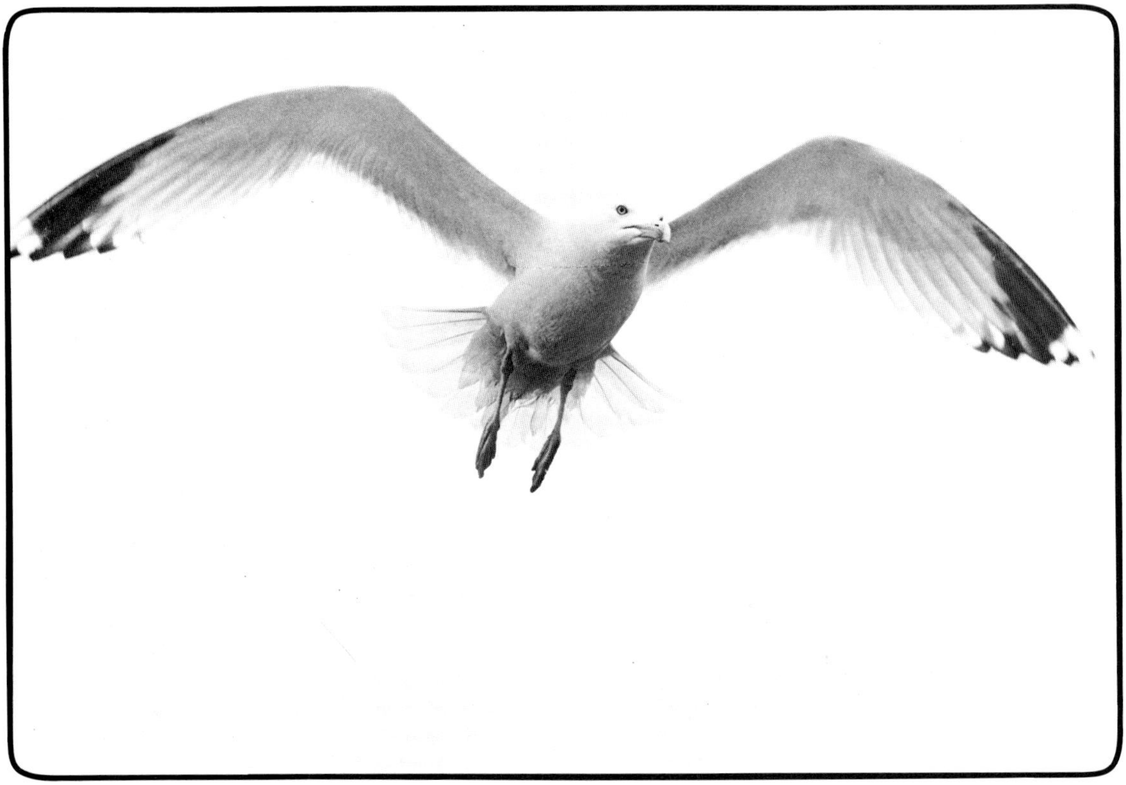

73 An obvious subject failure. A straight meter reading inevitably leads to underexposure. In these circumstances, a grey-card reading or the equivalent is a reasonable compromise.

but of varying densities succeeding one another on the screen.

A great deal of everyday photography consists of unthought-out shots of children, friends, eye-catching views, public buildings and monuments, events, street scenes, etc. shot on the move with family or acquaintances where the main aim is not pictorial. There just is not time to ponder the tonal value of this or that feature, to take careful readings and then calculate the exposure required for a particular effect. Is it really worthwhile in such cases, anyway?

Nevertheless, exposure is important. You cannot make gross errors without sacrificing something – generally definition owing to increased graininess in monochrome, together with a loss of detail in shadows or highlights. In colour, the same effects occur in exaggerated form, possibly together with loss or distortion of colour. So you need to adopt some method or system, however subconsciously, that protects you from such mishaps.

Subject failure

Most cameras in popular use have exposure meters, frequently the TTL type. These are, as we have already implied, almost perfectly suited to shooting on the run. Most of your pictures will integrate to grey, so you can happily follow the indications of the glowing LEDs, swinging needles, etc. The trick is to recognise the occasions when the mindless device misleads you, known as *subject failure*. Provided you can do that, you can keep exposure calculations within bounds and concentrate on the more important task of actually getting the picture. After all, a poorly exposed shot that captures the decisive moment is preferable to a technically superb shot that misses it.

The most common, and most often quoted, reason for subject failure is the inclusion of a large, light-coloured area in the picture – usually sky, but sometimes a background. In a view with a beautifully cloud-filled sky, the white clouds have a powerful effect on the meter. The ground area will inevitably be underexposed if you follow the meter reading blindly. The level of underexposure can be as much as two stops, giving you a cloud-filled sky with a very dark foreground. On a colour slide, your sky will look great, but the foreground is likely to look as if it were photographed in the late evening.

Maybe you are quite happy with that: it can sometimes be very effective. White clouds against a blue sky can look dramatic in colour with a stop or so underexposure. Generally, however, a mainly white or light grey sky can influence your meter unduly and you should exclude most of it while metering by pointing the camera slightly downward. Then disregard the meter indication when actually taking the shot.

A deep blue sky has considerably less effect. It is not far removed from the average mid-tone and should not affect your meter reading unduly. In a colour slide, if you wish to preserve that deep blue, it is in any case better to err slightly on the side of underexposure.

Auto-exposure cameras try to take care of some of these considerations. The first attempt was *centre-weighted* metering, in which the metering system takes more account of the central areas of the screen image than of the edges. That is rather more cosmetic than genuinely useful, but it was followed by the incorporation of *exposure compensation* devices. These generally override the film speed setting on the camera to allow the meter to recommend more or less exposure than it would for a normal scene. The user has to decide when to operate the exposure compensation control. Now, of course, Nikon have their system of the 'thinking' exposure meter, which decides whether or not the subject is 'average' and automatically imposes exposure compensation if it is not.

Those with the normal type of meter have to keep a watchful eye on the sky tone and the amount of it that is included in the viewfinder image. If it is more than about one-quarter of the image area, one stop should be added to the indicated exposure. Greater areas can call for up to two stops extra exposure. In black and white, you can afford to err on the generous side. In colour, particularly with colour slide material, it would be better to take the time needed for a substitute reading, excluding most of the sky area.

The same type of problem arises with backgrounds. Indeed, the sky might well be a background for a portrait, architectural feature, inn signboard, etc. If you are out on a trip when such a feature is likely to occur – and that includes almost any walk around an unfamiliar area – a useful trick if you feel that you cannot spend too much time on the shot is to keep your camera set for a normal shot in the prevailing conditions.

15.2 The background can influence a meter reading. In such cases, exposure compensation should be used to provide the exposure level indicated by a reading from a grey card or an incident light reading.

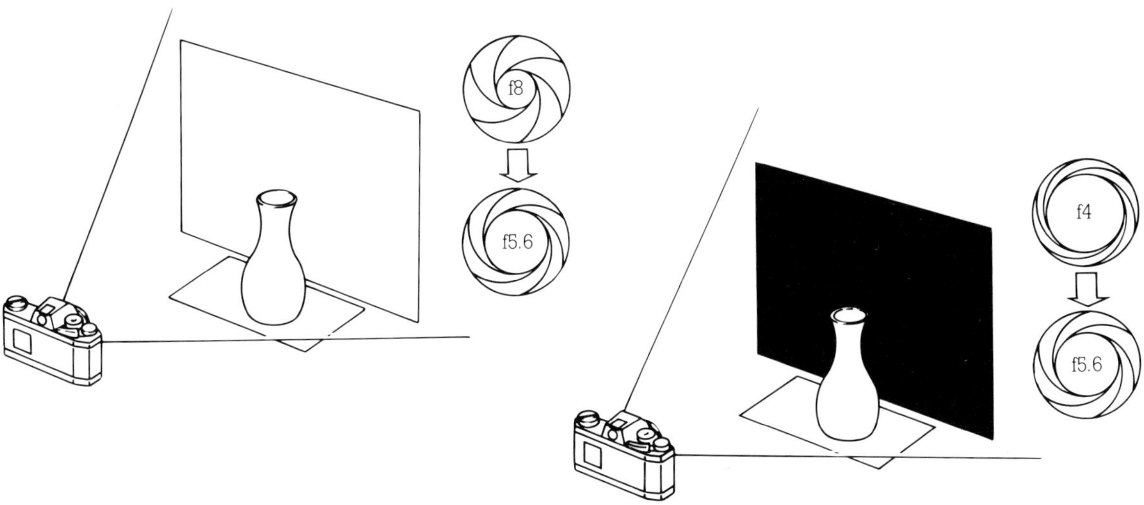

Average and non-average subjects

This is probably as good a place as any to point out that the 'average' and 'non-average' tags that crop up when we discuss exposure are a modern phenomenon. They are a product of the exposure meter age. The subjects are average or non-average only as far as exposure meter readings are concerned. If, for example, you pose a head-and-shoulders shot against a relatively large, light-toned background, or against the same sized dark-tone background, the exposure required is the same. Why would it not be? The subject has not changed. If you worked solely by the little slip of paper supplied with the film, you would give the same exposure in each case and not even think about the background. If, however, you were a more sophisticated photographer with an exposure meter (TTL or otherwise), or with an auto-exposure camera, you would get a different meter reading for each shot. And, if you were the unthinking type, you would use different exposures for each shot.

When shooting on the run, therefore, it is often wise to take a meter reading before you start shooting – preferably an incident light reading or a reading from a substitute mid-tone. That is the only meter reading you need unless the light changes. You can shoot any subject you come across with guaranteed success – in the sun, in the shade, backlit or whatever, provided the general light level does not change.

Background and foreground tone. To return to exposure meter usage, excessively light backgrounds or foregrounds that are large in relation to the subject always produce subject failure and cause the exposure meter to give a wrong reading. Whenever there are large areas of light-toned flowers, whitewashed wall, snow, sand, sea, etc. in the picture area, add at least one stop to the meter-indicated exposure. Preferably, in all such cases, take a substitute reading from a more balanced distribution of tones, from a grey card or from the back of your hand and use that exposure, rather than that indicated by a reading from the subject area.

Dark backgrounds and foregrounds lead your meter in the opposite direction. When the greater part of your picture is composed of very dark tones, an exposure meter always indicates over-exposure, as it tries to make the subject conform to its preconceived idea of an average subject. It believes the scene integrates to grey, no matter what its actual tonal average may be. So watch out for dark fencing, foliage, walls, etc. If your subject is in light clothing in such surroundings, over-exposure can cause serious loss of detail and, in colour, possibly even a total loss of any pastel hues in the clothing. In such a case, decrease the indicated exposure by at least one stop. If detail in the dark areas is not important, it is as well to err on the side of apparent underexposure in such cases.

Large areas of dark or light tone in the picture area are obvious causes of subject failure; most of us soon learn to recognise their effect. There are other, less obvious, culprits. One stems from virtually the same conditions, but is often overlooked because the offending areas are not included in the picture.

Hand-held meters commonly have a relatively wide angle of view (about 40°), and frequently read areas that are not to be included in the picture. The supposed advantage of the TTL meter, that it reads only the tones actually appearing in the picture area, is not always borne out in practice. Strong light from outside the picture area can affect the meter reading. However flare-free your lens may be, some of the light reaching its front surface (not all of which by any means is image-forming) does get through to the meter. Centre-weighting helps to reduce its influence, but it is still there.

Whichever type of meter you use, therefore, it is wise to take any available precaution (lens hood, shading with the hand, tilting the meter away from the light) to avoid the influence of such extraneous light.

Distance and atmosphere

Distance is another awkward factor. Distant scenes do not have large areas of shadow, except, perhaps, in the case of low sun on a mountain range. Such shadows as may be present are relieved by diffuse light scattered by the atmosphere. Consequently, most distant scenes integrate to a tone rather lighter than a mid-tone, again fooling an exposure meter into indicating under-exposure.

When you take an ordinary scene, including near, middle and far distance, a reflected-light meter reading tends to give an adequate exposure that shows a natural recession of tones, darker in the foreground, lighter in the background as distance increases. The distant scene, regarded as a picture in itself, is, in effect, overexposed and may show a certain loss of detail. In context, it looks perfectly natural, but if you try to enlarge up only the background detail, you tend to get a very unsatisfactory picture. You do not expect to see much detail in the far distance; but when the shot looks as if it was taken from

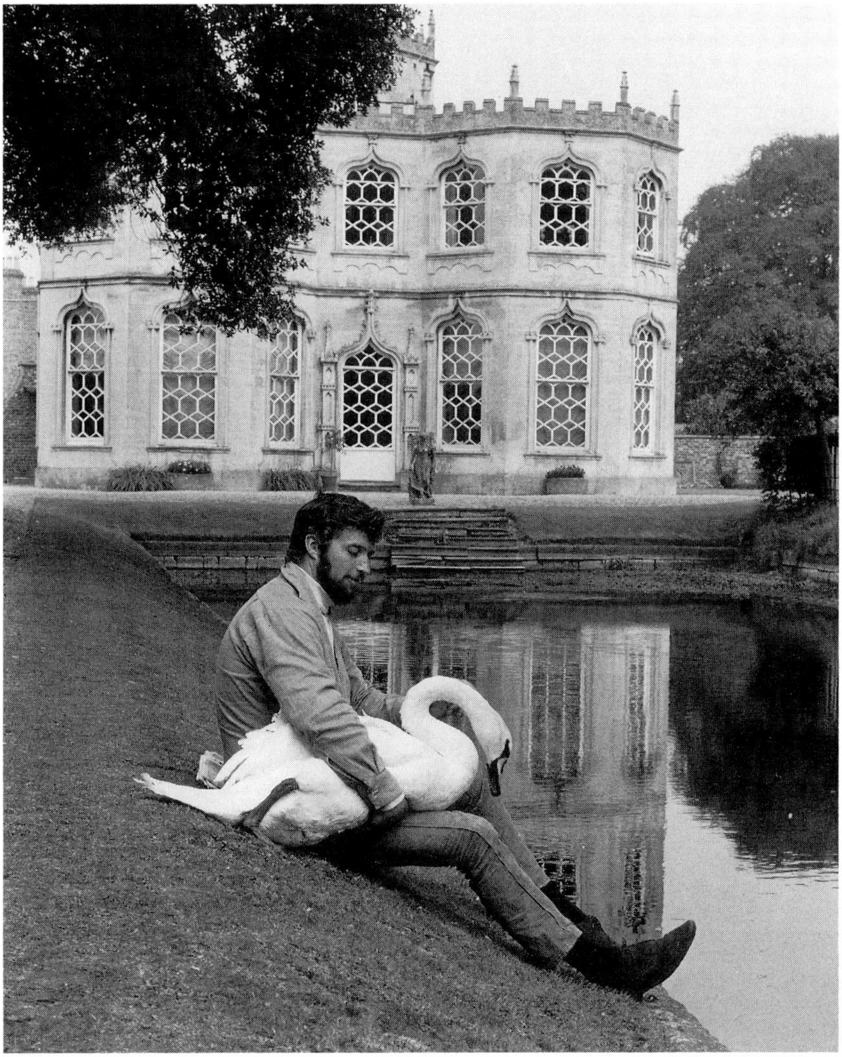

74 Such shots have to be grabbed. A camera set to a normal exposure for the conditions, or an autoexposure camera, would cope adequately with this shot and many like it.

much closer, the lack of detail can be disturbing.

Enlarging up the distant part is more or less the same as taking a long-range shot of that area with a telephoto lens. The difference is that the excessively enlarged portion will probably show extra loss of detail from increased grain size. A telephoto shot should show better image quality from that point of view, but it could also suffer even more from the effects of overexposure. The meter does not understand that it is metering a lower-contrast distant scene and will generally recommend rather more overexposure of the light-toned distant scene than it normally gets. In very few cases is it a reliable procedure to allow a long telephoto lens to control an exposure meter.

Colour sensitivity of film and meter

A less obvious source of subject failure is the colour of the prevailing light. Generally speaking, exposure meters (except selenium types) are excessively sensitive to red, while films are a little over-sensitive to blue. This is a broad generalisation and must not be taken too literally, but it can have a significant effect on your pictures. Flaming red sunsets, for example, are notoriously difficult subjects to expose satisfactorily, mainly because we would probably like to exaggerate them, and perhaps do exaggerate them in our mind's eye, but partly because of the high red content.

There can be no such thing as an average sunset, so it is difficult to talk of its tonal value. Does it integrate to a mid-tone? Quite often, it probably does, but the meter may still recommend underexposure because the relatively lower sensitivity of the film to red and yellow results in its receiving less exposure than the meter anticipates. We are thinking largely of colour film here, where moderate underexposure may not be a bad thing. It intensifies colour, reduces detail in the landscape, and concentrates interest in the sky. It is far preferable to overexposure, which puts unwanted detail into the foreground and desaturates the colours in the sky.

Thus, 'correct' exposure for sunset scenes is likely to be near that indicated by a direct meter reading of the subject area. Nevertheless, this is obviously a case for bracketed exposures. There is no reliable method of predicting the effect to be obtained from any method of meter usage that includes a reading from the sky area. The zone method can supply an alternative, however. Knowing that you want to avoid overexposure of the sky area at all costs, a reading can be taken from a prominent feature in the foreground that you hope to reproduce in virtual silhouette. If that tone is then placed at Tone 1 or 2, your requirements should be met. In other words, you give four of five more stops than the meter reading recommends. If that should coincide with, or be less than, a direct meter reading from the sky area, you should be assured of success.

Meter errors. There is a tendency in some forms of artificial lighting and with some meters for a normal reading to lead to underexposure, again possibly because the film is not as sensitive to the red content of light as is the meter. We put this at no more than 'possibly' because these conditions generally arise at low light levels and, as already noted, few meters give reliable exposure indications at the lower end of the scale.

The opposite condition, the film's over-sensitivity to blue, is rather less marked, but there is still a tendency for exposure meters to under-read the light level in bright blue sky conditions, particularly in shaded areas where the direct effect of the sun is excluded. In colour, the effect is not only a degree of overexposure, but the noticeably blue cast caused by the lighting conditions.

These fallibilities of the exposure meter must be borne in mind by those whose practice it is to rely heavily on the indication in their viewfinders to provide correctly exposed pictures. Those who make a real effort to correct exposure to the nearest half stop for every shot are heavily outnumbered by those who either rely on experience, have an unshakable faith in exposure meters, use a mixture of the two, or shoot first and ask questions afterwards. It will always be so. Very few people are prepared to make hard work out of their hobby. Nevertheless, a basic understanding of the ways in which exposure meters can be led astray is a necessity for any enthusiast who wants to be sure he will never have to say, "It didn't come out".

15.3 Readings from the whole screen area (A) can lead to significant underexposure if a large part of the image is light in tone. Carefully designed centre-weighted readings (B) can reduce the risk.

75 Sunsets are not average subjects, but a direct meter reading of the whole subject area generally provides a satisfactory sunset effect. To record the sun's disc sharply, the exposure level must be low.

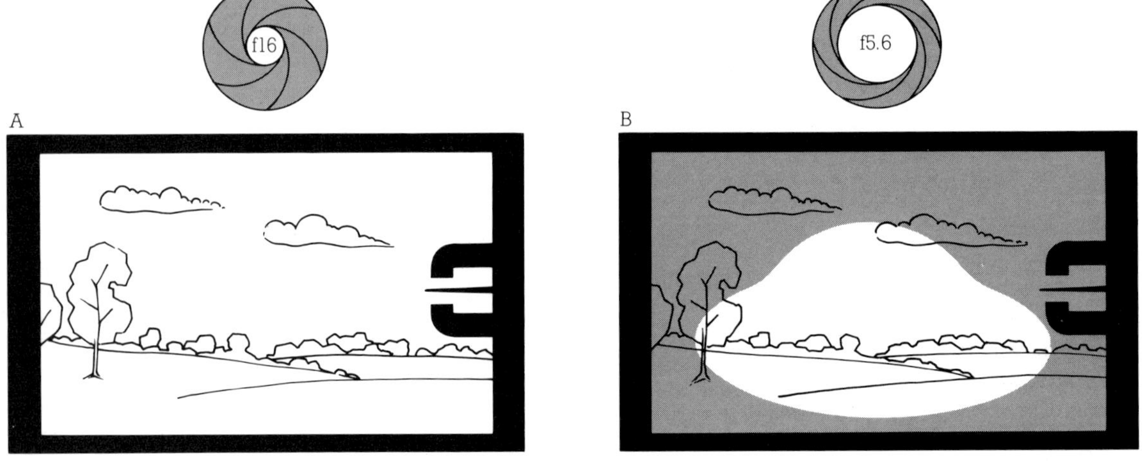

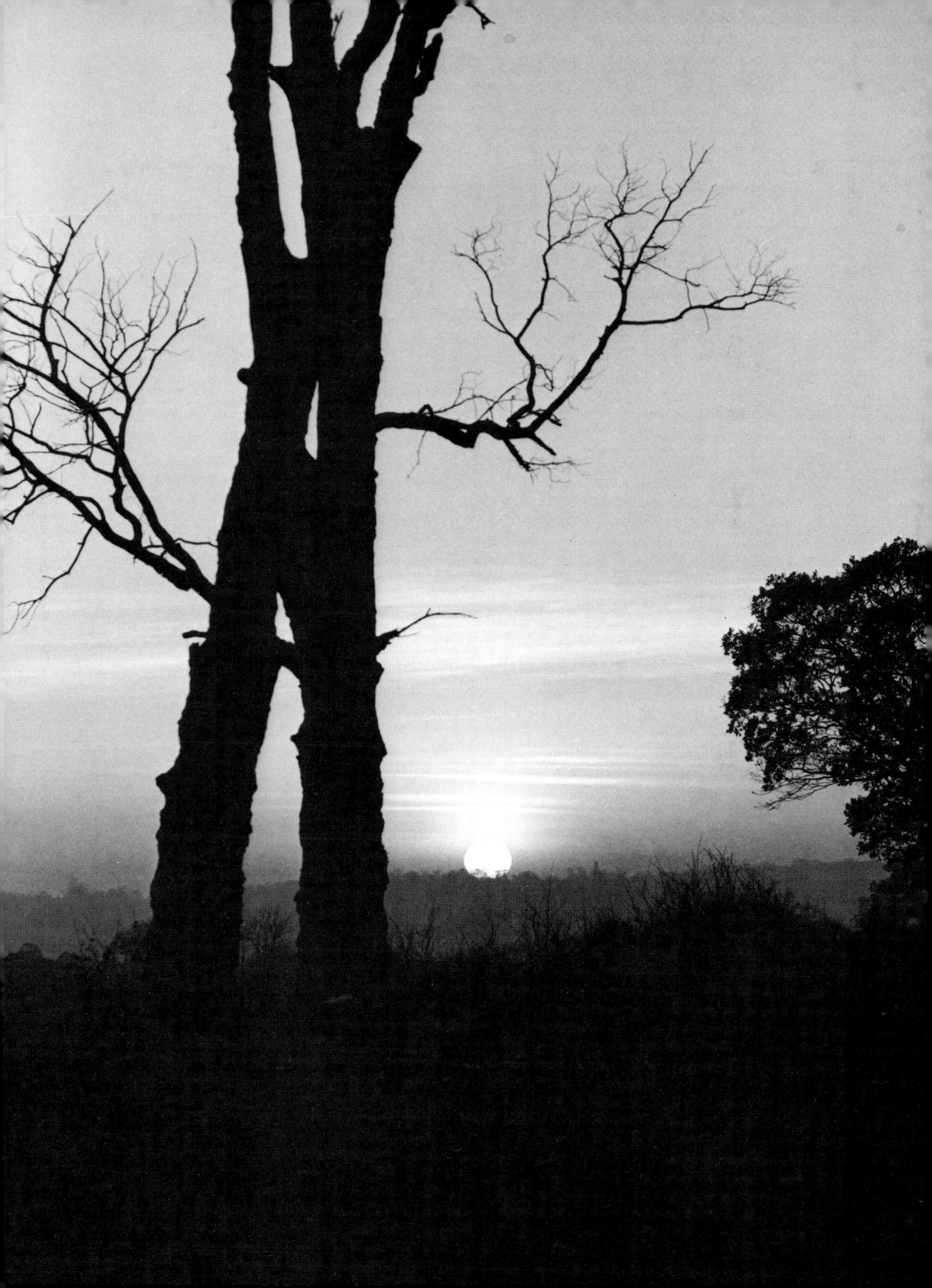

16 SPECIFICALLY COLOUR

The greater part of this book relates to monochrome work. This is inevitable because, despite the advances in user processing of colour materials, monochrome film still offers the greater opportunities in control of tonal values throughout the exposing, processing and printing stages. It deals only with tones, not hues, and there is no need to worry about the effect a particular variation of procedure may have on colour rendering. Additionally, a far greater proportion of colour film, particularly colour slide film, is commercially processed and depends on a standardised exposure method.

Nevertheless, or perhaps because of these limitations, colour film does have exposure problems that are specifically its own. All colour films have three light-sensitive layers, so light has to pass through the top layer to reach the second and through two layers to reach the third. As the layers are differentially colour-sensitised but as all are sensitive to blue, there has to be a filter layer, too, and, for technical reasons, there are many other layers. Thus, there is a delicate problem of balance, to ensure that each layer has the same effective speed or sensitivity. As almost every colour in nature is a mixture of at least two of those used by colour film, it is evident that inaccuracies in exposure can affect the layers differentially and so distort colour as well as affecting the overall density.

Colour-slide films pose an even greater problem because they undergo two development processes. The first produces a normal monochrome silver negative image, and the second puts colour into the parts that were not originally exposed, thus forming a positive image on the same film. Colour slides can handle a very wide range of tones because they are transilluminated for viewing, but they cannot maintain correct colour over the whole range.

Rules for exposure

The basic rules for exposing colour film are no different from those for monochrome. Effectively, your exposure must still be based on that required to render a mid-tone correctly. Exposure is based on tone, not colour. A subject can integrate to a mid-tone without integrating to grey. In such cases, exposure indicated by a straight reflected-light reading is correct even though the subject may be predominantly of one hue.

The limitations on colour exposure are almost entirely due to the lack of processing and printing controls. We are talking here of the processes and materials within the reach, and probably the inclination, of the average enthusiast. You *can* control colour processes, particularly in colour printing, by means such as altering the developer formulation, development time or temperature, by shading, burning in or pre-flashing while printing, and other methods. But all these techniques are considerably more complicated than with monochrome materials. Moreover, colour material characteristics are constantly changing as manufacturers introduce different chemistry to increase sensitivity, improve definition and colour fidelity, and to speed up processing. Each change can have its effect on processing and thus on processing variations. Most colour film users have to rely on the standard recommended process for their films, and have very little opportunity to vary exposures to handle contrast. Naturally, they can still use all the exposure variation techniques that do not call for adjustments in film developing or printing. But most of these 'variations' are not, of course, variations at all. They are simply corrections applied to uninformed recommendations made by rigidly-programmed exposure meters.

Most monochrome and colour print films now have so much exposure latitude that they can, perfectionism apart, afford to ignore the failings of exposure meters for the general run of subjects. Within two stops either side of 'correct' exposure, they may occasionally show more graininess, but they rarely show any loss in tonal range or colour. Colour slide film is far less tolerant. Even a one-stop variation can have a significant effect on the rendering of some colours. Overexposure, in particular, can totally destroy some of the paler colours. Underexposure can seriously distort

76 Opposite, top. Even colour transparency film has relatively wide exposure latitude in low contrast situations. A reflected reading is generally adequate but overexposure can be tolerated if the colour is subdued.

77 Opposite, bottom. Zoos can pose tricky exposure problems because you often have to take your reading from a distance. With an integrated reading, assess the overall tone value and adjust the reading accordingly.

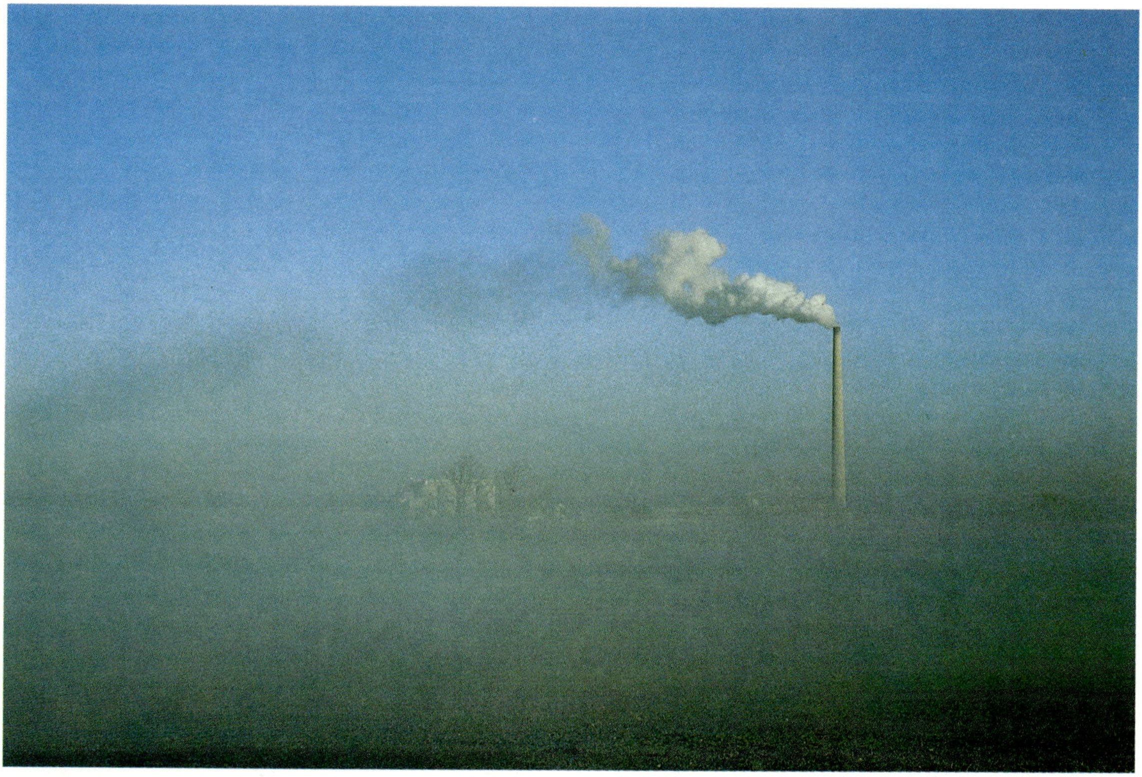

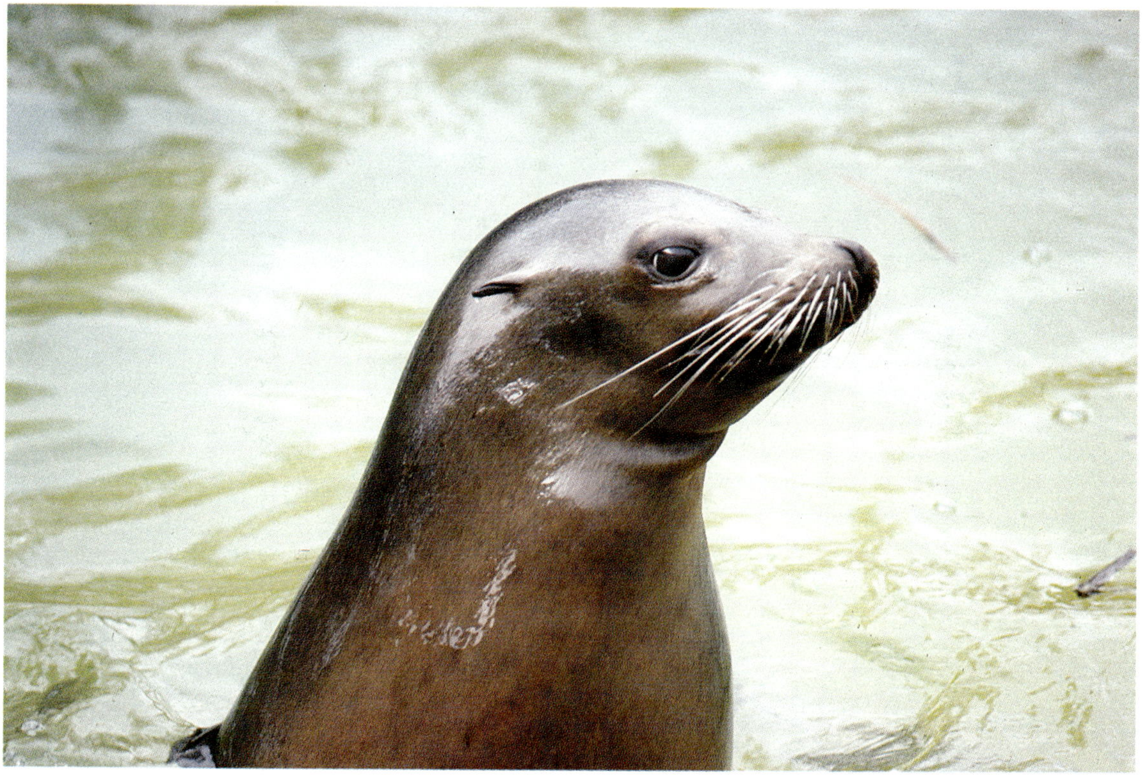

darker colours and cause unpleasantly purplish or greenish shadows. Where the subject has a long tonal range, therefore, even one stop departure from the ideal compromise can cause loss or distortion of colour.

Nevertheless, both variations can be used in a way that is peculiar to colour images. With the right type of subject (fairly low contrast) overexposure can turn reasonably light colours to pastel shades particularly appropriate to glamour photography, pictures of children and babies, lazy summer days, and so on. Underexposure can have the opposite effect, adding depth to colours and contrast, or apparent contrast, to dull-weather shooting.

Both techniques have to be used with great care. The treatment must suit the subject and it must be kept within bounds. A relatively low contrast subject is essential in the second case, while overexposure of a high contrast subject destroys all highlight colour.

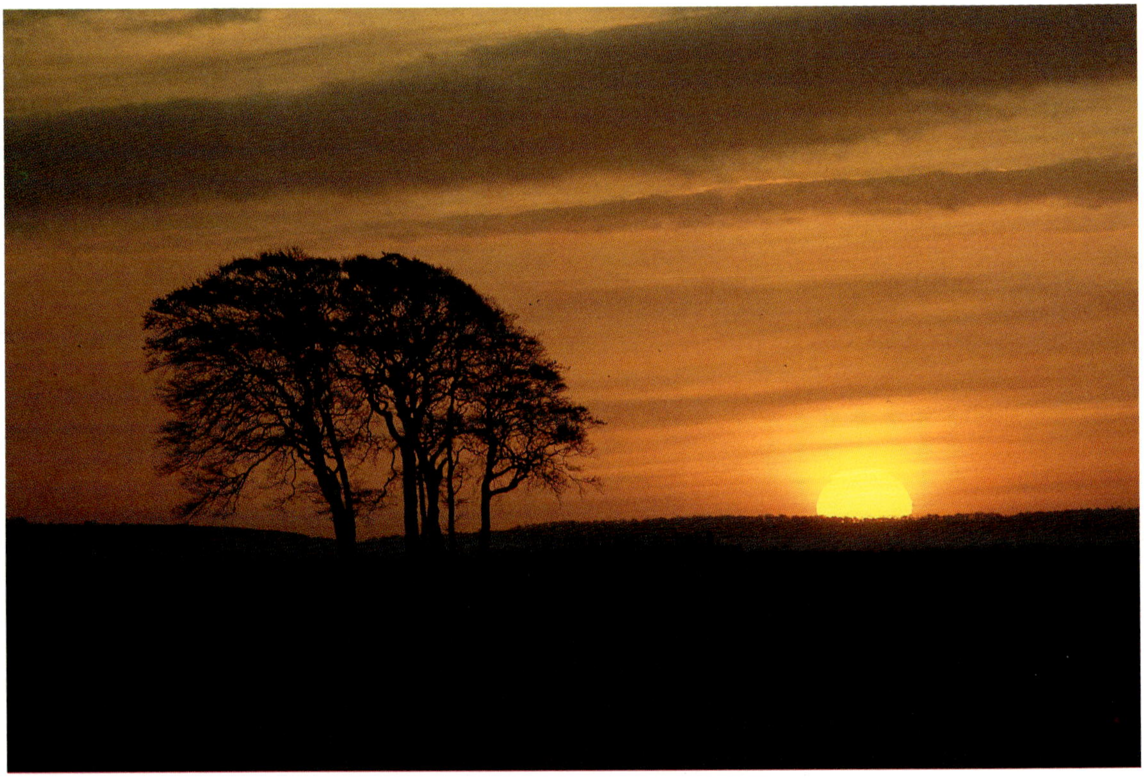

78 The classic silhouette. You base the exposure on maximum black for the trees. By progressively shortening the exposure you can then bring the sky tone to the required value, generally making it rather darker than it appears to the eye.

Colour temperature and mired values

Colour rendering is, of course, highly dependent on the colour of the light illuminating the subject. Most colour films are designed for use in sun and cloud conditions providing light of a colour temperature of about 5500 kelvins (K). Colour temperature is a method of defining the colour quality of light in terms of the colour temperature of a body that would give light of that quality when heated to a certain point on the Kelvin or Absolute scale. It is usually preferable, however, to think of colour quality in terms of *mireds*. This word is taken from the initial letters of the term *micro reciprocal degree*, which simply means one million divided by the kelvin figure.

By using mireds, we get a clearer idea of the difference between colour temperatures in the form of actual colour. A mired variation or *mired shift* of 50, for example, represents more or less the same extent of colour change anywhere along the scale, whereas a variation in colour temperature at the top (blue) end of the scale is much less significant than a numerically equal variation at the bottom (red) end. Daylight, for example, can vary from less than 5000K for a cloudy sky to 20,000K or more for a deep blue sky. The commonly encountered range, however, is from about 5000K to 10,000K, or 200-100 mireds. Most colour films can quite comfortably handle a 50-mired shift. With the daylight colour temperature at 10,000K, however, a noticeable blue cast would be produced.

Lower down the scale, a photoflood lamp gives a much yellower light with a colour temperature of about 3400K or 294 mireds. This is a long way from the 180 mireds or so for which a daylight colour film is balanced. As a result, a daylight-balanced colour film used in photoflood lighting will show a pronounced yellow-orange cast. Further down still, we have domestic lighting at about 2600 to 2800K or 384 to 357 mireds, sufficiently far removed from the balance of 3400K films to make colour rendering less than perfect. In fact, films for 3400K photoflood lighting have now largely disappeared. There are a few artificial light films, but they are generally for studio type lamps at 3200K or 312 mireds. These can give reasonable results with high-wattage domestic lamps and photofloods but are naturally best used in the light for which they are designed.

Flash is suitable lighting for all popular colour films in that all electronic flash units are designed to produce light of about 6000K and such flashbulbs as are still available are coated blue to provide light of a similar quality. Flash can therefore be used in conjunction with daylight outdoors or indoors. It cannot be used in conjunction with tungsten lighting, unless it is sufficiently powerful to swamp the effect of the tungsten lamps totally. Nor can tungsten light be used with daylight (window light).

The window light, on daylight film, gives a normal image, while the tungsten light overlays the parts it reaches with a very distinct orange-yellow cast.

The contrast limitation

The greatest limitation with colour film, particularly colour slide film, is contrast. Each individual emulsion has considerable exposure latitude. It is not unlike a monochrome emulsion in that sense. But each layer has a different function and it has to work together with one or more of the others. A red in the subject, for example, may contain a small amount of blue. It is vital that each layer receive just the right exposure so that each can produce the correct amount of colour. Over- or underexposure is bound to act differentially to some extent on the different layers so the latitude of the two layers is less than that of one. Thus, when the subject has a wide range of tonal values, with very pale yellow, perhaps, and deep blues, browns or blacks, the ideal exposure at one end may be only a fraction of that at the other. The compromise that we have to make by giving all parts of the film the same exposure time means that the colour at one or other end of the scale runs out of tolerance. Not only is it over- or underexposed but the separate layers receive different levels of over- or underexposure. That is why colour slides of brightly lit sunlit scenes with light tones and deep shadows tend to lose detail and colour at the highlight end.

There is no remedy for such conditions, short of putting more light into the shadow area to reduce the overall contrast of the scene. If the subject can be moved out of the direct sunlight, some improvement can be expected, but further difficulties may then be encountered. If the sky is very blue, it gives light of a very high colour temperature, well above that for which the film is designed. When you exclude the effect of the direct sunlight, you are likely to get a distinctly blue image, necessitating the use of a pale amber or 'skylight' filter. The ideal light for colour slides is that for which the film is designed – sunlight with a fair amount of white cloud to act as natural reflectors and to cover a large proportion of the blue sky. Even then, contrast can sometimes be a little high, and a light covering of cloud over the sun might be preferable with subjects of inherent high contrast. Lowering the contrast improves exposure latitude and makes underexposure, in particular, more acceptable.

In dull weather conditions, it is even preferable to give a little less exposure than the meter indicates because this increases colour saturation and allows colour contrast to compensate for lack of lighting contrast. The lack of tonal contrast in

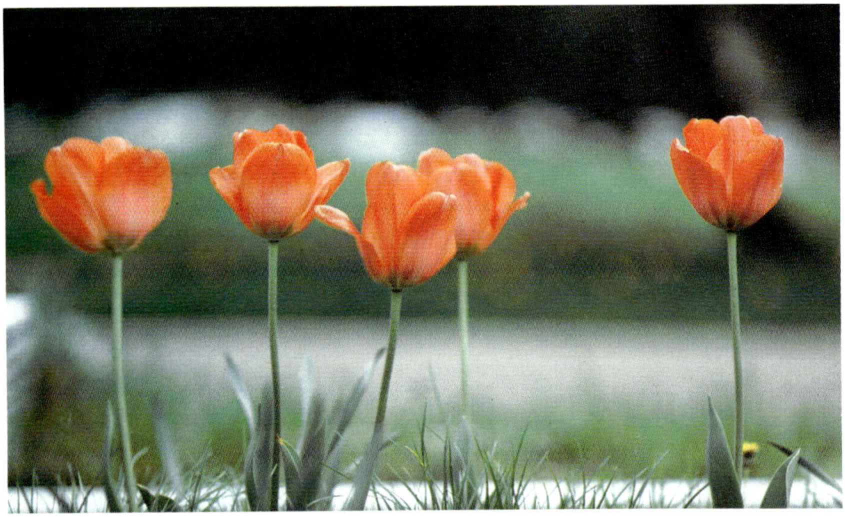

79 A chance for the aperture-priority camera to show its worth. A wide aperture must be set to achieve the required shallow depth of field: shutter speed is unimportant. As the subject should integrate to a mid-tone, automatic exposure or a standard reading should be adequate.

colour images (the type that is dealt with by filters in monochrome photography) can often be overcome by the careful use of colour contrast.

Colour in the dark

Night-time shooting with colour slide film raises problems that are not encountered in monochrome. Contrast is high because night shooting always requires some highlights; frequently they are highlights in which you want colour and detail. In monochrome, you can generally overexpose such highlights to retain detail in the shadows and yet still be able to print through them. Or you might be able to adjust the film processing. On colour slide film, overexposure is likely to send them stark white and lose all detail long before you have sufficient exposure to put detail into the shadows. Processing techniques to reduce contrast are not generally available.

Colour slide and colour negative

We have concentrated largely on colour-slide materials in this chapter because their exposure is much more critical than that for colour print films. Colour print, or colour negative, films are of similar construction to colour slide films, but their processing is different and considerably simpler. There is only one development stage, producing colour along with the silver negative image, which is then bleached and removed. The image is negative in both tone and colour, and is printed in a manner similar to a monochrome print, but the print is processed in virtually the same way as the film.

The printing process uses a three-layer print material, and wide variations of colour filtration can be inserted into the exposing light beam to adjust the colour balance. The duration of the exposure can be varied to provide the correct density. Thus, there is a great deal of exposure control over both colour and density, but only within the latitude of the film.

In monochrome printing, you are concerned only with getting the light through the negative. Provided the highlights are not totally blocked up and the required detail is visible in the shadow areas, you can make at least a passable print. A colour negative is a different proposition. At the highlight end, colour is likely to disappear before you reach maximum density and, although faint detail may be seen in the shadows, the colour can be severely distorted.

Colour print film can handle more contrast than colour slide film while still retaining highlight detail and colour fidelity, particularly with skilled hand printing. Nevertheless, high contrast is best

80 Transparency film can handle this sort of contrast only by making a feature of it. You base the exposure on the sunlit portions and allow the shadow areas to deepen. Any attempt to expose for the shadows would subdue the brilliant colour.

81 You can never be sure how your meter will respond to a single colour. Equally it is not easy to assess the tonal value of some colours. In this case, a direct reading would lead to too short an exposure. A grey-card or incident light reading is preferable, with suitable adjustment for any extra lens extension used.

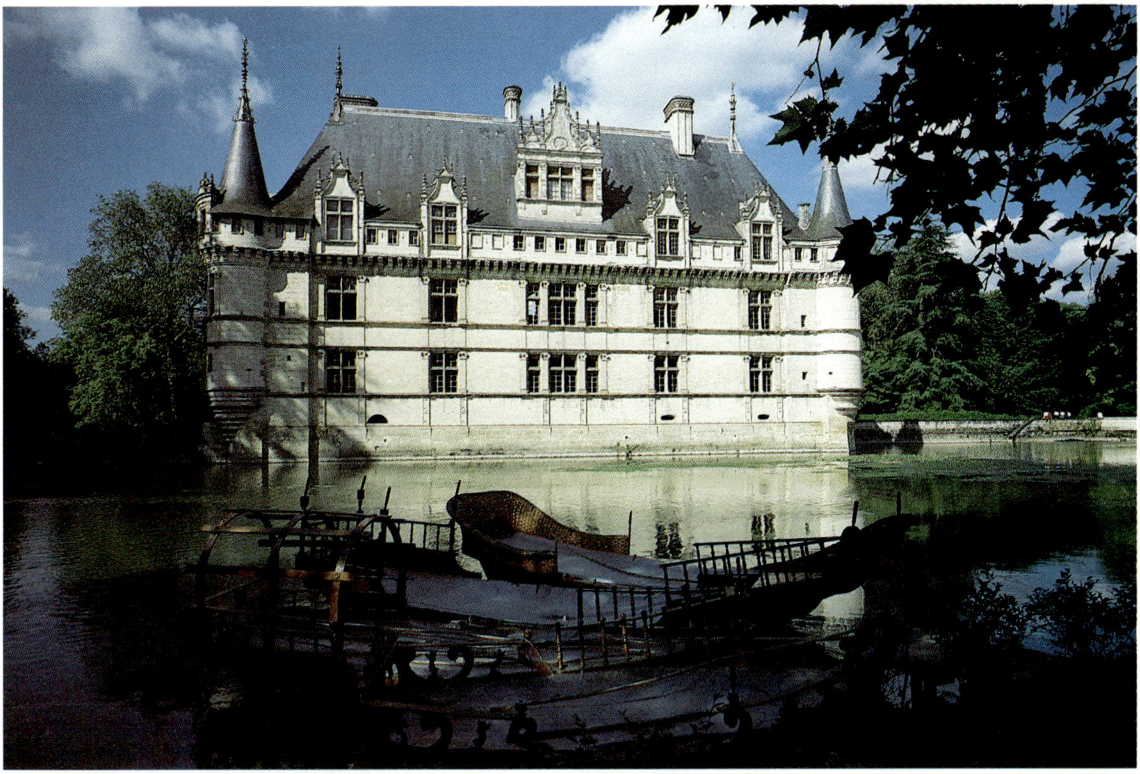

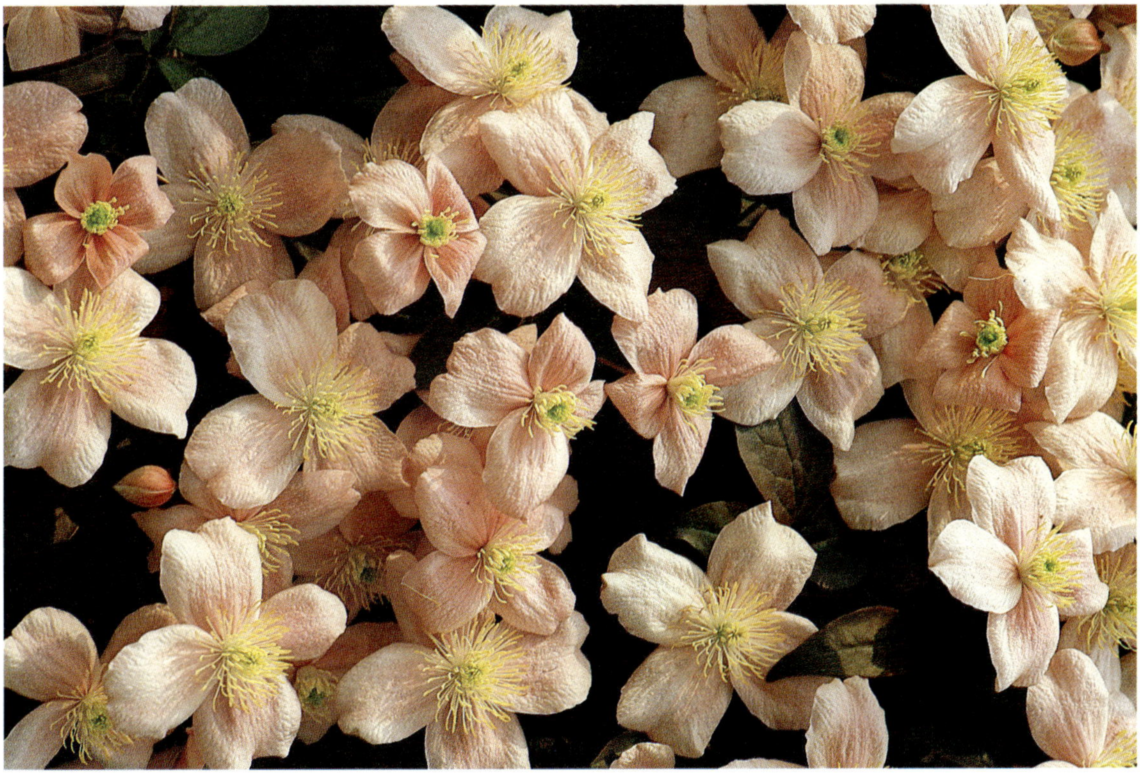

avoided because the danger of colour loss or distortion is still there. Lower contrast is acceptable because the colour itself can often compensate for the lack of tonal contrast that would mar a monochrome print. This is even more evident in later films, where an attempt is being made to separate colour saturation from tonal value.

Colour print film can also cope with 'unsuitable' lighting somewhat better than colour slide film. It is sometimes called 'universal' film because it can be used (at least theoretically) in either daylight or artificial light without filtration. The overall colour cast that tungsten light causes can be filtered out at the printing stage. A blue cast caused by shooting in the shade under a deep blue sky can be similarly dealt with. In fact, any overall variation of this nature can be eliminated at the printing stage provided its effect is not too drastic. However, any deviation from the designed colour temperature restricts the exposure latitude of the film.

On the other hand, no amount of filtering can put right the effect of using mixed lighting, eg, tungsten light with daylight in the same shot, or flash with tungsten lighting, or even a colour cast caused by a nearby reflecting surface. The filter needed to correct the 'wrong' colour rendering

84 Opposite, top. Panning and zooming simultaneously gives a startling effect on a fast bend. Exposure here is preset for the normal subject in the prevailing light conditions.

85 Extreme wide angle lens (20mm) taking in a fairly wide range of tones, but sufficiently well balanced and distributed to permit a reliable direct reading and satisfactory tones on a slide.

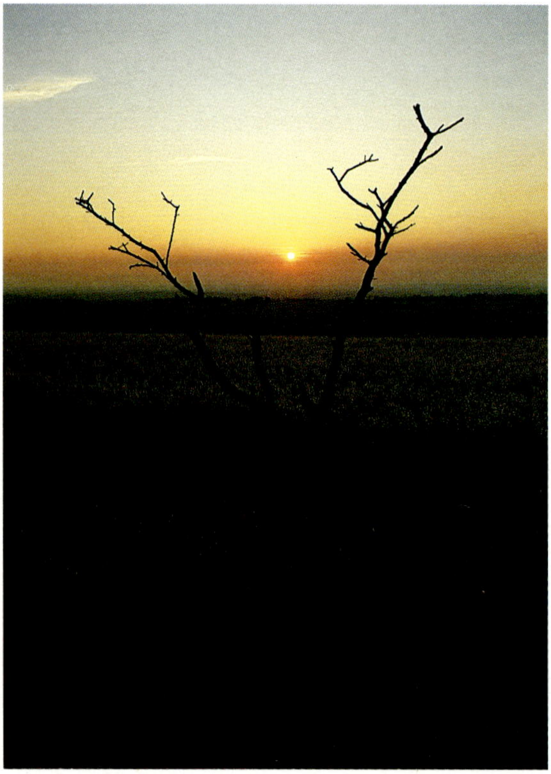

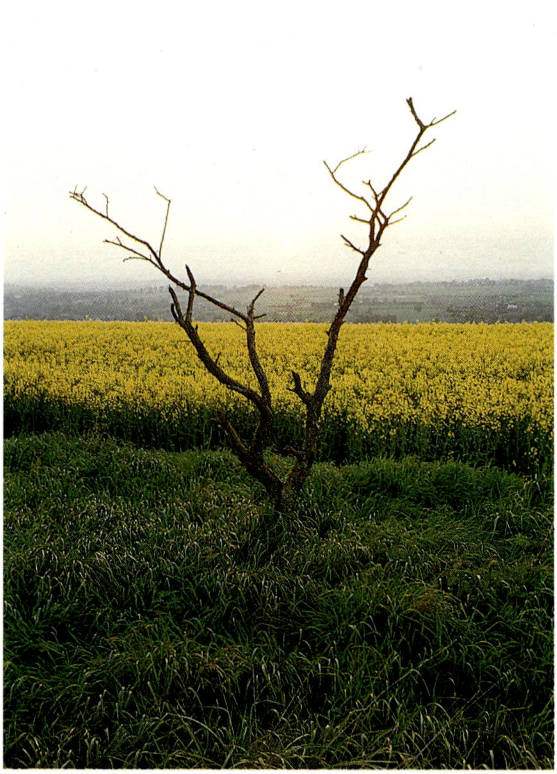

82,83 Wide-angle lenses can make TTL metering difficult if tonal masses are not reasonably well balanced. The light sky tone and distant mist could lead to underexposure, whereas the delicate tonal values are better rendered by moderate overexposure.

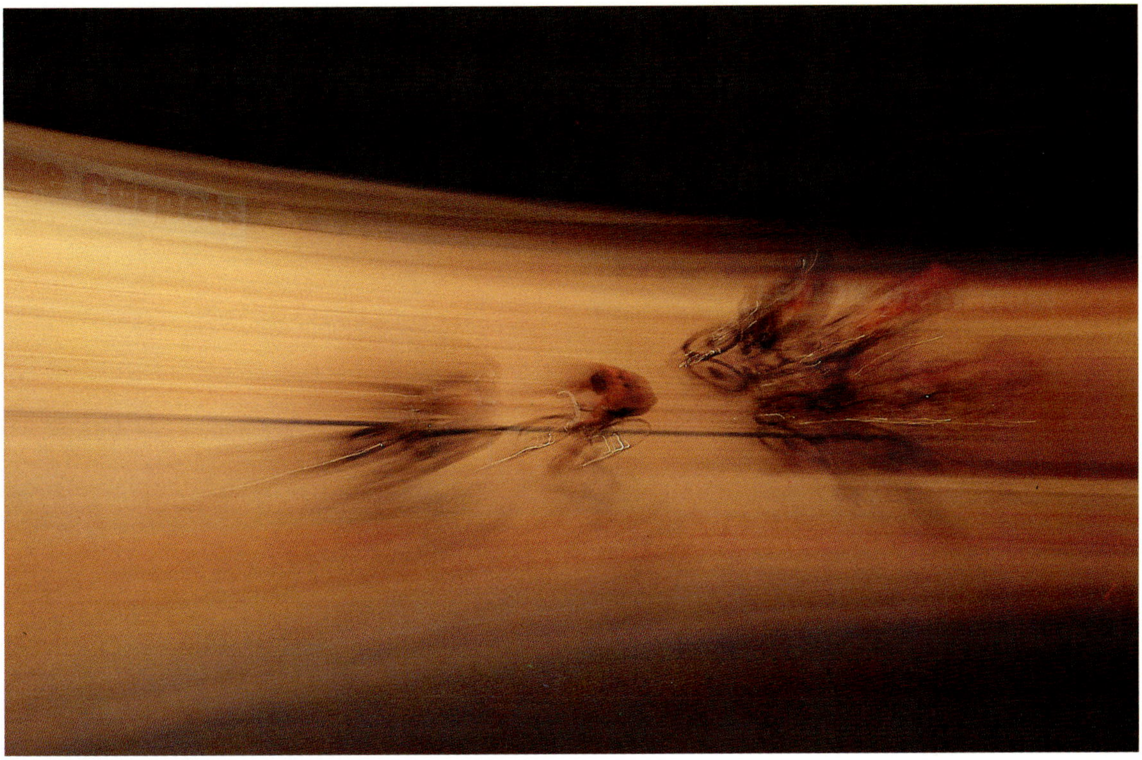

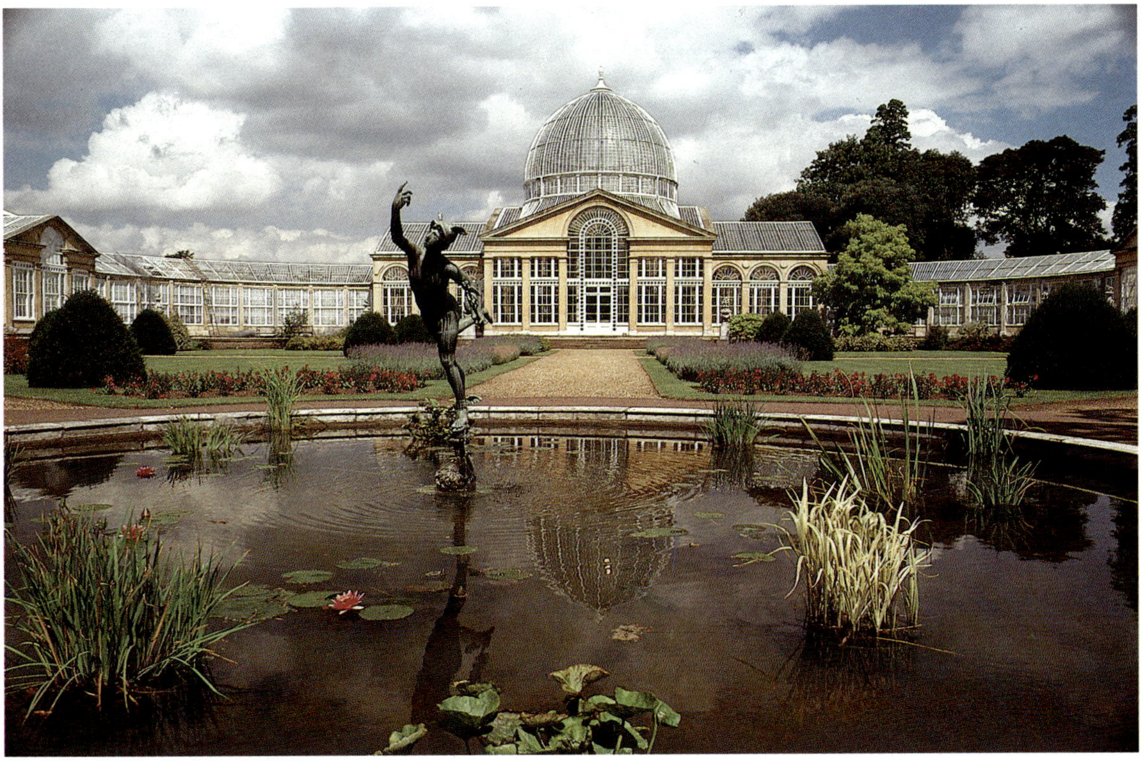

puts a cast of its own colour over the parts that were correctly reproduced.

Uprating colour film

The earliest colour films were very slow and, not all that many years ago, ISO 80/20° (ASA 80/20 DIN) was more or less the standard for colour print film and ISO 64/19° (ASA 64/19 DIN) was considered reasonably fast for colour slides. Now we have colour print speeds up to ISO 1600/33° (ASA 1600/33 DIN) and colour slides rated at ISO 1000/31° (ASA 1000/31 DIN). And faster films are on the way.

The relative slowness of their films irked many early colour enthusiasts and forced them to think of uprating. Despite the tremendous advances made, this is still a popular pastime, with constant new claims about the incredible speeds these new super fast films have been pushed to.

Uprating simply means setting your exposure meter to a higher film speed figure than the manufacturer has assigned to a particular film and then *push-processing* the film to compensate for the reduced exposure.

With a colour slide film, push-processing consists of extending the development time for the first (monochrome) developer. Colour development is not extended because it affects only the unexposed parts of the film and is generally taken close to finality. For that reason, uprating is not a recommended practice for colour print film. Both monochrome and colour images are produced in the same developer and extending the development time affects both colour and density. It can be done, but the results are largely unpredictable and will almost certainly show a greater colour shift than with a colour slide film.

Uprating inevitably leads to some loss of image quality. The form the loss usually takes is in poorer resolution, owing to increased grain size, and a lowering of both colour saturation and contrast. The loss of contrast is not acceptable, because it carries along with it a degradation of colour, ie, colour contrast suffers as well as tonal contrast. The technique cannot, therefore, be used as a form of contrast control. Indeed, as with all uprating techniques, it cannot satisfactorily be used with long tonal range subjects at all, because the first victim of underexposure is shadow detail and,

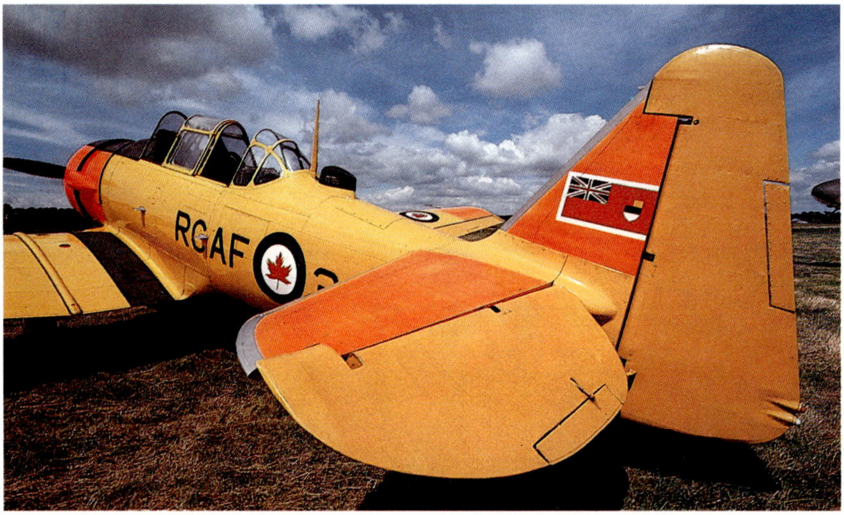

86 A wide-angle lens can give extreme depth of field even at moderately large apertures. With a static subject, you then have a choice of exposure settings from slow speed and smallest aperture if you can support the camera rigidly, to a hand-holdable speed at a mid-range aperture.

87 Skyscapes can be subjects in themselves or the starting point for combination pictures. Exposure depends on the result you want. You have to assess the tonal value required in the main part of the subject and adjust a direct reading accordingly.

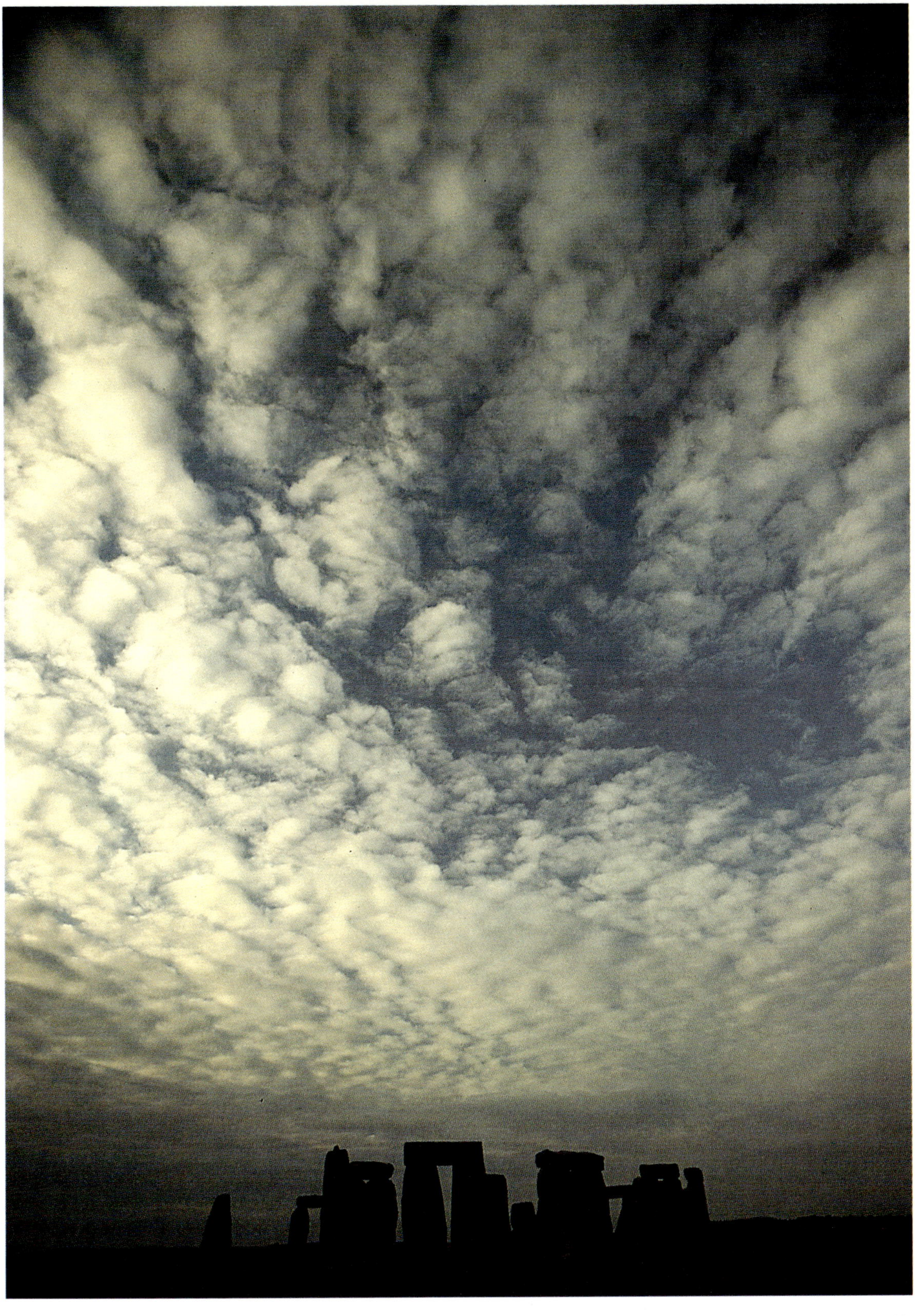

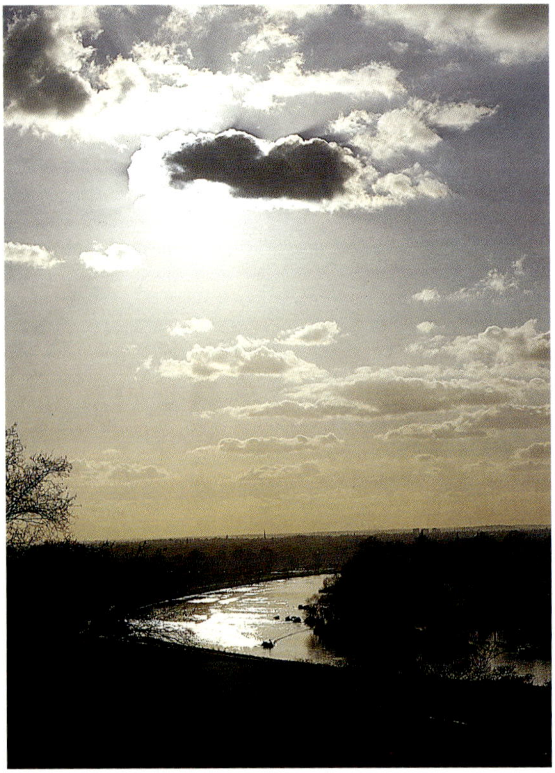

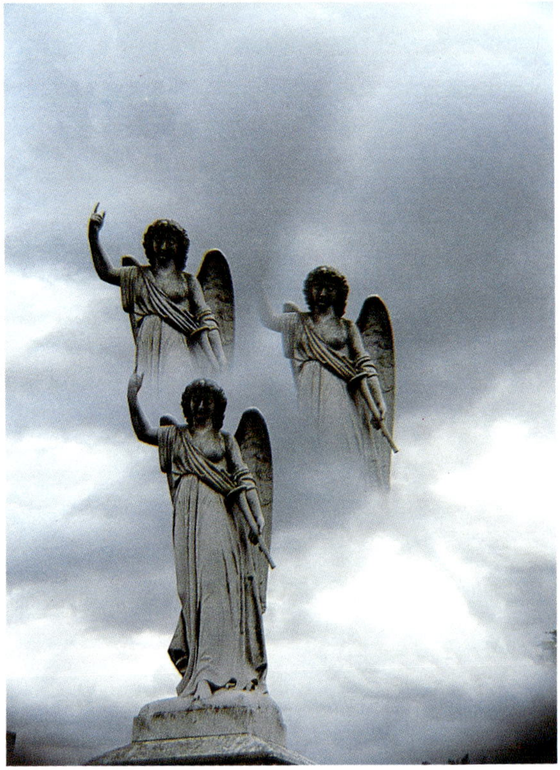

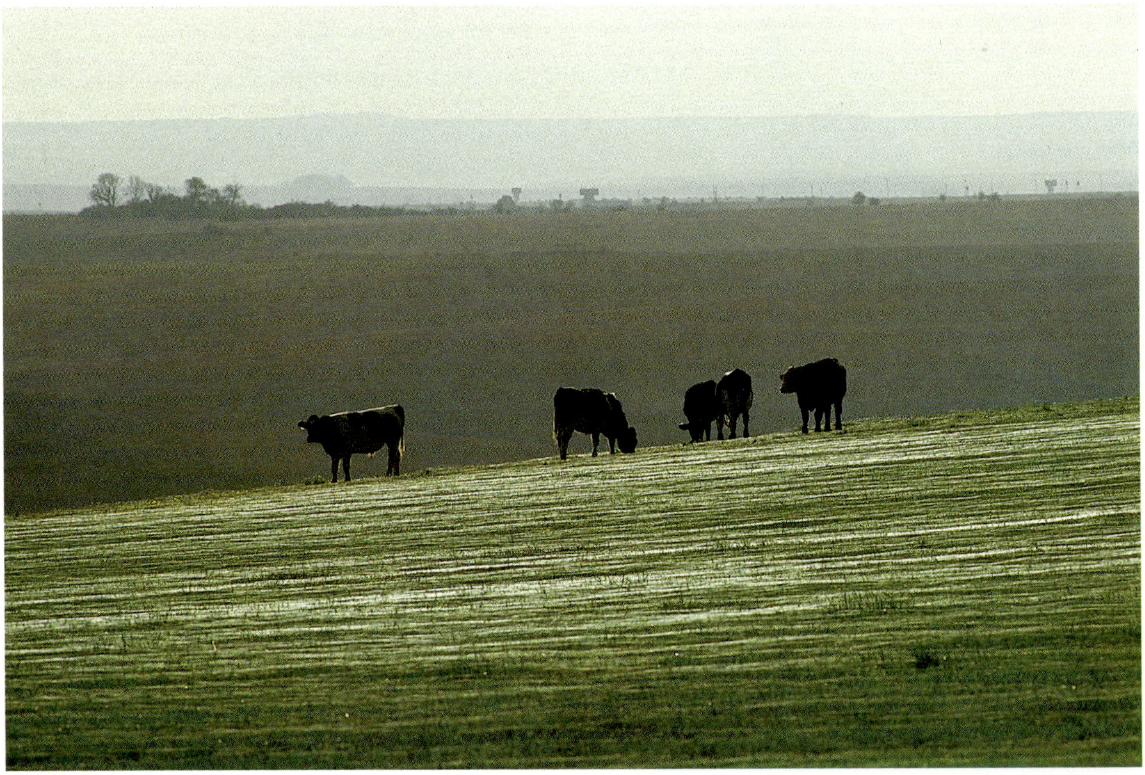

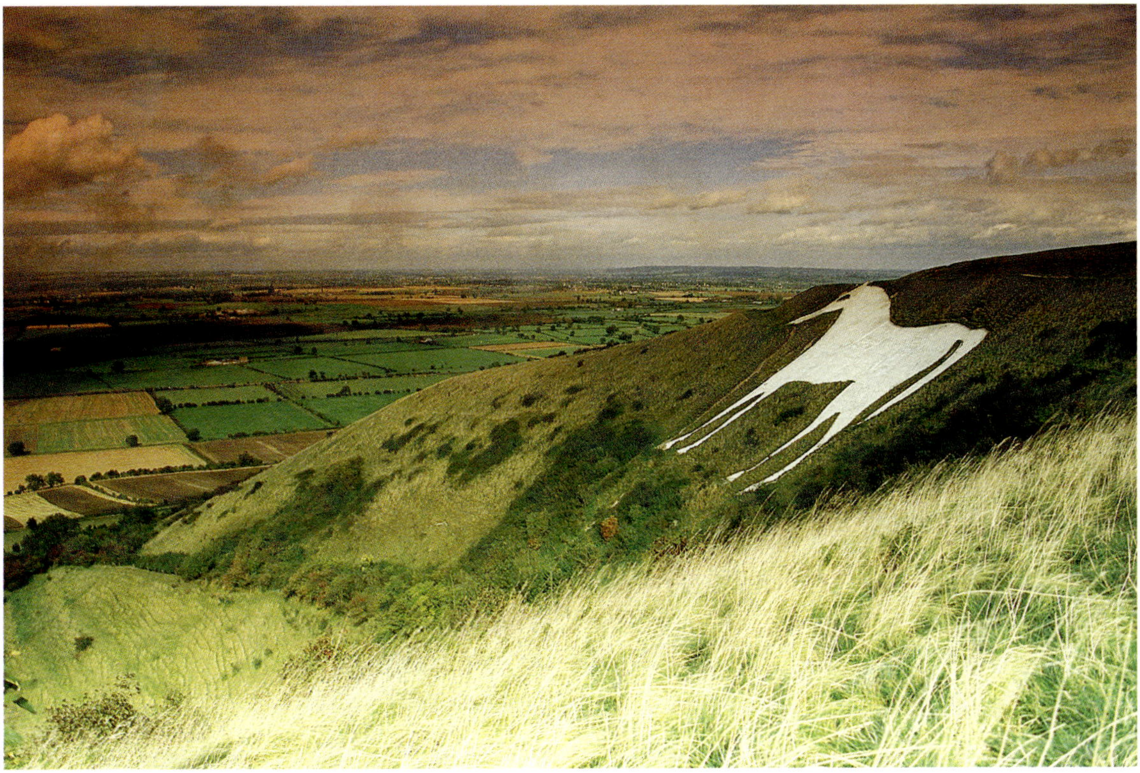

88 You may exploit the apparent increase in contrast with colour slides to pictorial effect. With exposure based on the sky area, the river seems extra brilliant against the darkened landscape.

89 Multi-images are created with prismatic attachments. A relatively small aperture is generally necessary to obtain reasonable sharpness in the secondary images but exposure is based on a normal reading for the main subject.

90 Cattle on a plain. Strong backlighting caught in gossamer webs makes a foreground 'highlight' in this scene. Exposure for these features render the cattle as outlined semi-silhouettes.

91 Graduated filters add not only colour but density to the picture. With slides in particular, and depending on the effect required, small adjustment to exposure may be called for in some cases to avoid repetitively darkened effects.

in colour films, shadow colour.

Nevertheless, uprating is a way of life for many photojournalists and others. Many laboratories are prepared to undertake the modified processing required, or you can follow one of the many published methods yourself.

Colour consistency

Colour film manufacture is a highly sophisticated process. The consistency of the end product is remarkably good, but it is not absolute. The emulsion is made in batches and films made from the same emulsion batch should produce virtually identical results, provided they have been stored correctly. There is no such guarantee with films produced from different batches of emulsion. Variations in colour rendering and effective speed can and do occur. Such variations are generally minimal and pass unnoticed by the average user. They tend to be less noticeable on 'amateur' films than on the larger format sheet or roll films designed specifically for professional use. This film is intended for immediate use and processing and should be kept in cold storage. 'Amateur' films are designed to 'settle down' to their optimum quality (ie, drift toward the norm) within about six months of manufacture, to take account of the likely shelf storage time at normal temperatures before use.

When colour rendering is highly critical and consistency from shot to shot is paramount, batch variations have to be taken into account. This is generally necessary only in high quality commercial work involving foodstuffs, fabrics, jewellery, cosmetics, art reproductions, etc. If a large number of pictures is to be taken, it is necessary to obtain sufficient material with the same emulsion batch number before shooting starts. The procedure then is often to use several test exposures and have them processed by a thoroughly reliable laboratory offering consistent processing. Exposure and filtration can then be worked out before shooting begins.

Clip processing

Some laboratories offer a modified version of this procedure, known as *clip processing*. They offer to process a few frames of your roll of 35mm film and send them to you for assessment and further instructions. If you are not too sure of the exposures you have given, or if you have uprated the film, or set the wrong film speed figure, you can ask them to clip off the first few frames of film for test processing and adjust the processing of the remaining frames as necessary.

17 PERFORMANCE TESTS

No matter how much care you take over camera exposure, you will get nowhere if you start from the wrong baseline. Your processing and printing technique must be good enough to translate the correct camera exposure into the required quality of negative and print.

We assume in these tests that you do your own processing, because if you do not, all your efforts at correct exposure can be nullified by the processing lab's automated production line. If you do not do your own processing, all is not lost. Follow the tests as far as possible and stick to one processing lab. In that case, you would do best to carry out the tests on colour slide film, which has less exposure latitude, shows up errors more clearly and goes through a single standardised process.

If you do your own processing, a few tests of procedure are worthwhile. How you make the various exposures required is a matter for your own ingenuity. It is not easy with 35mm film. You can space various exposures by shooting blank frames between them and carefully measuring and cutting the film in the darkroom. It is more reliable, however, to load short lengths of film into cassettes, say 10-12 exposures for each test.

Testing your basic technique

Choose a subject in reasonable daylight conditions, not brilliant direct sunlight, in which you can meter a light tone with some detail in it and a dark tone with similar characteristics just six stops away from it. Take a grey card or incident light reading and expose the film at that level. As this is a single-exposure test that will be processed normally, you can put it in with one of the other tests or on any film that will receive normal processing.

After processing the film, make the best possible print from the negative on your usual paper with your usual printing and processing technique, without shading or burning in. If you find that you have adequate tone rendering and detail in both of the metered areas, there is little wrong with your technique. If you cannot produce satisfactory detail in both areas in a straight print, there is something wrong with either your film speed setting or your developing procedure.

You might also try a pair of tones seven stops apart. The film can handle this without difficulty, but it is near the limit for a straight print on normal grade paper.

If your print is unsatisfactory, you need to identify the fault. If, when you print the lighter tone correctly, the darker tone is detailed but too light, the negative is lacking in contrast. This means either underexposure or underdevelopment. If, on the other hand, when you print the lighter tone correctly, the darker tone goes totally black and loses detail, your negative has too much contrast. That means overexposure or overdevelopment.

So far, so good. Deciding between underexposure and underdevelopment or overexposure and overdevelopment is not so easy, especially when, as should be the case here, the error is slight.

The best course is to review your technique and your equipment. Your exposure should be correct because you metered the two tones as well within the film's capability and gave a reliable grey-card-based exposure. The only way you could go wrong here is with a faulty exposure meter, using the meter wrongly, or with highly inaccurate exposure times on your camera. The second is most likely. You must make sure you measure only the area of the grey card and that the card is so oriented that light falls on it in the same way as it does on the subject. You must not allow a shadow to fall on the card as you take the reading. An incident light reading must be taken with the meter cell and diffuser pointing from the subject position to the camera lens, not the light source.

A possible source of error is the relationship between your film-speed setting and your film processing. There can be a variety of reasons, such as errors in your meter indications, shutter settings or lens aperture markings, or your processing thermometer or timer. These are not generally important, providing the degree of inaccuracy is consistent and not too great. Exposure times can vary by up to 20 per cent from the marked values with no significant effect on any normal film. A thermometer that over, or under-reads by a degree or so (and a great many do) is still usable provided the error is consistent. Some kinds of thermometer, particularly the dial-on-a-stem types, read differently in different depths of solution. Minor troubles of this nature can be ironed out in the next test, which is designed to ascertain whether you are using the correct film speed setting for your processing technique.

Determining your effective film speed
Choose a normal subject with a reasonable distribution of tones, including some deep shadow and highlight areas. Take a normal reflected light reading and a reading from a grey card to check that it is an average subject. The readings should agree within one stop.

Make your first exposure at the grey card level with your meter set to the marked film speed. Make four further exposures at half stop intervals either side, ie, half, one, one and a half and two stops more and less than the indicated exposure. Whether you use the lens aperture or exposure time as the variable is relatively unimportant with modern improved shutter design and electronic timing. Your aperture group should preferably range from *f*/2.8 to *f*/11 or *f*/4 to *f*/16, depending on the lens used. Avoid exposure times shorter than 1/250 sec. If you decide to use varying exposure times, it is best to take all your shots from a tripod.

As this is the test on which all others depend, it is worth taking some trouble with it. Make no more exposures of consequence on this roll. Unload the film and process it strictly in accordance with the developer manufacturer's instructions. Wait until the film is completely dry before examining it.

If you know the type of negative you want, check the nine exposures visually and determine which has given the result required. If you cannot decide that way (and it is not easy), put the strip of negatives aside until you can make prints. When you do so, take care to produce the best possible print from each negative on normal grade paper. Examine the prints closely when they are dry, paying particular attention to the rendering of shadow and highlight detail, maximum black and minimum white.

It is more than likely that two, three or even more of the prints are virtually identical. With most modern films, except colour slides, a one-stop exposure error on an average subject has very little effect on final image quality. With print films, make your choice of the best negative according to the density you prefer to print from.

When your choice is made, check the exposure given to that negative. If it was not the one that had the exposure recommended by the meter, your 'personal' speed for that particular film, processed in your particular manner, differs from that of the maker. If it is the +1 stop negative, you should in future set your film speed to half the manufacturer's figure. If it is the −1 stop negative, you should set the film speed to double the manufacturer's figure. If you choose one of the half-stop negatives, then you should use one of the intermediate one-third positions normally marked between film speed figures.

Thereafter, this will be your film speed for the camera, lens, film and developer you used for the test – and for your darkroom equipment, materials and printing technique. Change any one of those and your film speed figure may also change. Ideally, you should retest if you make any change. If you work with 'professional' materials, such as colour film in sheet form and professional rollfilm, you may carry the tests further. In general, if you work exclusively with monochrome or so-called amateur colour materials, you can be reasonably satisfied with a single test for each brand and speed of film, unless the test runs into exposure difficulties. When working in colour, it is advisable to repeat the tests from time to time because colour emulsions are often changed without publicity.

The film developer is important. The safest method of use for consistency is the one-shot, throwaway system. You use fresh developer for each film or for each batch of films developed together. If you do not do this, follow precisely the manufacturer's instructions about the prolongation of development time for each subsequent film. Without absolute consistency in processing, the tests are useless.

Effect of variations in exposure
Having determined your basic effective film speed, you can proceed to test the effect of varying exposure and processing to control contrast. This entails quite a lot of work and you may finish with little worthwhile data. Nevertheless, there is nothing like finding out for yourself and it just may be that your particular film/developer combination gives useful results.

Uprating technique. Load three short lengths of film into cassettes (or take three rollfilms). On each film, take a series of pictures in relatively low-contrast lighting. Suitable subjects are buildings with a reasonable variety of tones, some weak shadows from window sills and some white paint. Space your exposures as before, one at the standard grey card level and four at half-stop intervals up to two stops underexposure. Thus, you have five more or less identical shots on each roll of film, or multiples of five if you have shot

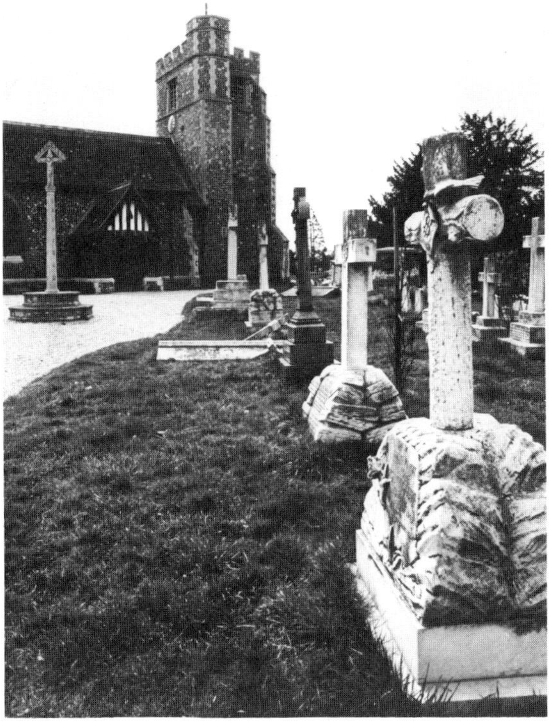

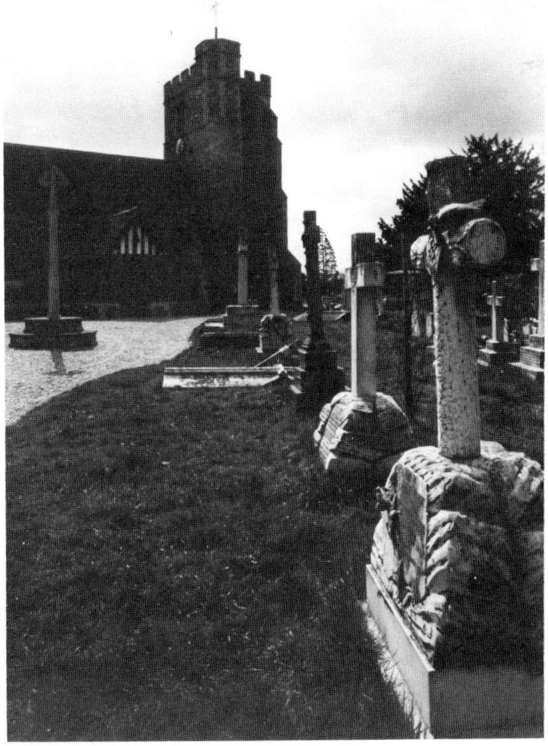

92-94 Exposure latitude. The print above is from a 'correctly' exposed negative. The other negatives had two stops less exposure (top) and two stops more (bottom).

more than one subject. Take one film and develop it as standard. Develop another for 30 per cent longer than the standard time and the third for 50 per cent longer than the standard time. Now you have three films showing 15 different treatments of the same subject.

Shot	Exposure	Development
1	standard	standard
2	½ stop under	standard
3	1 stop under	standard
4	1½ stops under	standard
5	2 stops under	standard
6	standard	30 per cent increase
7	½ stop under	30 per cent increase
8	1 stop under	30 per cent increase
9	1½ stops under	30 per cent increase
10	2 stops under	30 per cent increase
11	standard	50 per cent increase
12	½ stop under	50 per cent increase
13	1 stop under	50 per cent increase
14	1½ stops under	50 per cent increase
15	2 stops under	50 per cent increase

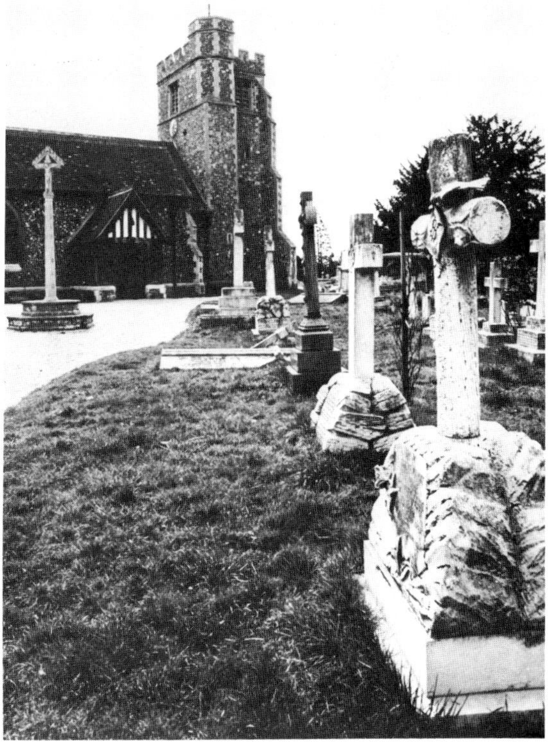

If you have not carried out this sort of test before, the first thing that will strike you is that you have 15 negatives that are almost identical – a situation that certainly did not exist some years ago. There will probably be surprisingly little difference between No 1 and No 5 and virtually no difference between No 1 and No 15. You are likely to find that every one of these negatives can produce at least an acceptable print. Only if your subject was of rather higher contrast than envisaged will you perhaps find that fine highlight detail has been lost in Nos 11 and 12 or very weak shadow detail has disappeared in Nos 4 and 5.

You will find it very difficult to decide which is the best negative without making prints. Try making the best possible print on normal grade paper from each of them. Then select those that seem to be the lowest in contrast, and print them on a higher contrast grade of paper.

You should now be able to come to some conclusions about increasing contrast by reducing exposure and extending development, or placing a tone lower on the curve and bringing it up again by increased development. Study all your 15 prints carefully from this point of view. Has overall contrast increased in any of them? Are the shadows deeper or the highlights brighter? Are the middle tones better separated? You will probably not see any dramatic differences, because modern films are not made that way; but you might see some subtle effects you could make use of, to add that little extra quality to your prints.

One thing you certainly will notice is that you have discovered the origin of the uprating technique. If your subject has no extreme highlights or shadows, you can underexpose most monochrome films by up to two stops and over-develop by 50-75 per cent to produce a negative very similar to that produced by normal exposure and normal development. When you come to make the print, you may find that the quality is not quite as good. Graininess will have increased marginally. Overall contrast may be slightly higher. But you will have apparently increased film speed by a factor of 4. This is a valid operation when it is used with the right kind of subject and for a specific purpose, ie, to cope with movement in dim lighting, or to obtain greater depth of field etc.

If you repeat the test in bright sunny conditions on a subject with weak highlight and shadow detail, you will find a different story. You will certainly lose the shadow detail at two stops underexposure and normal development, and the highlights are very likely to block up completely at normal exposure and 50 per cent overdevelopment. But, more important, extended development is not likely to bring back the shadow detail lost by two stops underexposure, and the highlights may become too dense to print easily. Overall contrast can also increase (but that was not the object of the exercise).

Downrating technique. Now we move to the next test. Can we reduce contrast by generous exposure and curtailed development – or placing a tone higher on the curve and bringing it down again by adjusting the development time? You need another three short lengths of film with at least five exposures on each. This time, however, you want a high contrast subject; you will supplement your normal exposure with four others at half-stop intervals up to two stops overexposure. This is the technique that used to be known as 'exposing for the shadows and developing for the highlights'. At the processing stage, develop one film normally, one at 15 per cent less development time and one at 30 per cent less.

Again, you have 15 treatments:

Shot	Exposure	Development
1	standard	standard
2	½ stop over	standard
3	1 stop over	standard
4	1½ stops over	standard
5	2 stops over	standard
6	standard	15 per cent decrease
7	½ stop over	15 per cent decrease
8	1 stop over	15 per cent decrease
9	1½ stops over	15 per cent decrease
10	2 stops over	15 per cent decrease
11	standard	30 per cent decrease
12	½ stop over	30 per cent decrease
13	1 stop over	30 per cent decrease
14	1½ stops over	30 per cent decrease
15	2 stops over	30 per cent decrease

Again, your results will look remarkably similar. Repeat the assessment and printing procedure, and see what conclusions you come to this time. Look for the subtle effects. Can you improve your negatives sufficiently by this technique to make it worthwhile (particularly with 35mm film, where it is not easy to separate subjects by contrast on to different cassettes)? Rollfilm workers can weigh up the balance more critically. What may offer only a marginal advantage for 35mm workers may be worthwhile for them.

If you do manage to produce significantly improved negatives by one or other of these techniques, it is worth pursuing. It is always preferable to get the quality into the negative if possible and to aim at printing everything on the same grade of paper. You cannot always do this, but the nearer you can get to it, the easier it becomes to produce first class prints.

Darkroom tests

In monochrome and, to some extent, with colour print film, exposure must be related to the whole process of picture-making, right through to the final print. It may be unacceptable to the purist, but it remains true to say that different photographers like to print from different types of negative. Some like a 'meaty' negative with noticeable density even in the darkest shadows: others prefer to print from the thinnest negative possible. Enlarger characteristics can also affect the type of negative that prints best. Even colour slide materials do not have a single correct exposure. There is sufficient latitude to allow you to produce a denser slide for powerful projector lamps.

So it is advisable, unless you know the type of negative you are looking for, to take all tests through to the final print stage. The theoretically perfect negative may not be perfect for you. By striving to make the best print from a given negative, moreover, you learn a lot about print quality.

Performance of materials. A useful exercise, rather than a test, to start with is to check the behaviour of your usual print material and developer combination. How many different recognisable tones can you reproduce? What is the minimum exposure to produce maximum black through clear film – a frame of unexposed, fully processed film? With test strip type exposures of 2, 4, 6, 8 etc. seconds at a moderate aperture on a 10 x 8in sheet of paper, you should be able to make out 30 or more different tones, any of the last half-dozen or so of which you might have considered to be maximum black until you tried this experiment. This range of tones gives you a clearer idea of the capability of your paper than the normally-quoted 60:1 ratio. When you see all the tones and the barely discernible differences between them, in fact, you may wonder what all the talk of restricted tonal range is about. What it is actually all about is fitting as many as possible out of the longer range of tones in the negative on to the paper. And that is largely a matter of emulsion chemistry.

Another useful piece of information can be obtained from the experiment. Suppose you were using the enlarger lens at *f*/11 and you found that you did not get a maximum black until you reached an exposure of 70 sec. Then you know that no print of that size made from a normal negative can show a maximum black anywhere with an exposure of less than 70 sec at *f*/11, or its equivalent.

The effect of using different paper contrast grades is well illustrated if you repeat this test on as many different grades as possible. If you want to be really industrious, try it with different developers, too – or with developer well below the recommended temperature, say at 13°C.

Personal performance. Darkroom tests relate largely to checking your own technique. Take your best negative and make your best print from it by your usual methods. Use fresh materials and solutions at the manufacturer's recommended temperature. Set your best print aside and then give another sheet of paper exactly the same exposure through the same negative. This time, however, develop it for twice the recommended time. (This is for monochrome only, of course.)

When both prints are fixed, washed and dried, examine them carefully. There should be little, if any, detectable difference. If the second print is noticeably darker than the first and the highlights are not clean, your enlarger exposure was too long. Make another pair of prints, and a third if necessary, with shorter exposures until you can develop two identically exposed prints, one for the recommended time and the other for twice the recommended time, and not see any significant difference between them. Then compare both prints with your first (your best) print. There is every chance that they will look brighter, with better tonal separation and richer blacks.

Overexposure in the enlarger is a common fault, often leading you to remove the print from the developer before it has fully developed, because you can see that it is going to be too dark. Such a 'snatched' print can never be the best. It will be lower in contrast than it should be and will not show a maximum black anywhere.

Underexposure is even more common, especially among those who believe they can judge the quality of a print in safelight conditions and while it is still immersed in the developer solution.

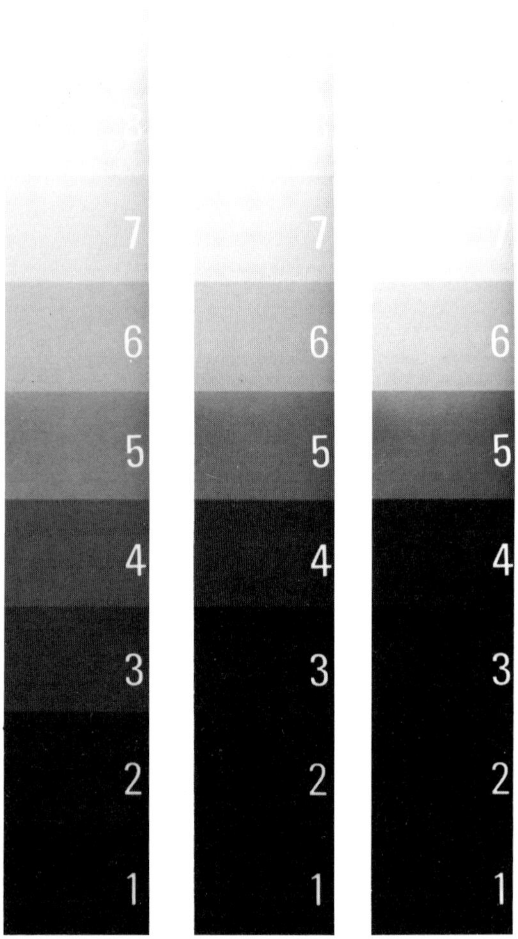

95 The range of tones available on, from left to right, Grades 0, 2 and 4 paper.

This will show up in the test, but not so noticeably as in the case of overexposure. If the second print looks just a little darker than the first but rather higher in contrast, try increasing the exposure until you can produce two identically exposed prints that look near enough the same whether you give them normal or twice-normal development time. Compare them with your best print. Again, they should look stronger, with considerably increased contrast caused mainly by a deeper shadow tone.

Exposure estimation. Despite all the electronic aids now available for the darkroom, the test strip method is still the most reliable for judging the correct exposure required for any particular negative. For the best possible print, however, a single test strip is rarely enough.

The normal test-strip method is to take a generously-sized piece of printing paper – at least 35mm wide – and to lay it across the image area on the enlarger baseboard so that it covers as wide a range of tones as possible. Moving a piece of black card across the strip (also oriented to take in as many tones as possible at each exposure) give three or four doubled up exposures through your chosen negative – say 5, 10, 20, 40 sec.

Process the strip and examine it after blotting it dry. Ideally, it should be completely dry, but at least take the water sheen off. Use strong light, preferably daylight, to examine the strip. If all the segments are too dark or too light, you will need to start again with a different series of exposures or a larger or smaller lens aperture. Assuming that the results run from too light to too dark, check the shadow and highlight areas in the middle segments. Provided the negative does not have too much contrast, you should be able to see detail in both areas, while deep shadow should be maximum black or very close to it. You may have to test again, with more closely spaced exposures, before you are certain that you have the right one.

That is the normal test-strip procedure. It generally gives enough additional information to tell you whether any special treatment such as shading or burning-in may be necessary. This means giving the extra exposure that a highlight area is shown to need, because its best rendering is in a segment other than that containing the best shadow area rendering; or giving the exposure that renders the highlight correctly while shielding the shadow area.

There are expert printers who can carry out all shading and burning in procedures with their hands, but to begin with it is easier to use pieces of black card, fixed to a length of thin wire. The card must be kept gently moving throughout the operation to avoid forming a sharp edge between tones.

A more refined type of test strip concentrates on single tones. If you have an area that you want to reproduce as maximum black, for example, lay your test strip over that tone only and find the minimum exposure required to produce the tone required. You can do the same for any other tone, of course. If you test two important tones in this

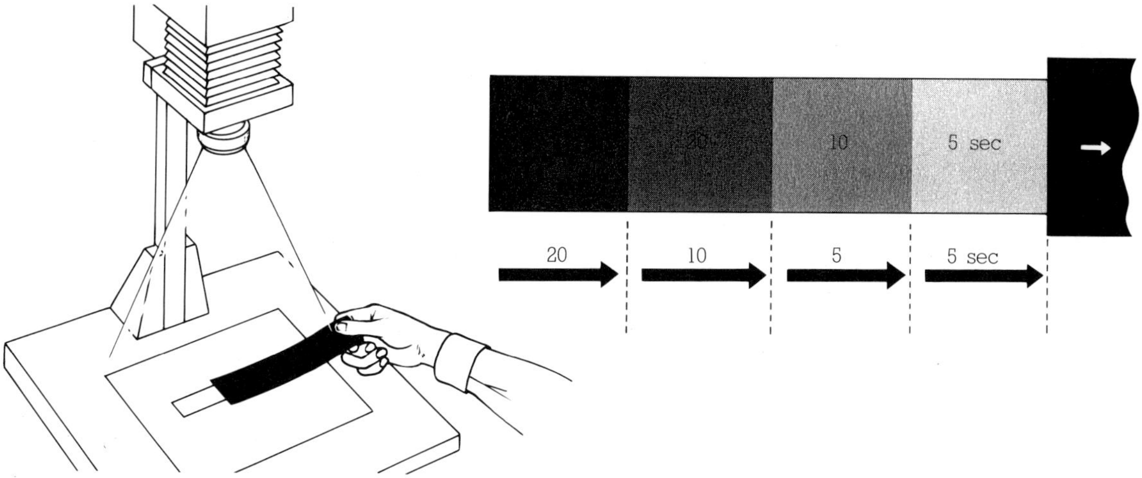

17.1 Lay the test strip across the image area to cover as many tones as possible and hold a piece of black card just above it. Switch on the enlarger lamp and draw the card back to give the exposures indicated (A). The actual exposures of each portion of the strip are then as shown (B). Naturally other figures can be substituted in the light of experience.

way and the indicated exposures are the same or very close, you know that you are well on the way to producing the kind of print you want. If the two indicated exposures are slightly different, a change of paper grade should solve the problem. If they are markedly different, selective exposure treatment is likely to be necessary.

Exposure meters for printing

Various forms of exposure meter have been produced for darkroom use. They fall into two basic groups: those using a light-sensitive probe placed on the baseboard and accepting light directly from the enlarger lens, and those held at a fixed position above the baseboard and reading the light reflected from the paper surface.

The latter are commonly automatic exposure types, ie, they meter the exposure as it is given and switch off the enlarger lamp at the appropriate time. They can work very well for the rapid production of a series of prints from different negatives at different degrees of enlargement. They read a large area of the image, however, and work on an integration-to-grey principle. The precise area read is not immediately obvious and they are easily misled by 'non-average' images.

The probe sensor is much more versatile. It generally works in conjunction with a timer so that as you turn the timer dial an indication is given when you have set the correct exposure time. Light-emitting diode (LED) indicators are now commonly used. The advantage of this type of meter is that it can measure a small area directly or work on an integrated reading in conjunction with a diffuser over the enlarger lens. The diffused reading works on an integration-to-grey principle and is satisfactory in most cases. The 'spot-reading' facility enables you to assess the exposure required for maximum black or for a flesh tone or any other key tone you like to select.

All such meters have to be calibrated by the user to his own materials and techniques. Naturally, different papers have different sensitivities, and developers vary in their action. The meter has a 'paper speed' dial which needs to be reset for each set of circumstances – paper, developer, lens and, in the case of spot readings, the type of reading required. Alternatively, there may be a simple 'exposure compensation' dial for calibration purposes.

To effect the calibration, you must first produce a top-quality print from an 'average' negative. Then, with the enlarger at the same setting of the lens and head height, you set the exposure time given on the timer dial. Place your probe on the baseboard to give the type of reading required, and adjust the paper speed or exposure compensation dial of the timer until correct exposure is indicated. The meter is then set for all subsequent operations in the same conditions. It will vary, of course, with the type of reading you use: you need to keep a record of the calibration settings for

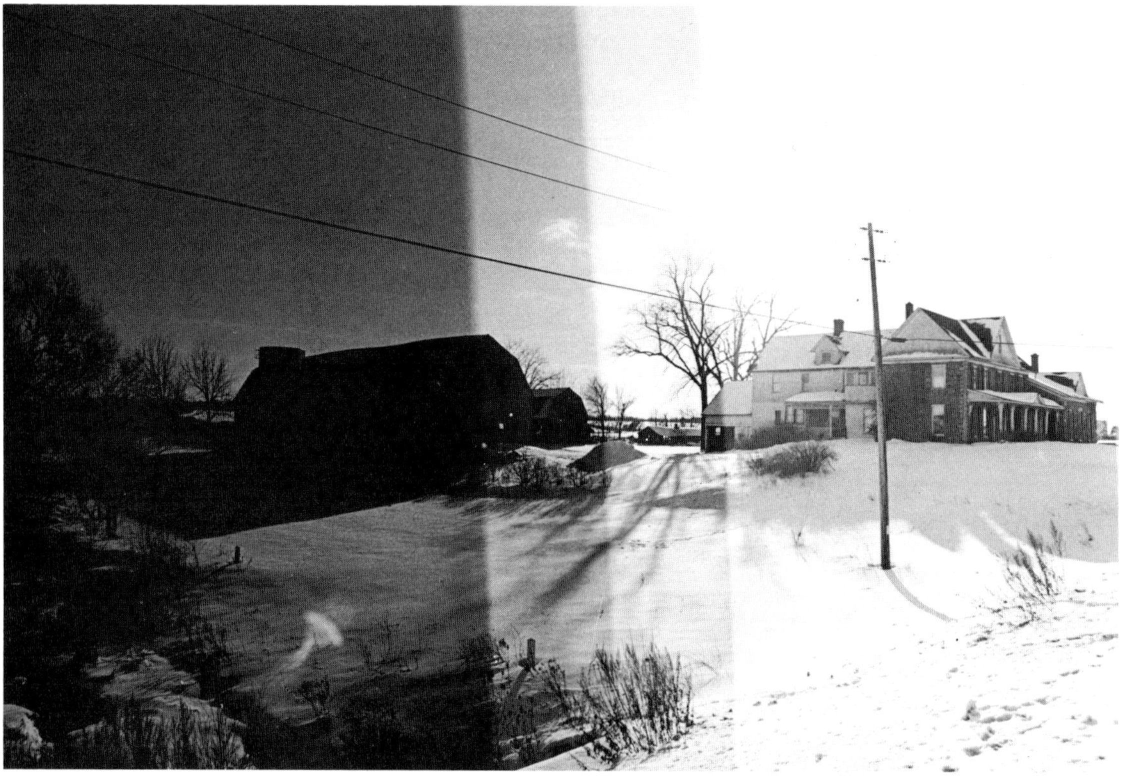

97 Print exposures of 5, 10, 20 and 40 seconds. Note that each strip covers a wide range of tones.

each type of reading you intend to use – flesh tone, highlight, shadow, maximum black, average, etc.

No enlarger meter can give you anything but approximate results. According to the expertise you acquire in using it, it can produce prints ranging in quality from acceptable to very good. Perhaps, by the law of averages, it may occasionally give you a perfect print. Generally, however, it gives you a starting point. If you have calibrated the meter correctly, it should give you a starting point close to the correct exposure. A popular method of using such meters, therefore, is to make a full-sized print at the recommended exposure and use it as a deluxe test strip. For the experienced worker, it is then relatively easy to assess the adjustments required to make the best possible print.

The importance of print quality

It is not much use taking infinite pains over the exposure of a negative if you are not able to do justice to it in the darkroom. To get the exposure right, the answer is careful and intelligent making of test strips, aided (if you wish) by an exposure meter, and a reluctance to be satisfied with the first print. The perfectionist regards the first print as the last test-strip, or even the last but one. On it he re-assesses the exposure for the whole print and notes the areas, if any, that need special treatment.

No matter how careful you are with exposure, you will not get perfect prints unless everything else in the darkroom process is working efficiently. Always use fresh paper, properly stored away from damp, heat and chemicals. Your developer must be fresh and at the correct temperature.

The fixer must be fresh and the print adequately washed after fixing.

Safelight and stray light testing. Above all, your safelight must be really safe, and there must be no significant light leaks into your darkroom. Light safety is easily tested. Set the enlarger to make a print with all blackout arrangements in place and the safelight on. Position the printing paper on the baseboard. Place a coin over an area that is to be reproduced as a light to mid-tone. Leave the paper and coin in place for two or three minutes, then remove the coin and make your print in the usual way. When you examine the final print, there should be no trace of where the coin lay. If your lighting is unsafe, you will find that the position of the coin is visible as a lighter area.

It is essential that you make the test in this way, because your lighting may be only marginally unsafe. If you develop the paper without making a print, you might see no evidence of the coin, but the extra exposure given by making a print is enough to bring any latent fogging up in the final print. The result of any such stray light in the darkroom is that your prints lack that extra 'bite' that is associated with clean whites and good separation between the delicate lighter tones.

INDEX

ACKNOWLEDGEMENTS

All photographs by Ed Buziak except:
Paul Petzold, 102, 104b, 121b, 124t, 130t, l and r.
Jack Taylor 21